THE

INFLUENCE OF THE ROMAN LAW

ON THE

LAW OF ENGLAND.

BEING THE YORKE PRIZE ESSAY OF THE UNIVERSITY OF
CAMBRIDGE FOR THE YEAR 1884:

BY

THOMAS EDWARD SCRUTTON,

M.A. LL.B. (LOND.), B.A. LL.B. (CAMB.): BARRISTER AT LAW; PROFESSOR OF
CONSTITUTIONAL LAW AND HISTORY IN, AND FELLOW OF, UNIVERSITY COLLEGE,
LONDON: LATE SCHOLAR OF TRINITY COLLEGE, CAMBRIDGE: AUTHOR OF
"THE LAWS OF COPYRIGHT," BEING THE YORKE PRIZE ESSAY
FOR 1882.

———————

"Tu regere imperio populos, Romane, memento."
VERG. *Aen.* VI.

———————

THE LAWBOOK EXCHANGE, LTD.
Clark, New Jersey

ISBN-13: 9781584779841 (hardcover)
ISBN-13: 9781616190354 (paperback)

Lawbook Exchange edition 2010

The quality of this reprint is equivalent to the quality of the original work.

THE LAWBOOK EXCHANGE, LTD.

33 Terminal Avenue
Clark, New Jersey 07066-1321

*Please see our website for a selection of our other publications
and fine facsimile reprints of classic works of legal history:*
www.lawbookexchange.com

Library of Congress Cataloging-in-Publication Data

Scrutton, Thomas Edward, Sir, 1856-1934.
  The influence of the Roman law on the law of England : being
the Yorke prize essay of the University of Cambridge for the year
1884 / by Thomas Edward Scrutton.
      p. cm.
  Reprint. Originally published: Cambridge [Cambridgeshire] :
University Press, 1885.
  Includes index.
  ISBN-13: 978-1-58477-984-1 (cloth : alk. paper)
  ISBN-10: 1-58477-984-5 (cloth : alk. paper)
  1. Law--Great Britain--Roman influences. 2. Law--Great Britain--
History. 3. Roman law. I. Title.

KD540.S37 2009
349.42--dc22

                                    2009025477

Printed in the United States of America on acid-free paper

THE

INFLUENCE OF THE ROMAN LAW

ON THE

LAW OF ENGLAND.

BEING THE YORKE PRIZE ESSAY OF THE UNIVERSITY OF
CAMBRIDGE FOR THE YEAR 1884:

BY

THOMAS EDWARD SCRUTTON,

M.A. LL.B. (LOND.), B.A. LL.B. (CAMB.): BARRISTER AT LAW; PROFESSOR OF
CONSTITUTIONAL LAW AND HISTORY IN, AND FELLOW OF, UNIVERSITY COLLEGE,
LONDON: LATE SCHOLAR OF TRINITY COLLEGE, CAMBRIDGE: AUTHOR OF
"THE LAWS OF COPYRIGHT," BEING THE YORKE PRIZE ESSAY
FOR 1882.

"Tu regere imperio populos, Romane, memento."
VERG. *Aen.* VI.

CAMBRIDGE:
AT THE UNIVERSITY PRESS.
1885.

𝔊𝔞𝔪𝔟𝔯𝔦𝔡𝔤𝔢:

PRINTED BY C. J. CLAY, M.A. & SON,

AT THE UNIVERSITY PRESS.

PREFACE.

THE Yorke Prize of the University of Cambridge, to the establishment of which this work owes its existence, was founded about twelve years ago by Edmund Yorke, late Fellow of St. Catharine's College, Cambridge, and, under a scheme of the Court of Chancery, is given annually to that graduate of the University, of not more than seven years' standing from his first degree, who shall be the author of the best essay on some subject relating to the "Law of Property, its Principles, and History in various Ages and Countries." The subject prescribed for the year 1884 by the Adjudicators, (Arthur Cohen, Esq., Q.C., M.P., and R. Romer, Esq., Q.C.), was "The Influence of the Roman Law on the Law of England". The prize was awarded to the Essay bearing the motto: "*Tu regere imperio populos, Romane, memento,*" which is now published in accordance with the conditions of the Award.

The history of English law has yet to be written, but one of the most interesting chapters in that work of the future will be the one which deals with the subject of this Essay. I am far from imagining that the following pages afford an exhaustive or even adequate treatment of so important and difficult a question. To expect such a work to be written in ten months by a young man within seven years of his first degree would, I think, be asking too much even of "the omniscience of youth." Except in one instance, I do not pretend to have done more than collected and, to the best of my ability, criticized what has been written on the subject by my predecessors in the field, though this possibly may lighten the labours of my successors.

The question is a very difficult one for three reasons. As to many of the critical periods in the growth of the English law, especially the centuries immediately following the Saxon invasion and the Norman Conquest, we have but slight evidence as to even the nature of our institutions and laws. In those periods on which we have more information, the growth of the law by judicial decisions is frequently influenced through personal, and as it were underground, channels, which leave but scanty traces of their existence to subsequent students. Lord Holt's borrowings from the Law of Rome are on the surface, but what can we say of the methods of his forerunners who made and moulded the Common Law of England? And thirdly, some of the principal sources of knowledge on the history of English law are still of such an inaccessible nature as to discourage and repel any but students most patient and prodigal in time. The Year-Books are still enveloped in the darkness in which their original editions enshroud them, though I learn with pleasure that there is prospect of a satisfactory edition of these treasure-houses of English Law, for which Mr Pike's recent volume affords an admirable pattern.

Part of the chapter on Bracton, (in which I claim to have accomplished at least some original work, though much remains to be done in the same field), has already appeared, under a slightly altered form, as a separate article in the *Law Quarterly Review* for October, 1885. In that article I have criticized that wonderful production, the edition of Bracton by Sir T. Twiss in the Rolls Series, more freely than it was possible to do in this Essay. John Selden must have had a prophet's pen when he wrote that Bracton has been "basely handled by his editors." But on this edition, or on the foundation of its text, the corrupt edition by Tottell, the

ordinary English student, who cannot collate all the Bracton
MSS., has still to rely.

To these causes we perhaps owe it that the most startling
divergences of opinion on particular parts of the subject exist.
One writer ascribes everything to Roman influence; another
finds Roman materials almost entirely wanting in our law.

> *Hic liber est, in quo quaerit sua dogmata quisque,*
> *Invenit et pariter dogmata quisque sua.*

That patriotic maxim "An Englishman's house is his castle"
is traced back to Justinian's Code, and the Twelve Tables of the
Roman Law are discovered to be "plainly referred to" in the
Sermon on the Mount.

But the interest of the subject to the student of our law
is at least equal to its difficulty, and I only hope that I may
have lessened in some degree the difficulties, for those who
feel the interest. For the rest, the words of Sir Henry
Spelman are still true and to the point : "I wish some worthy
lawyer would read the law diligently, and show the several
heads from which these laws of ours are taken. They beyond
the seas are not only diligent, but very curious in this kind;
but we are all for profit and *Lucrando pane,* taking what we
find at market, without enquiring whence it comes."

T. E. S.

TABLE OF CONTENTS.

LIST OF WORKS CITED.

(Other than Reports and Text Books.)

ANGLO-SAXON LAW : Essays in. Boston, 1876.

ARNOLD, WILHELM : *Ansiedelungen und Wanderungen Deutscher Stämme.* Marburg, 1881.

AZO : *Summa* of. Venice, 1596.

BALE : *Scriptorum Britannorum Centuriae.*

BIENER : *Das Englische Geschwornengericht.*

BIGELOW, M. M. : *Placita Anglo-Normannica.* Lond. 1879.

,, ,, : Leading cases on Torts. Boston, 1875.

BLACKSTONE, SIR W. : Commentaries on the Law of England. 1st ed. Oxford, 1765.

BRACTON, H. DE : *ed.* Tottell. Lond. 1569.

,, : *ed.* Sir T. Twiss. Rolls Series. 6 vols. Lond. 1878—1883.

BRENTANO, L. : On the History and Development of Guilds, and the Origin of Trade Unions. Lond. 1870.

BRICE, SEWARD : Public Worship. Lond. 1875.

BRITTON : *ed.* Nicholls. 2 vols. Oxford, 1865.

CALLIS, R. : Reading on Statute of Sewers ; delivered, 1622 : 2nd ed. Lond. 1686.

CAMPBELL, LORD : Lives of Lord Chief Justices. 2 vols. Lond. 1849.

COKE, SIR E., UPON LITTLETON : ed. Hargrave and Butler. 2 vols. 19th ed. Lond. 1832.

COKE, SIR. E : Institutes. 4 vols. Lond. 1817.

COLLYER, J. : on Partnership. Lond. 1840.

COOTE, H. C : A neglected Fact in English History. Lond. 1864.

,, : Romans in Britain. Lond. 1878.

,, : Ordinances of the Secular Gilds of London. Lond. 1871.

,, : Ecclesiastical Practice. Lond. 1847.

,, : Probate Practice. 8th ed. Lond. 1878.

CORPUS JURIS CANONICI : A. L. Richter. 2nd edit. by Friedberg, 2 vols. Leipsic, 1876—1881.

COWELL, JOHN : *Institutiones Juris Anglicani ad seriem Institutionum Imperialium Digestae.* Camb. 1605.

DOCTOR AND STUDENT : 18th ed. Lond. 1815.

DOMAT, J. : *Loix Civiles dans leur Ordre Naturel.* 2 vols. Paris, 1777.

DUCK, A. : *De Usu et Authoritate Juris Civilis Romani.* Lond. 1679.

ELLIS, SIR H. : Introduction to Domesday. 2 vols. Lond. 1833.

ELTON, C. : Origins of English History. Lond. 1882.

FINLASON, W. F. : ed. Reeves' History of the English Law, *q. v.*

FITZHERBERT, A. : Grand Abridgment. 1516.

FLETA : 1618.

FORTESCUE, SIR J. : *De Laudibus Legum Angliae.* Lond. 1616.

FOSS, E. : The Judges of England. 9 vols. Lond. 1848—1864.

FREEMAN, E. A. : Norman Conquest. 5 vols. Oxford, 1867—1876.

FULBECK, W.: A Conference of the Civil, Canon and Common Law of England. 1601.

GLANVIL, R. DE : *Tractatus de Legibus et Consuetudinibus Angliae.* Lond. 1673.

„   „   : translation of, by Beames. Lond. 1812.

GODOLPHIN, J. : View of the Admiralty Jurisdiction. Lond. 1661.

GÜTERBOCK, C. : Bracton and his relation to the Roman Law : trans. and ed. Brinton Coxe. Philadelphia, 1866.

HALE, SIR M. : History of the Common Law : pub. 1713 : 5th ed. Lond. 1820.

HANSSEN : *Agrar-Historische Abhandhlungen.* Leipsic, 1880.

HARGRAVE, F. : Law Tracts. Lond. 1787.

HARTWIG : *Untersuchungen über die ersten Anfänge des Gildewesens.* Gottingen. 1863.

HOLMES, O. W. : The Common Law. Lond. 1882.

HOUARD, D. : *Traités sur les Coutumes Anglo-Normandes.* 4 vols. Paris, 1776.

IRVING, D. : Introduction to the Study of the Civil Law. Lond. 1837.

JUSTINIAN : *Digesta,* ed. T. Mommsen. Berlin, 1870.

„   : *Codex,* ed. Krueger. Berlin, 1877.

KEMBLE, J. M. : The Saxons in England : ed. Birch. Lond. 1876.

KENNY, C. S. : On Primogeniture. Lond. and Camb. 1878.

„   „   : On Effects of Marriage on Property. Lond. and Camb. 1879.

LANDAU : *Die Territorien in Bezug auf ihre Bildung und ihre Entwicklung.* Hamburg, 1854.

LITTLETON : On Tenures. ed. Tomlins. Lond. 1841.

LOFTIE, W. J. : History of London. 2 vols. Lond. 1883.

LONG, G. Discourses introductory to Jurisprudence and Civil Law. Lond. 1847.

LYNDWOOD : *Provinciale, seu Constitutiones Angliae.* Paris, 1505. Oxford, 1679.

MACKELDEY : Modern Civil Law, ed. Kaufmann. Lond. 1845.

MADOX, T. : History of the Exchequer. 2 vols. Lond. 1769.

MAINE, SIR H. S : Ancient Law.   8th ed. Lond. 1880.

    „   „   : Village Communities in the East and West.   Lond. 1871.

    „   „   : Influence of Roman Law.   Cambridge Essays.   1856.

MALYNES, G. : *Lex Mercatoria.*   1st ed. 1622, 3rd ed. 1685, Lond.

MEITZEN, A. : *Georg Hanssen, als Agrar-Historiker.*   Tübingen, 1881.

MIRROUR OF JUSTICE : by Andrew Horne.   Lond. 1642.

PALGRAVE, SIR F. : Rise and Progress of English Commonwealth.   Lond. 1832.

PANNIER : *Ruines de la Coutume de Normandie.*   Rouen, 1856.

PARDESSUS, J. M. : *Collection de Lois Maritimes.*   4 vols.   Paris, 1828.

PARK, ALAN : Insurance.   7th ed.   Lond. 1806.

PEARSON, C. H. : History of England in Early and Middle Ages.   2 vols. Lond. 1867.

PIKE, L. O. : Preface to Year-books, 12 & 13 Edw. III. Rolls Series, Lond. 1885.

POLLOCK, F. : Land Laws.   Lond. 1883.

POTHIER, R. J. : *Des obligations:* trans. and ed. Evans.   2 vols.   Lond. 1806.

RECORD COMMISSION :

    Ancient Laws and Institutes of England.   ed. Thorpe.   Lond. 1840.

    Ancient Laws and Institutes of Wales.   ed. A. Owen.   Lond. 1841.

    General Introduction to Domesday Book, by Sir H. Ellis.   2 vols. 1833.

REEVES, J. : History of English Law.   3 vols.   ed. Finlason.   Lond. 1869.

REPORT OF CITY GUILDS COMMISSION : Parl. Papers, 1884.   R. 4073.

ROLLS SERIES :

    No. 70.   Bracton, ed. Sir T. Twiss.   6 vols.   1878—1883.

    No. 55.   Black Book of Admiralty.   ed. Sir T. Twiss.   4 vols.   1871 —1876.

    No. 51.   R. de Hoveden.   ed. Stubbs.   4 vols.   1868—1871.

SAVIGNY, F. C. DE : *Geschichte des Romischen Rechts im Mittelalter.* Heidelberg.   1815—1831.

SEEBOHM, F. : English Village Community.   Lond. 1883.

SELDEN, JOHN : *Dissertatio ad Fletam.*   Lond. 1618.   Trans. by Kelham. Lond. 1771.

    „   „   : Notes on Fortescue, *de Laudibus.*

SHELFORD, L. : on Marriage.   Lond. 1841.

SOMNER, W. : on Gavelkind.   Lond. 1660.

SPELMAN, SIR H. : *Archaeologus seu Glossarium.*   Lond. 1687.

    „   „   : The Law Terms : Posthumous Works.   ed. Gibson. Lond. 1723.

    „   „   : *Concilia in Re Ecclesiarum Orbis Britannici.*   Lond. 1639.

SPENCE, G. : Equitable Jurisdiction of the Court of Chancery. 2 vols. Lond. 1849.

STAUNFORD, SIR W. : Pleas of the Crown. Lond. 1607.

STEPHEN, SIR J. F. : History of Criminal Law. 3 vols. Lond. 1883.

STUBBS, W. : Constitutional History. 3 vols. Oxford, 1874.

    „   : Select Charters. 3rd ed. Oxford. 1876.

    „   : Preface to *R. de Hoveden*. Rolls Series. 4 vols. 1868—1871.

THORPE, B. : Ancient Laws and Institutes of England : Record Commission. Lond. 1840.

VACARIUS : Article on, in Penny Encyclopaedia. Lond. 1843.

VINOGRADOFF, P. : "Text of Bracton." Law Quarterly Review. April, 1885.

WAITZ, G. : *Deutsche Verfassungs Geschichte*. Kiel, 1865—1866.

WARREN, S : Introduction to Law Studies. 3rd ed. 2 vols. Lond. 1863.

WENCK, C. F. C. : *Magister Vacarius, Primus Juris Romani in Angliae Professor*. Leipsic. 1820.

WILDA : *Das Gildewesen in Mittelalter*. Halle, 1831.

WRIGHT, SIR M. : On Tenures. 2nd ed. Lond. 1734.

WRIGHT, T. : Municipal Privileges under the Anglo-Saxons. Archaeologia, XXXII. pp. 298—311. Lond. 1847.

ZOUCH, R. : Jurisdiction of Admiralty of England asserted. Lond. 1686.

THE INFLUENCE OF THE ROMAN LAW

ON

THE LAW OF ENGLAND.

"Tu regere imperio populos, Romane, memento."

INTRODUCTION.

ANY discussion of the influence exercised in England by the Roman Law will naturally fall into two divisions, separated by the arrival in the year 1143 of Vacarius on our shores in the train of Archbishop Theobald[1], and his lectures on Roman Law at Oxford in and after 1149; for these events, which in European history form part of the current of Roman influence which sprang from the enthusiastic studies of the Law School at Bologna in the 12th century[2], begin a new era in the history of English law and of its connexion with the legal system of Rome. We have then in our survey to deal with two great periods. Investigating in the first place, if such a search be possible, what traces of its influence the Roman occupation of Britain had left on its inhabitants, their institutions and customs, we may study both the law before the Conquest, and that law as influenced by the Norman invasion, to ascertain, if possible, how far its leading features at either period are attributable to Norman or to Teutonic influences. The period is one of custom, not of written law; of vagueness rather than of precision; and it will afford no matter for surprise if in the legal obscurity of

---

[1] Kaufman's Mackeldey, p. 72.   [2] Ibid. p. 66.

those early centuries we find very little ground for confident assertion in matters peculiarly difficult.

With our second period we find more light. From the teaching of Vacarius in 1149 we pass at once to authoritative text books by masters of the law. The treatises of Ranulph Glanvill, Justiciar, composed in 1190, and of Sir Henry de Bracton, one of the King's judges, written in the few years before 1259, the works called Briton and Fleta, compiled about 1290, the Year books, the legislation of Edward I., all combine to illumine the dawn of the historical period of English law. Though great industry, ingenuity, and learning may yet be necessary to unravel the tangled skein, we are not left without material for such a task. We are not asked to make our legal bricks without straw, to compile our laws without sources. We are able to trace, under the guidance of Spence[1], the rise of the Court of Chancery, Roman to the backbone; we can study the efforts of the great Lord Mansfield to construct a scientific code of Mercantile Law on principles largely Roman, and we can follow through the Ecclesiastical Courts the learning of the clergy in the laws of the mighty Rome.

To the first of our periods, however, we may now turn, if not with hope, at least with the knowledge that where success is all but impossible, failure has in it nothing of disgrace.

Equitable Jurisdiction of the Court of Chancery, Lond. 1849.

PART I.

ROMAN INFLUENCES ON ENGLISH LAW BEFORE THE COMING OF VACARIUS.

CHAPTER I.

THE SOURCES OF THE ROMAN LAW.

THE Romans under Julius Caesar landed on these shores in B.C. 55, and in A.D. 43 the serious conquest of Britain commenced under the Emperor Claudius: the Roman legions were finally withdrawn in A.D. 410 under the Emperor Honorius. During this period, while the adventurers or puppets who ruled the Western Empire exercised very little direct control over Britain, it is probable that the greater part of the island was governed on the Roman provincial system, and the Roman law was administered with more or less strictness. Into the details of this system we do not propose to enter. " The details of the later Roman Provincial system, and of the economic condition of the German and British provinces, remain so obscure, even after the labours of Mommsen, Marquardt and Madvig, that he who attempts to build a bridge across the gulf of the Teutonic Conquests between Roman and English institutions still builds it somewhat at a venture[1]." The nature of the Roman provincial government is too obscure, the Roman law is too well known, to justify any lengthy exposition here of either of them. We may however remark that it is recorded by Dio Cassius[2] that the great Papinian, the Fearne of Roman Law, whose works it was

---

[1] Seebohm on *English Village Community*, Lond. 1883. Pref. p. xii. Mr Coote in his *Romans in Britain*, London, 1878, has attempted such a reconstruction, but with more ingenuity than success.

[2] Selden, *Dissertatio ad Fletam*, c. 4 § 3. Duck, *De Usu*, II. 8, 2. 4.

1—2

presumption to profess to understand under three years' study, not only accompanied the Emperor Severus to Britain, but also filled the judicial office in the City of York, evidently administering the Imperial law in Britain.

We may accept it as probable that, for the century or so preceding the withdrawal of the legions, the actual influence of Rome on Britain was very slight, whilst the withdrawal of those legions in A.D. 410 did not mean the entire withdrawal of Roman institutions, customs, and culture. But the vestiges of Roman influence can hardly have endured with any permanence in face of the anarchy of invasion which swept over them. The incursions of Teutonic invaders had been frequent even during the Roman occupation, and that part of the coast exposed to their ravages had acquired the name of the *Littus Saxonicum*[1], with special officers to guard it, as early as A.D. 300. There are traces also of the permanent transplanting of certain Gaulish or Teutonic tribes as legionaries in Britain during the Roman era[2], a fact not without its importance in view of subsequent investigations. But historical materials are very scanty[3], as authentic records entirely disappear from A.D. 418 to A.D. 473. It is clear that during the last half of the 5th century the Saxon invasions resulted in settlements of some degree of permanence and power; Hengist in Kent, Ella in Sussex, Cerdic in Wessex, established themselves in force. During the 6th century the old settlements grew into Kingdoms, and new conquests were made in Essex, Northumbria and East Anglia. In the year 600, we obtain the first written code of English Laws, which purports to be issued by Ethelbert, King of Kent[4]. This code (which, with the other Kentish laws, is only preserved to us by the *Textus Roffensis*, a MS. of the 12th century) contains 90 short clauses, many of which are of great obscurity. It is clear that as a code of law the document is utterly inadequate, and presupposes a vast mass of custom regulating the ordinary relations of life.

---

[1] According to Palgrave (*Commonwealth*, pp. 359, 384), on account of the Saxons already settled there. The Bishop of Chester prefers the explanation given in the text *Hist.* i. 59).

[2] Palgrave, i. 355, 356, 377.

[3] Elton, *Origins of History*.

[4] Thorpe, *Ancient Laws and Institutes of England*, p. 1.

Many of the clauses[1] relate to the particular fines to be paid for damage to the person, which are set out with great minuteness: e.g.

§ 58. If there be a bruise...a shilling. § 59. If the bruise be black in a part not covered with the clothes, let *bot* be made with 30 *scaetts*. § 60. If it be covered with the clothes, let *bot* be made with 20 *scaetts*.

About the year 680 we have a second Kentish code[2] of Kings Hlothaere and Edric, composed of 16 clauses, which relate mainly to procedure, and recite that the two kings "augmented the laws which their elders had before made by these dooms." In 696 a further Kentish code[3], issued by Wihtraed, recites that "the great men decreed, with the suffrages of all, these dooms, and added them to the lawful customs of the Kentish men." This code consists of 28 clauses, and has, as compared with its forerunners, a distinctly Christian and clerical character.

The first Wessex code appears about the year 700 in the shape of Dooms issued by King Ina[4] "with the counsel and teaching of his Witan." These consist of 76 clauses, and, when taken in connexion with the laws of Alfred, give much greater insight into the early law. But for a period of 300 years after the Roman legions left Britain, 300 years filled with wars and rumours of wars, raids of Angles and Saxons, Picts and Scots, bloodshed and burning, there are, with the exception of three scanty codes of one small kingdom, scarcely any materials for even the knowledge of early law and custom, let alone any satisfactory traces of its history. The Roman system is for nearly 400 years exposed to such an ordeal of fire and sword that it would be indeed strange were any considerable part of its principles to survive in a recognizable shape.

The Laws of King Alfred[5] commence with nearly 50 sections representing the Mosaic law, followed by 77 actual English laws of considerable importance. Alfred has himself described his method of framing them as follows[6]: "I then, Alfred, King, gathered these together and commanded many of those to be written which our forefathers held, those which to me seemed

---

[1] E.g. §§ 32—72.
[2] Thorpe, p. 11.
[3] Ibid. p. 16.
[4] Thorpe, p. 45. Ina, A.D. 688-725.
[5] Circa, A.D. 900. Thorpe, p. 20.
[6] Thorpe, p. 27.

good, and many of those which seemed to me not good, I rejected them by the counsel of my Witan, and in other wise commanded them to be holden: for I durst not venture to set down in writing much of my own, for it was unknown to me what of it would please them who should come after us. But those things which I met with, either of the days of Ina my kinsman, or of Offa[1], King of the Mercians, or of Ethelberht,...those which seemed to me the rightest, those I have here gathered together and rejected the others."

Here, as throughout the early history, we are forced to recognise that the written laws are but crystallizations on the surface of a mass of custom, which varies in nature with race and place, and which holds in solution all the real institutions of the English people. The possible elements in fusion have up to this time been: (1) British or Celtic, (2) Roman, (3) Teutonic. Each tribe that landed from the German warships brought its peculiar customs to blend into "those things which our forefathers held;" while, fourthly, it is probable that some institutions and customs of South German tribes, who had come more under Roman influence than their North German brethren, have had influence on at least the English Land system[2].

From the beginning of the 9th century the *Dane-lagu* brings a new element to the compound, that Dane-law which the Northmen who had settled after successful raids in the North-east of England obeyed, as embodying the customs they had brought from their Northern homes. And these customs took form in written legislation in the "Peace of Alfred and Guthrum" in 878, and the Laws of Edward and Guthrum[3] (*circa* A.D. 900). Not to elaborate this account of our scanty sources, we have the Laws of Edward, of Athelstan, of Edmund, of Edgar (especially his famous ordinance of the Hundred)[4], and of King Ethelred[5]. This latter code is more lengthy than those of Ethelred's predecessors, and shows many traces of clerical influence.

---

[1] These laws have not survived except as embodied in Alfred's code.

[2] Seebohm, *English Village Community*, see *infra*, pp. 30, *et seq*.

[3] Thorpe, pp. 66, 71.

[4] Ibid. pp. 68—119.

[5] Ibid. p. 119.

The Laws of Cnut[1] again indicate the reintroduction of the Norse element. There also exist several detached documents of some importance, such as the *Penitentials* of Canterbury and York[2]; the *Rectitudines Singularum Personarum*[3], containing much information as to ranks and status; the Dooms of the City of London[4]; detached fragments on Oaths, and on *Were*[5] and other similar sources. Some information as to customs and institutions is gained from the wills, land-grants and records of suits collected by Thorpe, but any account of Anglo-Saxon law founded on these sources alone cannot but exhibit large *hiatus*. These gaps may be to some extent conjecturally supplied by collation with the written sources of law of the kindred German tribes on the continent[6].

Some evidence as to British and Saxon customs may also be obtained from the laws of Wales, although these only exist in MSS. of the 13th and 14th centuries[7], and purport to date from the codification of Welsh custom by Howel Dha about the year 950. But when these laws are put forward as strong evidence to show the customs of Roman Britons, it will not be sufficient, as is done by Mr Finlason[8], to extract those small parts which suggest a Roman origin, while entirely omitting to consider those portions which, while different from what we know of Saxon institutions, are also completely unlike the Roman system on which they are supposed to be founded. The Welsh land and family law especially suggest, in the first place, that Roman civilization had either never very deeply affected British institutions, or that, if it had, the traces of its influence had been destroyed during the anarchy that followed the Roman withdrawal. While, secondly, if the Welsh institutions are unlike the Saxon in important points, either the ancient British system has been modified in Wales in an entirely different way to that in which it has changed in Saxon England, a result which can

---

[1] Thorpe, p. 153.

[2] Ibid. p. 277.

[3] Ibid. p. 185.

[4] Ibid. pp. 97, 127.

[5] Ibid. pp. 75, 76.

[6] The Visigothic, Salic, Burgundian, Ripuarian, Allemannic, Bara-rian, Frisian, Saxon, and Thuringian, Law Collections; originating between the 5th and 8th centuries. Mackeldey, Kaufmann, p. 78.

[7] *Ancient Laws and Customs of Wales:* Record Commission.

[8] Finlason's Preface to Reeves.

only be due to the laws and customs of the Saxon invaders. or, which is far more probable, while British customs have survived in Wales with but small change, the Saxon invaders have in England altogether replaced them by their own.

To put the argument in another form, the Welsh land and family law is entirely different, as far as we can gather, from the laws of the Romans and Anglo-Saxons on kindred subjects. Now either the Roman law was the source of both Welsh and Saxon law or it was not. If it was the source of neither, *cadit quaestio*. The question is also answered if it was the source of Welsh law only, the Saxon system being independent, while it can only have been the source of Saxon law by being also the origin of the law of the Welsh or Romanized Britons, which forms the alleged connecting link between the 5th and 7th centuries. If then it was the source of both, the two laws, Welsh and Saxon, had on important points become entirely unlike. Now the law of Wales, i.e. of the Romanized Britons, was subject to no special disturbing influences but the retreat before the Saxon invasion, while the law of England was, or may have been, largely affected by the importation of Teutonic customs and institutions in the Saxon keels. From every point of view therefore, the dissimilarities as well as the similarities of Welsh to Roman and Saxon law, should be included in our study.

But from that study, so widened, our greatest historian expects but little. "If," says Mr Stubbs[1], "the agreement between the local machinery of the Welsh laws and the Anglo-Saxon usages were much closer than it has ever been shown to be, if the most ancient remains of Welsh law could be shown not to be much younger in date than the best established customs of Angle and Saxon jurisprudence, the fact would still remain that the historical civilization is English and not Celtic. The *cantred* of Howel Dha may answer to the *Hundred* of Edgar, but the *Hundred* of Edgar is distinctly the *hundred* of the Franks...The Welsh may in late times have adopted the institutions from the English, or in all the nations the common

---

[1] *Const. Hist.* I. 63.

features may be the signs of a common stage of civilization; but the kinship is between the English and German forms."

The early sources of our investigation have been dwelt on at this length in order to show the difficulties of our task and the slight materials on which our conclusions must be based. Several of the sources are unfortunately not to be depended on as evidence. Thus the so-called "Laws of Edward the Confessor[1]," which purport to be the result of the inquiries made in or after the 4th year of the Conqueror through 12 sworn men from each shire, bear traces on their face of a much later date, and are considered by modern historians, as possibly founded on a report of the jurors of 1070, but in their existing form not earlier than 1180 and put forward by Glanvill[2]. A passing reference may also be made to the "Mirrour of Justice," a work of the time of Edward I. purporting to give authentic information as to the laws of Alfred, and information to be found nowhere else. Of this it is sufficient to say here that Palgrave considers it "a curious specimen of the apocrypha of the law[3]," and Sir J. F. Stephen treats the part relating to Alfred as "merely an invention[4]." It is moreover an undoubted fact that many of the existing charters are monkish forgeries for the purposes of subsequent suits.

Though it is unnecessary and even misleading to draw a definite line between law before and after the Conquest, since on the one hand Norman influences had been at work during the reign of Edward the Confessor, and on the other hand the customary law was not changed in any direct or immediate way by the Conqueror, yet as undoubtedly the development of feudalism under Ranulf Flambard and the changes in procedure wrought by the introduction of the sworn inquest and the procedure by appeal did affect English law, the Conquest forms a convenient halting ground in our first period.

We have thus enumerated the English sources of laws and charters, and the extra-English sources of Continental Teutonic, and Welsh laws, from which the early law of England may be

---

[1] Thorpe, p. 190.

[2] Stubbs: Preface to R. de Hoveden, II. 44.

[3] *Commonwealth*, Proofs, p. 113.

[4] Stephen, *Hist. Crim. Law*, I. 52.

gathered. It only remains to state briefly what Roman law was available as a modifying, (as opposed to an originating), influence during the period before the Conquest.

The legal compilations of Justinian did not come into existence until A.D. 565: prior to these, the only systematic collections were the *Codices Gregorianus* and *Hermogenianus*[1], both compiled about A.D. 450, and the *Codex Theodosianus*, published in A.D. 438; and these, besides being published after the Roman legions had left Britain, only extended in operation over the Eastern Empire. This, the Justinianean body of law appears to have had no force in Western Europe[2] and indeed, with the exception of a partial and temporary application in Italy, to have been almost unknown until the revival of its study by the Bolognese Law School about the year 1150.

The Collections of law in the Western Empire, which was overrun by Goths, Vandals and Huns, were as follows:

I.[3] The *Edictum Theodorici*, issued at Rome, A.D. 500, and imposed on the conquered Romans, and conquering Ostrogoths. Though this was derived almost entirely from the Roman Law, and especially from the *Codex Theodosianus*, the sources were used so arbitrarily and with such freedom, that the character of the Roman Law can scarcely be traced in them.

II. The *Breviarium Alaricianum*, current among the Visigoths; published in 506 by Alaric, and also derived, with modifications, from Roman sources.

III. The *Lex Romana Burgundiorum*, published between the years 517—534; and largely compiled from Roman Law; intended for the Roman subjects of the Burgundian Empire.

This Roman law, ante-Justinianean in character, and much altered in the different collections[4], was the only source, which could modify, by Romanizing, the Saxon institutions. Into the laborious task of tracing these modifications, if any, we cannot enter in detail. It may suffice at present to have pointed

---

[1] Mackeldey: Kaufmann, p. 45.
[2] Selden *ad Fletam*, c. VI. § 1. Mackeldey, pp. 37, 64.
[3] Mackeldey, p. 48.
[4] Selden *ad Fletam*, c. V. § 5.

out that the comparison, until the 12th century, is not with the *Corpus Juris* of Justinian, but with a much mutilated code of earlier date, largely added to from barbarian sources[1].

[1] The Roman Law never seems to have been very popular among the early Western Nations. King Cindaswinthus, in A.D. 650, prohibits by express edict the use of the Roman Law among the Wisigoths. Selden *ad Fletam*, v. 5.

CHAPTER II.

THE CLAIMS OF THE ROMAN LAW.

THERE are two ways in which the influence of the Roman on the English Law previous to the 12th century may be discussed. One, and the most exhaustive, method would give a complete account of the Saxon Polity and Law, comparing it step by step with its supposed Roman prototype. Such a method, while most satisfactory if thoroughly carried out, would far exceed the bounds or possibilities of this Essay. The other and more feasible course would set out the claims that have been made for Roman Law by its most pronounced advocates, with the evidence by which those claims are supported, and would endeavour by independent criticism and investigation to adopt or reject them, or to add to or diminish their extent. For this task fortunately materials exist, and such a method does not appear an unfair one. It is not pretended that the fact that energetic advocates have not ventured to claim some particular part of the Anglo-Saxon polity as of Roman origin proves conclusively that no such claim can fairly be made. That even so zealous and daring an advocate as Mr Finlason[1] does not allege the English criminal procedure to be Roman in its source, need not preclude us from attempting to give a few conclusive proofs that its leading features are purely Teutonic. But we can thus concentrate our attention on those points for which a Roman origin is specially asserted.

The writers who make definite and precise allegations as to the Roman influences at work during the period before the

[1] Finlason's Reeves, p. 2, note. Mr *Romans in Britain*, pp. 303—313. Coote however does make the claim.

Conquest are few.   Sir Fras. Palgrave[1] is mainly concerned with his unfortunate theory of the English kings as Roman Emperors. He however declares the feudal system to be partly Roman[2] in its origin, and asserts that the Craft-Gilds descend in a direct line from the Roman *collegia opificum*[3] : though he admits that only scanty traces of Roman Municipal institutions can be discerned, and that we cannot, as in Gaul, deduce the political existence of Cities from the Roman era[4].   Noticing of course the undoubted fact of the Roman and ecclesiastical parentage of Wills[5], he also traces a rather shadowy line of descent from Rome for English parliamentary proceedings[6].   Mr H. C. Coote, in a small work entitled, *A Neglected Fact in English History*, afterwards expanded into his larger work, *Romans in Britain*, makes what the Bishop of Chester calls " a very learned and ingenious" contribution to the question, which certainly deserves more than a passing notice[7].   He finds the chief traces of Roman influence in : (1) the division into privileged and unprivileged classes ; *thegnas* and *ceorlas* : (2) the land system, especially the *trinoda necessitas*, and an alleged right of resumption, (3) the Municipal system, (4) the general civilisation and institutions of the people.   Any argument that Mr Coote urges demands the most careful attention, though the ingenuity with which he makes bricks without straw, and describes institutions without evidence, almost conceals the entire lack of foundation for some of his statements.

Mr Finlason is more daring, though his materials hardly warrant the boldness of his claims.   In editing in 1869 the learned work of Mr Reeves, who, writing during the last century, had taken the purely English view of the common law, he found himself constantly opposed to the results arrived at by his author, and was therefore led to sum up his own views in a Preface of 128 pages, avowedly directed to maintain the theory of the prevailing influence of Roman Law in this country.   The

[1] Palgrave's *Rise and Progress of English Commonwealth.*
[2] Ibid. 77; Proofs, p. 205.
[3] Ibid. 628.
[4] Ibid. 629.
[5] Ibid. ; Proofs, 358.
[6] Ibid.; Proofs, 418.
[7] Mr Coote's lack of acquaintance with the recent German investigations into early English civilisation is however very marked.

conclusions in the essay are plainly stated though it is sometimes a little difficult to discover on what evidence they have been reached. We cannot but notice the great importance Mr Finlason attaches to the "Mirrour of Justice," of whose genuineness he apparently entertains no suspicion. There seems now a complete concurrence of opinion among historical students[1] as to the apocryphal character of this work, so far as it professes to be anything more than a private compilation, made in the reign of Edward I. by Andrew Horne, Town Clerk of London, Citizen and Fishmonger. It has been alleged that the account of Saxon Law is taken from some earlier work to which Horne had access in the Guildhall Library, but such a work is no longer in existence and the materials supposed to be derived from it are so curious as to render its actual existence at any time very improbable. Horne continually cites the "Rolls of Alfred," a set of documents probably invented by analogy to the then-existing Pipe and other Rolls. Statements like the following:—"He (Alfred) hanged Markes, because[2] he judged During to death by 12 men who were not sworn : he hanged Thurston because he judged Thuringer to death by a verdict of inquest taken *ex officio* without inquest joined: he hanged Friburne because he judged Harpen to die whereas the jury were in doubt of the verdict, for in doubtful cases one ought rather to save than to condemn :"—statements so contrary to all that is known, from authentic sources, of Saxon procedure, do not suggest that any reliance is to be placed on the number of strange names of judges, and the confidence with which their alleged decisions are cited. Neither does the manner in which Mr Finlason deals with the statements of the work increase our confidence in his own power of estimating evidence. Two instances will suffice. The *Mirrour* says (s. 22) :—"Thurmond ordained that criminal actions for revenge should cease at the year's end": on which Mr Finlason comments :—"a passage which is evidently most ancient, for the name of the judge is Saxon, and the notion of any limitation of criminal prosecution was not known in later times[3]." This method of proof would

---

[1] Palgrave, Proofs, 113. Stephen, *Hist. Crim. Law*, I. 52, note.

[2] Cited in Finlason's Reeves, pref. p. 64.

[3] Ibid. pref. p. 64, note.

demonstrate the antiquity of any decision, ascribed to a judge with a Saxon name, and out of accord with all known law. In other words, it assumes the *Mirrour* to be an accurate work, and then proves the antiquity of the statement by the fact that it is inaccurate as applied to any period of which we have any knowledge. But this is not all: our advocate, having proved the antiquity of the decision, performs the same kind office for Thurmond himself, as follows[1]: "Now Thurmond was clearly neither a Saxon nor a Norman king, neither was he a judge after the Conquest, for the names of the judges since then are known. He was therefore (!) some Saxon judge or sheriff." Surely there is another and more probable alternative; he is an altogether imaginary person. But Mr Finlason, assuming his existence, proves his antiquity by showing he did not exist during the times when records of the judges are available.

The *Mirrour* also cites a number of decisions in the present tense; "Turgis saith"; "Billing saith", in commenting on which Mr Finlason excels himself in logical acumen[2]:—"'Billing saith', as if the judge were still alive at the time it was written." Billing is proved by the above method to be of great antiquity; consequently his decision is ancient; therefore the Mirrour was written in times of great antiquity, the writer remarking of a recent decision, "Billing saith." This would prove every book in which occurs the common phrase, "Lord Eldon lays down"; "Lord Mansfield says"; to have been written in the time of Lord Eldon or Lord Mansfield; while to apply it to the very work before us, Mr Finlason's Preface can be by his own method conclusively proved to have been written in the times of Lord Hale, Montesquieu, Guizot, Lingard, and St Augustine, all of whom are cited in the present tense in the same manner in which the apocryphal Turgis, Billing and their brethren are cited in the "Mirror of Justice."

Leaving however this "curious specimen of the apocrypha of the law" as Palgrave calls it, and with it a large portion of Mr Finlason's evidence, let us consider the grounds on which this most daring advocate of Roman Law bases his claims. His methods of procedure appear to be two. We have first the

---

[1] Finl. Reeves, p. 65.   [2] Ibid. p. 63, note.

proof by negation : the English Law must be Roman, because there is no other source from which it can have come. Apparently from some sense of weakness in this line of argument, we have the second method, consisting of positive statements as to specific branches of the law attributable to Roman sources.

The first method is carried out by Mr Finlason with great daring. The question is as follows. Let us assume a Romanized civilization existing in Britain in A.D. 400 : the next 200 years, the Roman legions having withdrawn, are filled with anarchy, and the invasions of North German tribes, who had in Germany well defined institutions and customs of their own, which have had a great influence in continental history. In A.D. 600 the first written laws remaining to us are composed, and by A.D. 850 the island has become tranquil and united. A system of law is then found in existence which can be compiled with some precision from written laws, references to customs, and our knowledge of continental legal codes. This system has been alleged to bear a distinctly Teutonic stamp. Mr Finlason desires to prove it of Roman origin.

He first disposes of the aboriginal Britons : "That the Britons were in a state of barbarism on the arrival of the Romans is clear...and it is idle and absurd to talk of their laws[1]." The maintenance of Roman institutions after the departure of the legions is then asserted with considerable confidence when we consider the almost entire absence of evidence as to Britain in the 5th century[2]. But the coming of the Saxons is an undoubted fact, and their peculiar institutions can hardly be denied. How does Mr Finlason deal with them? The method is simple. "The Saxons, being little better than savages, had no civilized institutions of their own......they did not bring any institutions or laws worthy of the name with them. They brought only rude barbarian usages, as will be seen in their written laws, which express for the most part their own usages....It is manifest that they created nothing civilized[3]." Noting the admission that the written laws are

---

[1] Reeves, Finl. pref. p. 1, note.

[2] Elton, *Origins of English History*, pp. 358—362.

[3] Reeves, Finl. pref. pp. 39, 40, 42, 44. The whole passage (pp. 39—44) is curious.

not Roman, but Teutonic, we find Mr Finlason recognizing the existence of a large mass of custom; "the most valuable rights of the people were embodied in customs, which were unwritten[1]." Are these then Teutonic or Roman in origin? Mr Finlason's answer is extraordinary. After admitting that much unwritten law was mentioned in, and its existence implied by, the written law, he continues: "but its origin is not to be found in any of the written laws, and it therefore could only have been derived from the Roman law[2]." Why? we wonderingly ask: and the answer seems to be that as the Saxons were barbarians and brought nothing worthy, in Mr Finlason's opinion, of the name of law, any system of unwritten law, which Mr Finlason may subsequently think worthy of the name, can only have arisen from Roman sources. Such an argument suggests a great ignorance of historical progress, and lack of appreciation of the value and fertility of early customs and institutions, "barbarous" though they may seem to an enlightened Romanist. The whole of the argument requires the assumption that no Saxon customs had in them even the germs of later institutions, an assumption incorrect, as Mr Finlason admits, with regard to criminal law, and without foundation, as will be seen, in many other portions of the English legal system.

For, having dealt with the negative side of Mr Finlason's argument, we may now turn to his positive claims. Though these are often of a shadowy nature, involving the assertion that certain very general principles pervade both laws and must have been derived by one from the other, we yet find our author definitely committed to the claim of a Roman origin for, *inter alia*[3]: I. The Manorial system. II. The Municipal system. III. A regular judicature and judicial tribunals with skilled judges of the law and jurors, or sworn *judices facti*, for the matters of fact. In short, as Mr Finlason vaguely puts it: "the general scope of our civil procedure and the whole scope of our law, so far as it relates to civil matters[4]." IV. The political organization, and divisions of the country.

[1] Finl. Reeves, Pref. p. 65.
[2] Ibid. p. 5, note.
[3] Finl. Reeves, Pref. p. 92; Text,
p. 2, note.
[4] Finl. Reeves, I. 2, note.

With these specific claims and those of other writers, notably Mr Coote[1] and Mr Seebohm, we may best deal by treating the Anglo-Saxon Law, under four heads, as follows:

    I.   Land Law.

    II.   Family Law.

    III.   Law of Courts and Procedure, Civil and Criminal.

    IV.   Law of Organization: (*a*) Territorial.

                            (*b*) Municipal.

---

[1] Mr Coote has summarised his matured positions in the Preface to *The Romans in Britain*, pp. vi. viii., and in the Introduction, pp. 2—5.

CHAPTER III.

ROMAN LAW IN THE EARLY LAND LAW.

THE researches of recent German writers and of Mr Seebohm have thrown a flood of new light on the English and German land systems, and Mr Finlason's remarks on this point have become out of date. He laid special stress on the resemblance of the *folc-land* to the *ager publicus*, on the system of military services, and on the connexion of the manor, with its *villani* and manorial court, with the Roman *villa* and *coloni*[1]. On this point he contented himself with a simple statement that, "the Saxons established themselves in the manors and adopted the manorial system[2]." There was, he said, no trace in the written laws of the establishment of such a system by the Saxons. The Latin translation of the Laws of Ina used the terms "*colonus vel villanus*[3]," the original words being *geneat* and *ceorl*, and this choice of words in translation was supposed to prove the Roman character of the institution[4]. There was also a most extraordinary argument that because copyholds were held of the manor "by immemorial usage", therefore manors were of Roman origin, an argument which, if it proves any thing, would prove that manors originated with the aboriginal Britons. But on this point we may safely leave Mr Finlason for conclusions more modern both in date and spirit.

The real question in dispute among historical students at the present day is as to the origin of manors[5]. Were the village

---

[1] Reeves, I. 10, note.
[2] Ibid. Pref. p. 46.
[3] *Laws of Ina*, Thorpe, §§ 19, 22, 40, 42.
[4] Reeve, Pref. p. 51.
[5] Seebohm, *English Village Community*, Pref. p. ix.

communities living in the *hams* and *tuns* of England at the out-set of English history free village communities, or communities in serfdom under a manorial lordship ? If the first alternative is accepted, English history and the English land law begin with free village communities, gradually degenerating into mediaeval serfdom; and, as the free village community is an essentially Teutonic institution, the germs of the English land system are seen to be Teutonic, and not Roman. If, on the other hand, English history commences with a population, perhaps themselves freemen, tilling the soil in serfdom to a lord, and gradually freeing themselves from servile tenure, it has been suggested, though the evidence is not very clear, that such a system, similar to the later manorial one, has elements in it derived, in all probability, from the Roman system of *coloni*.

Until quite recently the weight of opinion has been in favour of the former view. G. L. von Maurer in Germany united the system of common husbandry which he found there, and the village community which inhabited it, into the conception of the "Mark," as the unit of Teutonic civilization. Kemble, in his "Saxons in England," built up the English polity as an aggre-gation of Marks, communities of freemen tilling the land in common; while Nasse, in Germany, showed the similarity between the English and German land-systems. Mr Freeman adopted in full Kemble's view of the Mark system, although its existence in England is largely a matter of conjecture[1]. Prof. Stubbs, with his usual caution, has recognized this conjectural character, and contents himself with saying that "it cannot safely be affirmed that the German settlers in Britain brought with them the entire system of the Mark-organization[2]."

But recent German investigations[3], notably those of Dr Landau and Professors Hanssen and Meitzen, and the admirable work of Mr Seebohm have thrown great doubt on many of the previously accepted conclusions of the advocates of the Mark.

---

[1] See also Sir H. Maine on Village Communities, c. 5.

[2] Stubbs, *Hist.* i. 83.

[3] Landau, *Die Territorien*, etc. Hamburg, 1854.

Hanssen, *Agrarhistorische Abhand-lungen.* Leipzig, 1880.

Meitzen, *Georg Hanssen, als Ag-rar-Historiker.* Tubingen, 1881.

Seebohm, *Village Community*, p. 371.

Mr Seebohm, for instance, in an elaborate analysis[1] of the early evidence of the existence of Marks, produced by Von Maurer, shows that evidence to be at least equally consistent with the hypothesis of a manorial villa with serfs as tenants. It is again a little startling to find that the well-known "three-field" system, hitherto confidently asserted to be the common possession of English and German Saxons, is really a South German system[2]; and that the North German lands, from which our Saxon and Anglian ancestors came, were, and still are, tilled by marl and manure on a one-field system. Investigation[3] of the Welsh and Irish land systems has shown a very early species of land-culture existing among them, and, in the case of the Welsh, certainly showing no traces of Roman influence. The solution of the question is very difficult and involved, and we can only profess to state briefly the way in which Roman influences are alleged to have acted on our Land system.

The advocates of the Mark allege that England, by the Saxon invasion, was portioned out among communities of freemen[4], who held their land in common and tilled it according to strict customs of cultivation. These freemen, their land and their village organization, constitute the Mark. Each freeman holds his homestead or *alod* as his own property: the arable and pasture-lands are portioned among the freemen at stated intervals, and cultivated or grazed according to fixed rules of agriculture. The woods or waste, which surround the cultivated land, belong to the community in common; and each community is embedded in unappropriated forests or moors, which in time are held to belong to the *folk* or nation into which the Marks have amalgamated.

We have thus three classes of CUSTOMARY ESTATES[5], held, not by any writing, but by customary rules.

I. *The estate of the Family or Individual; Family Land or Heir-land; the ethel or alod*[6]. This is essentially an estate of

[1] Seebohm, pp. 329—335.
[2] Hanssen, pp. 190 et seq. Seebohm, p. 372.
[3] Seebohm, pp. 181—213.
[4] Kemble, *Saxons in England*, I.
p. 54. Stubbs, *Hist.* I. 49.
[5] *Anglo-Saxon Law*, p. 57.
[6] Ibid. pp. 68, 72, 73. Pollock, *Land Laws*, p. 191. Note B.

inheritance, being originally inalienable, and descending in the family according to fixed rules. It rested primarily on the needs of the family, and was subject to rights and limitations in favour of the family. Thus, originally inalienable, it became alienable, at first, within the limits of, and by the consent of, the family; then the consent of the King and witan sufficed; at last no consent for alienation was necessary. It was primarily an untaxed estate[1], full, free, and unburdened. For the test of the presence of taxation is the appearance in charters of grants of immunity; and before A.D. 798 no grant of any family land, freed from taxation, is to be found, while such lands only gradually become subject to taxation after the time of Alfred. Family land gradually dies out by conversion into Boc-land.

II. *Estates of the Community, or Common Land*[2]. These were those lands of the Mark, which were divided among its members according to customary rules, and held for a limited period. Assuming the Mark, one of the most interesting questions in early English History is the reason of its change into those Manorial Communities, which undoubtedly were most numerous at the time of the Conquest[3]. The community settled on and tilling this land, might either be dependent on a superior or independent. If dependent, their lord might be the King, on whose private demesne they were settled; the state, if they occupied the *folc-land;* or some private landowner. While thus dependent as a community, within their bounds there would still be *alods* or homesteads as separate property, strips in the arable fields, held from year to year, and common pasture lands. And the advocates of the Mark point to this common land in manors, as the relic of the community of freemen who, often remaining free themselves, have sunk into copyholders or villeins, holding lands by servile tenure.

III. *Estates of the People, or Folk-land*[4]. Though but slight evidence exists, we can confidently infer that estates of *folc-land* could, and did, exist, held by private individuals: such

---

[1] So Maurer in opposition to Kemble; Stubbs does not meet the question clearly. *Anglo-Saxon Law*, p. 78.

[2] Ibid. p. 81.
[3] Ibid. p. 83.
[4] Ibid. pp. 91, 93.

estates, though alienable as to the tenant's interest therein, were neither heritable nor the subjects of devise[1], but reverted to the nation, if not re-granted by the King and witan, who alone could so deal with them. The great feature of the *folc-land* was the taxation[2] which originated in, and always, in the absence of an express grant of immunity, accompanied it. For early grants of folc-land almost always contain a grant of immunity from taxation, early grants of family land never do. During the period from Cnut to William I. the *folc-land* became *terra regis*, granted by the King alone.

Before dealing with *Boc-land*, we may treat shortly of the much-misunderstood *laen-land*. This was not in any sense leasehold estate in the modern meaning; i.e. an estate for a fixed term of years: for only one such case, and that a very late one, can be found. The Anglo-Saxon *laen*[3] was simply an estate in which possession and title were separated;—a loan of land, usually for life. *Laens* might be *booked* or *unbooked*, that is held on definite written terms, or orally; and the class of *unbooked laens* included all estates of folc-land[4], and all land held in a manor from the lord.

In broad opposition to these Customary Lands, was the later and more rigid tenure of *Book-land*, or land held by *book*, which originates in a written instrument[5], charter or grant, the land being in theory held in strict accord with the conditions of the *book*. Such land always, probably, reverted to the donor, in cases of escheat or intestacy[6]; and the charters, or books, gave to their possessor an all-important advantage in litigation. The introduction of " books " and Book-land is undoubtedly owing to Church influence, the exclusive object of all the early grants being the endowment of the Church[7]. Its great result is the steady destruction of customary holdings and forms of procedure

---

[1] *Anglo-Saxon Law*, p. 98.

[2] Ibid. pp. 78, 94.

[3] Ibid. p. 95.

[4] Prof. Stubbs speaks (I. 77) of *folc-land* " held according to the terms of the grant," on which the authors of " Anglo-Saxon Law " comment rather severely, that if it were so, it would be bookland, but presumably Prof. Stubbs does not refer to a written grant, since he expressly, on p. 76, sets out *book-land* as being held by writing, *folc-land* being outside it. On unbooked *laens*, see Pollock, *Land Laws*. Note B, p. 194.

[5] *Anglo-Saxon Law*, p. 109.

[6] Ibid. p. 111.

[7] Ibid. p. 101.

in favour of the exact tenure by a writing. The growth of book-land involved the decay of customary tenures, which survived mainly in the manors and common lands.

At least two examples of mortgages of land appear in the charters, and the second bears a distinctly Roman form: "*quam videlicet terram Sigericus archiepiscopus dedit mihi in vadimonium pro pecunia quam a me mutuo accepit*": but it is impossible on the slight evidence to affirm more than the existence of mortgages[1].

The Saxon laws of inheritance to land are of some interest. Tacitus expressly declares that the Germans had no wills[2], and it is admitted that the Saxons and Angles did not develope the testamentary power until urged to the step, for interested motives, by ecclesiastical influence. Book-land is specially designated as "*terra testamentalis*." But the new documents gained ground very slowly : there are only four Saxon wills in existence dating from before A.D. 950, and none of them refer to the permission of the King or lord, as do the later wills[3]. Duke Alfred wills " his *boc-land* and his *yrfe-land*[4]" (i.e. family land which was alienable to members of the same family). The same will shows that *folc-land* could not be left by will: "and I grant to Aethelweard my son, 3 hides of *bocland*, and if the King will give him the *folcland* in addition to the *bocland*, let him have it."

In the absence of wills, family land followed the custom of inheritance, *book-land* followed the *book*, *folc-land* reverted to the Crown or nation. The custom of inheritance in family land was to all the sons equally, and failing them to all the daughters[5]. Women were only conditionally, not absolutely excluded[6]. Special customs, such as Borough English, or the succession of the youngest son, existed in various counties and towns.

Such is a brief sketch of the Saxon land-law, as developed by the later authorities. But, before we proceed to deal with claims of Roman origin, we may note the apparent confusion resulting from the fact that the division of lands is not exclusive.

[1] Cod. Dip. 499, 690. *Anglo-Saxon Law*, 106, 342.

[2] Tac. *Germ.* § 20.

[3] *Anglo-Saxon Law*, p. 107.

[4] Ibid. pp. 76, 93. Cod. Dip. p. 317.

[5] Ibid. p. 113.

[6] Ibid. p. 132.

Folc-land granted to a great lord as an *unbooked laen* may have imposed upon it a village community of freemen, with all their communal rights. As between the members of the community family and common-land exist, all being to the lord unbooked laens, while he may, by a suitable grant, convert portions into book-land as regards himself. The same land may therefore bear several different characters.

Admitting then the clerical and Roman origin of wills, and of *books* or charters, and *book-land*, we open a great field for clerical influence. Learning being almost a clerical monopoly, the Church would acquire great influence over all legal relations involving a written form. But, owing to the isolated and almost independent character of the early English Church, it was less influenced by Roman learning, and less likely to spread the dominion of Roman legal notions, than the continental ecclesiastics.

The chief points of resemblance which Mr Coote alleges to exist between the Roman and Saxon land-systems include[1] :— (1) an alleged imperfect ownership in the landholder and power of resumption in the Sovereign, which are not Teutonic, but Roman. This resumption, as a Roman institution, is alleged to have been a special feature of the *possessio*, or Bonitarian ownership of land, as distinguished from the *dominium* or Quiritarian ownership: and *possessio* was a provincial tenure, inalienable except by leave of the magistrate. The Agrarian laws, and the grants to military colonies in Italy, are alleged to be special examples of this resumption.

The evidence as to Anglo-Saxon land by which Mr Coote supports his position consists of those charters in which it is recited that the leave of the King was given for such an alienation. He cites no example earlier than A.D. 759, and most of his examples are of the 10th and 11th centuries.

But Mr Coote neither mentions nor explains the fact that, while a certain number of charters recite the license of the King a far larger number do not contain such a recital. Our preceding pages have shown that family land at one stage of its

---

[1] Coote, *Neglected Fact*, pp. 23, 173 ; *Romans in Britain*, pp. 247—251.

history was alienated with the consent of the King in order to bar the claims of the family[1]. Whether then the principle be true of Roman Law, or not, its application in English Law is certainly not universal, and its supposed examples may be explained by other considerations. Indeed Mr Coote has himself recognized the existence of other kinds of land[2]: he refers to land in Huntingdonshire :—"*tam libera quae per forisfacturam non possit iri perditum*"; and to those estates and even hundreds referred to in Domesday[3], and omitted from the *Textus Roffensis*, as exempted from the *trinoda necessitas*. In these he finds that *ager privatus* which, by special Imperial favour, existed in a very few cases in the Roman provinces. A more obvious and consistent explanation would refer these to the same rapidly disappearing class of family lands, allodial and, originally, free from taxation.

In the second place[4], Mr Coote claims Roman origin for the well-known tax called *trinoda necessitas*, or *threo nede*, the liability to contribute to *burhbot*, or town-fortifications, *brycg-bot*, or repair of bridges, and possibly roads, and the obligation to serve in the *fyrd*, or national militia. He finds the Roman *onera patrimonalia* paid by all provincial lands for "*pontium refectio, arcium munitio, viarum munitio, et tironum productio,*" services apparently identical with the *trinoda necessitas*. On the other hand such services would naturally be required in any country exposed to war, and with a certain amount of traffic. Owners of land in the Frankish Empire were liable to repair bridges, roads and fortifications, and to maintain the host and the watch, an obligation described by Charles the Bald, as, "*antiquam et aliarum gentium consuetudinem*[5]. But the *trinoda necessitas* in its origin does not appear to be a land tax at all, but a personal tax, universally imposed on freemen[6]. No genuine

---

[1] *Anglo-Saxon Law*, p. 77.

[2] Coote, *Neglected Fact*, p. 45 ; *Romans in Britain*, p. 244.

[3] Ellis, Domesday, p. 18.

[4] Coote, *Neglected Fact*, pp. 33, 177 ; *Romans in Britain*, pp. 244—247, 259—261. *Anglo-Saxon Law*, p. 61 ; Stubbs, *Hist.* I. 77, note. The Bishop refers to Mr Coote's argument on this point as displaying "great learning and ingenuity", but the only answer he makes to it is that it "wants both congruity and continuity."

[5] Stubbs, I. 77, note. Waitz, *D. V. G.* IV. 30, 31.

[6] *Anglo-Saxon Law*, p. 61.

charter contains an exemption from this tax; indeed no genuine charter before A.D. 740 contains any mention of it, and references to it only become common in the 9th century. The charters which do refer to it speak of it as the "burden common to all people" (not to all lands). These facts suggest that the tax, originally personal, became connected with the land as the progress of feudal ideas inseparably connected the freeman and the landowner. But this personal character is fatal to the Roman origin of the tax, the *patrimonalia munera* being essentially taxes on the land. The undoubted and curious coincidence between these *munera* and the *trinoda necessitas* cannot therefore be placed higher than a coincidence.

A third ingenious argument of Mr Coote's[1] attempts to trace to a Roman origin the *hide,* and the qualification of 5 hides as the holding of a *thegn.* The Roman *agrimensores,* in parcelling out a colony, allotted to each family 200 Roman *jugera,* being the amount which could be cultivated *ab uno possidente :* this amount was called a *centuria.* Further, the *Leges Licinia et Sempronia* allowed no citizen to hold more than 1000 jugera, and that amount only if he had two or more sons. Mr Coote does not pretend that these laws were strictly adhered to : indeed he says himself that they remained in force to the end of the Empire[2], "if not as laws, as measures"; (whatever that may mean). His chain of argument then appears to be that, the soldiers being the chief recipients of land grants, only distinguished officers would receive the full *modus* of 1000 jugera, which would therefore become associated with the idea of personal distinction. We may pause here to ask where the " two sons " of the Lex Sempronia have dropped out of the argument: for if the laws remained in force, the *maximum* holding of 1000 *jugera* could only be held by citizens with two children ; while if they did not remain in force, it is difficult to see how the limit of 1000 jugera, which the needs of Mr Coote's argument compel him to cling to, survives. For his next step is to establish a connexion between this 1000 *jugera,* a *maximum* holding, and the 5 hides, which were the *minimum* holding of

---

[1] Coote, *Neglected Fact,* 37—42; [2] Ibid. *Neglected Fact,* p. 41.
Romans in Britain, pp. 267—270.

an Anglo-Saxon *thegn*. But Mr Coote is here in a difficulty. To explain his 5 hides, he needs the Lex Sempronia, allowing 1000 *jugera*, and he also needs that the hide should equal 200 *jugera*. But the normal English hide was composed of 120, occasionally of 240 acres[1]. Even assuming that the *hid*, (a word having some connexion in meaning with "family"), is related to the *centuria*, the normal holding of the free Roman citizen, we have still the difficulty that the 5 hides will not equal the 1000 *jugera* from which Mr Coote is anxious to derive them, but will contain 600 or 1200 acres. Mr Coote is therefore compelled to accept as his *hide* a measure of 200 acres, existing only in Kent and Sussex, and not universally adopted in those counties[2].

We may therefore dismiss Mr Coote's arguments on this point, to deal with Mr Seebohm's theory of the connexion of the *centuria* and the hide[3]. His reasons for assuming, or suggesting, a Roman origin for the hide, are briefly as follows :—

(1)   The Roman unit of taxation was the *jugum*, which was connected in some way with the amount of land ploughed by a team of oxen, though finally it was merely a hypothetical unit of assessment. The English hide in the same way is connected with the amount ploughed by a full team of oxen, and ultimately becomes a unit of assessment.

(2)   The *centuria* consisted of either 200 or 240 *jugera*, and 30 jugera were connected with the plough-work of a yoke of oxen. The hide was 120 or 240 acres, and 30 acres were the plough-work of a yoke of oxen.

(3)   The lord of a Roman *villa* paid the *tributum* for his own land and that of his *coloni*. The lord of the English manor paid *hidage* for the whole of the land of his manor.

This evidence, though not convincing, certainly suggests some connexion, but it is so involved in the strength or weakness of Mr Seebohm's theory of the growth of manors that we may defer comment on it for the present.

Mr Coote's attempt to trace Roman influence[4] in the

---

[1] Seebohm, pp. 37, 76.

[2] Mr Seebohm finds hides of 240 acres in Sussex, p. 51.

[3] Seebohm, pp. 289—295.

[4] Coote, *Neglected Fact*, p. 57.

succession to land is more ingenious than convincing. The Anglo-Saxon law of succession was to the sons equally, and, failing male issue, to the daughters equally, being the rule surviving in the Kentish tenure of gavelkind : in some places the youngest son succeeded to the original homestead, by the English custom of Borough English, analogous to the continental *Jüngsten-Recht.* Mr Coote alleges both rule and exception to be Roman, the rule of gavelkind apparently on the ground that the Roman division among unemancipated children may have been relaxed to include all the children[1], the exception of Borough English because if only the youngest son were unemancipated, he might succeed to the property by Roman Law. But the fact that in a particular case the succession under the Roman Law is the same as that of Anglo-Saxon Law cannot explain the remarkable local distribution of the custom of *Jüngsten-Recht,* as noted by Mr Elton and Mr Seebohm[2]. They find the custom to have been universal in Wales, and in the Welsh settlements in Somersetshire ; also in a district nearly corresponding with the *Littus Saxonicum,* Kent, Sussex, Surrey, the environs of London, and East Anglia, while on the Continent it is localized with curious precision. In Ireland[3] the custom of gavelkind appears without the *Jüngsten-Recht,* while in many English manors, and frequently on the Continent, the *Jüngsten-Recht* appears without the succession in gavelkind. As to this Mr Seebohm conjectures that when the tribal household became manorial, the division among heirs, or gavelkind, being stopped by a necessity of maintaining the holding undivided, the *Jüngsten-Recht* remained to settle which of the sons should be the heir. It is abundantly clear that the theory

---

[1] Gavelkind divides amongst all sons, not all children.

[2] Elton, *Origins of History,* pp. 188, 189 ; 197, 198. Seebohm, pp. 352—354.

[3] The Welsh and Irish "gavelkind" is widely different from the Teutonic custom in Kent.

  In *Ireland and Wales*

(1) bastards were included,

(2 daughters were excluded,

(3) no dower was allowed to the widow.

  In *Kent*

(1) bastards were excluded,

(2) daughters succeeded in the absence of sons,

(3) dower was allowed.

  In Ireland the land was partible among the clansmen. Kenny on *Primogeniture,* p. 27.

of Roman origin is insufficient: it in no way explains the curious local distribution of the custom, and is content with the mere accident of the youngest son alone remaining unemancipated, as the explanation of a local custom of the succession of the youngest son. Both Gavelkind and *Jüngsten-Recht* are more probably survivals of the Tribal household.

We have thus enumerated the chief points in the English land system before the Conquest, which Mr Coote and Mr Finlason ascribe to Roman influences; and we may therefore turn to the more important theory developed by Mr Seebohm of the growth of manors from Roman and South German institutions.

Mr Seebohm's theory of the Roman Origin of Manors.

We have rather assumed so far that English Economic History begins with a free people who gradually degenerate into serfdom under the pressure of the growing manorial system. The poorer freemen find the protection of a lord invaluable, and the tie of land tenure gradually becomes inseparable from the tie of fealty. This theory of the manorial system Mr Seebohm attacks with great vigour and research, and with some success; and as his counter-theory involves the assumption of another source of Roman influence in England, and alleges a partly Roman origin for the English manor, it may well claim our careful attention.

Mr Seebohm's position[1], broadly stated, is that English Economic History begins with the serfdom of the rural population, who lived in village communities, each under a manorial lordship. His method of proof is to trace back the existing manor, century by century, and to show that the services required from the *villein* become more and more uncertain, more and more servile, the nearer we approach the early centuries of Saxon rule, while the manors appear at all times equally numerous. This investigation completed, he endeavours to discover the origin of this manorial community, and finds it

---

[1] Seebohm, Pref. p. 9. It is not clear how far Mr Seebohm appreciates the fact that a servile tenure of land did not involve loss of freedom by the tenant. See on this, Pollock, *Land Laws.* Note C, pp. 196—206.

ultimately in a mixture of Roman and South German institutions: finally, he suggests, (for evidence is almost totally
absent), a South German series of military colonies, by which
such a system might have been introduced.

We need not set out in any detail the steps by which Mr
Seebohm traces back manors to the time of Domesday. He
finds the manor to consist of: (1) the lord's demesne: (2) land
held in villeinage, laid out in three large fields, cultivated in a
customary rotation, and divided into parallel strips of an acre in
extent[1]. The holding of each villein is made up of a number of
these strips scattered about in apparently irregular order. The
Enclosure Acts were intended to destroy this system, and
between 1760 and 1814 these Acts were passed for 4000 out of
10,000 parishes in England. A very ingenious investigation
proves that the ordinary holding of a *villein* was a "*yard-
land*," or holding of 30 acre-strips of land, otherwise called a
virgate[2]. These holdings were probably customarily hereditary
by primogeniture[3], and are connected with the hide of 120 acres,
and the plough-team of 8 oxen, to which each villein furnished
two oxen, his original outfit from the lord[4]. In approaching
Domesday: (1) we find fewer irregular holdings: (2) the com-
mutations of services for money payments become less common:
(3) the services themselves become more severe and at the will
of the lord[5].

From Domesday onwards the evidence, for the purposes of
this essay, becomes more interesting. Hitherto Mr Seebohm,
on common ground with his opponents, has but given further
elucidation of points of difficulty: before the Conquest his
theory professes to carry back the existence of manors to a far
earlier date than that suggested by the advocates of the English
Mark. Both parties agree in the widespread existence of
manors under the Norman kings: they differ as to the time at
which they became thus common.

---

[1] Seebohm, p. 15.

[2] Ibid. p. 26. Cf. *Saxon Chronicle*,
cited ibid. p. 92. That not a hide nor
"an gyrde landes" was omitted from
Domesday. Mr Seebohm is the first
to satisfactorily explain the "yard-
land."

[3] Ibid. pp. 23, 24, 133, 176.

[4] Ibid. p. 60.

[5] Ibid. p. 75.

The Domesday Book, which records also the state of the land under Edward the Confessor, shows that England at the Conquest was manorial. The King alone has 1422 manors[1]: the division of manorial land into the lord's demesne, and land held in villeinage is common; and the usual manorial incidents appear everywhere. Moreover in the Domesday survey for the greater part of England there is not even a mention of free tenants, *liberi homines* or *liberi tenentes*[2]. *Socmen* and *liberi homines* form only 12 per cent. of the recorded population, and they are almost entirely settled in East Anglia and the Danish districts, a fact which may confirm the opinion of historians as to the effect of the Danish inroads as perpetuating early customs of freedom and free institutions. The *servi* or slaves in Domesday only number 2 per cent. of the people, being distributed over the West and South-west of England and on the Welsh Marches, or precisely where we should expect to find the descendants of the aboriginal Britons, driven west and enslaved by the Saxon invaders. In the Danish districts, Yorkshire and Lincolnshire, scarcely a slave is recorded. On the other hand the *villani, bordarii* and *cotarii*[3], who are distinctly manorial, form the mass of the population: between them they make up 70 per cent. of the population of England, forming 45 per cent. of the people in East Anglia where they are weakest[4]. Mr Seebohm seems justified in concluding that, except in East Anglia and the Danelagh, the class of free tenants was at the time of Domesday practically extinct.

[1] Seebohm, p. 82. Ellis, Int. I. 225.

[2] Ibid. p. 86.

[3] *bordarii* and *cotarii*, manorial tenants with holdings inferior to the typical *yardland*.

[4] The following is a list of counties in which they form more than 75 p.c. of the people, compiled from Seebohm, p. 86:

Rutland	97 per cent.	
Sussex	88 ,,	
Yorkshire	} 86 ,,	
Hertford		
Middlesex	} 85 ,,	
Derby		

Kent	} 83 per cent.	
Stafford		
Berks	82 ,,	
Surrey	81 ,,	
Oxfordshire	} 80 ,,	
Warwick		
Huntingdon	} 79 ,,	
Bucks		
Cambridge	78 ,,	
Hants	} 76 ,,	
Somerset		
Essex	75 ,,	

The lowest counties are Lincoln 46 p.c. and Suffolk 44 p.c.

But Domesday also records the condition of the land "*tempore regis Edwardi*[1]," i.e. as the Saxons left it. It shows that at least half the land then in cultivation was held in their customary holdings by the *villani, bordarii* and *cotarii,* while they probably tilled another quarter of the land as their lord's demesne[2]. And these customary holdings were composed of strips of land, assigned in a rotation bearing some relation to the number of oxen contributed to the village plough-teams[3]: this is confirmed by the grant of tithes in the laws of Ethelred and of Cnut[4], "as the plough traverses the 10th acre." A similar state of things existed in Wales, where the land ploughed was allotted in fixed proportions, according to the number of oxen and implements contributed to the common plough, the acre being probably the measure of a day's ploughing[5].

Before Domesday the word *manerium* disappears, (even in Domesday it is sometimes replaced by *mansio* or *villa*); and the places called in the Saxon records *hams* and *tuns,* are frequently, if not always, manors[6]. The lord is the *thegn* or *hlaford;* the *demesne land* the *thegn's inland;* the *villeins* are *geneats* or *geburs;* their land, *geneat-* or *gesettes-* or *gafol-land,* composed of *yard-lands,* tilled by *geburs,* and smaller holdings occupied by cottiers. The document called *Rectitudines Singularum Personarum*[7] contains a full account of the rights and services of the *thegn* and the *gebur,* which are of a clearly manorial character. The *gebur,* or *villein,* did three classes of work for his lord: (1) *gafol* or payments in money or kind: (2) *week-work,* work on the lord's demesne land for so many days a week, varying with the season of the year: (3) *precariae* or *benework,* extra and special services. From the Laws of Ina[8] we infer that the full *gebur* received a homestead from his lord, and it may be that the *liberi tenentes* of Domesday were those who had rented a *yard-land* from the lord, without, by receiving the

[1] Stubbs, *S. C.* p. 86.
[2] Seebohm, p. 102.
[3] Ibid. p. 117.
[4] Thorpe, pp. 144, 156.
[5] Seebohm, p. 124.

[6] Ibid. p. 127.
[7] Thorpe, p. 185.
[8] § 67. Thorpe, p. 63. Seebohm, p. 142.

homestead, becoming *geburs*, liable to the customary services in full, or holding by servile tenure.

So far we have nothing more than evidence of the existence of an institution similar to a manor in the 7th century. Now a comparison of the services on the manor of Tidenham, adjoining Wales, in the years 950 and 1307, shows that the earlier services were far more indefinite and servile than the later ones. The *villein* of the 13th century works "5 days in every other week from Michaelmas to Midsummer, 2½ days every week from Midsummer to August, 3 days a week from August to Michaelmas," for his lord: the *geneat* of the 10th century "shall work as well on land as off land, whichever he is bid," there being no limit of time. And it is suggested that as Tidenham was a royal manor in A.D. 950, its tenure and services had probably undergone no change during its previous history as a royal manor, which is assumed to date back to the Welsh Conquest[1]. Similarly the *ceorls* at Hysseburn in A.D. 900 "every week do what work they are bid[2]." The expressions in the Laws of Ina have been referred to, and Mr Seebohm relies on a number of passages in the Laws of Ethelbert[3] of this character: "If the king drink at *a man's ham*," and contends that the *hams* and *tuns*, so referred to as belonging to the king, an *eorl* or "*a man*," were in fact manors.

As evidence of extensive manorial tenures before the Laws of Ina this is very slight; and the Laws of Ina are consistent with a small or large acreage of lands tilled as manors. The interest of the theory for our present purpose lies in the steps by which Mr Seebohm endeavours to trace his manorial community to a partially Roman origin.

Welsh agriculture from the 7th to the 10th century was probably not manorial, but of the nature of a tribal and pastoral free community, paying food rents to its chief, and with a mode of tillage much simpler than the Saxon three-field system[4]. Irish and Scotch evidence shows an earlier form of tribal free community than the Welsh[5]. We have thus evidence of the

---

[1] Seebohm, pp. 148, 157.
[2] Ibid. p. 162.
[3] Ibid. p. 174.
[4] Seebohm, p. 181.
[5] Ibid. p. 214.

tribal free community in the West of Britain, and of the manorial community in the East; and Mr Seebohm contends on the authority of Caesar, Zosimus, Pliny and others, that even in pre-Roman times the South-east of Britain was under a system of tillage of some degree of fixity and development[1]. This, he urges, continued during the Roman occupation, in the open field system, which, as it is divided irregularly, cannot be Roman[2], and which is not brought by the Saxon invaders, for it is also found in Wales and Scotland. It must therefore have preceded the Roman occupation.

In order to trace the three-field system to its source, Mr Seebohm enters into an elaborate discussion[3] of the Roman provincial land system, and the German tribal system, into which we need not follow him minutely. Place names yield some interesting conclusions: the suffix -tun, -ton seems peculiar to England[4], a result held by Mr Coote to be due to the numerous enclosures of the Roman land-system. The suffix -ham corresponds to the -heim, -hem, of the Continental manors, and is chiefly found in the South-east of England. King Alfred's will disposes of his "land" in the West of England, his "hams" in the South-east. On the Continent the -heims are most prominent in those German districts which first became Roman provinces, in which also the termination -wyl, -weiler (villa), unknown in England, is found. The possessions of the abbeys are found to be often manorial before they come into monkish hands.

Mr Seebohm then examines the constitution of the Roman villa[5], which was originally the estate of a lord, worked by slaves under a villicus. Coloni, or freemen, though sometimes indigeni, or bound to the manor, are frequently found tilling it. And in

---

[1] Seebohm. p. 246. See Elton, Origins of History, pp. 33, 119.

[2] Seebohm, p. 411. Mr Coote shows clear evidence of centuriation in some parts of England, but probably only in cases of land actually assigned to the soldiers of a colonia. See Romans in Britain, pp. 42—121.

[3] Seebohm, p. 252.

[4] Stubbs, i. 82, note. "The tun is originally the enclosure or hedge." Seebohm, p. 255. Coote, Neglected Fact. Mr Coote does not explain why these enclosures should be peculiar to England.

[5] Seebohm, p. 264.

many continental cases the historical connexion between the *villa* and the *manor* can be traced[1].

Veterans settling on vacant land of the Empire received an outfit of oxen and seed to enable them to till the land. But the pure Roman field-system was one of straight lines and regular holdings; the irregular holdings of the open-field system may probably be attributed to Germanic customs and to joint ploughing.

It is believed that German military colonies were settled in Britain by the Romans, as for instance the Marcomanni, deported by Marcus Antoninus[2], and the Burgundians, Vandals and Alamannic tribes from the Rhine valley, by Probus[3]. There was a vigorous trade in corn between Britain and Gaul, involving the constant intercourse of their inhabitants.

Now the German system, apart from Roman influence, appears to have been of an early tribal type[4], like that of the Welsh and Irish; a system of open-field ploughing, which had not then developed into the "three-field" culture, but which tended in Germany, though not in Wales, to become manorial. With regard to German agriculture in its more developed form the researches of the latest German authorities[5] appear conclusively to establish that "the Angles, Saxons, Frisians, Low Germans and Jutes who came to England cannot have brought the 'three-field system' with them into England, because they did not themselves use it at home in North-west Germany and Jutland[6]." For in those parts a simple "one-field" system of crops grown every year on the same land, by marl and manure, still exists, and has existed for centuries past. A "three-field" system similar to the English one is found in South Germany, within the Roman *limes*, especially in Baden, Wirtemberg, Swabia, Bavaria, Elsass and the Moselle valley; and its details show a remarkable resemblance to the English system[7].

---

[1] Seebohm, p. 269.

[2] Gibbon, c. 9, quoting Dion Cassius 71, 72. Seebohm, p. 283.

[3] Ammianus Marcellinus, 18. 2. 3, and Zosimus, quoted in Elton, *Origins of History*, and Seebohm, p. 287.

[4] Seebohm, p. 336.

[5] G. Hanssen; A. Meitzen. *Vide ante* p. 20, note.

[6] Hanssen, *Agrar-Historische Abhandlungen*, p. 496. Seebohm, p. 373.

[7] Ibid. p. 410.

A study of the distribution of places terminating in -*ing*, -*ingen*, leads to interesting conclusions[1]. These places are usually supposed to be the original free settlements of families or clans, -*ing* being a patronymic. But such a suffix would seem primarily to imply *settlement*. Before a place can be called after people, the people must live there with some regularity. In England the -*ings* occur with the greatest frequency in the district called the Saxon shore, in which also Mr Elton has found the *Jüngsten-Recht* surviving. Similarly, on the Continent the succession of the youngest son to the homestead and the -*ings* are found together. And the "three-field" system is found in the same parts of the Continent, and in the South-east of Britain, as distinguished from the North-west and West.

Now Professor Wilhelm Arnold is of opinion[2] that the suffix -*ing*, -*ingen* invariably denotes an Alamannic settlement. And further, a striking resemblance, amounting in many cases to identity, exists between these English and German -*ings* or so-called "personal names:" of such names in Picardy 80 per cent. are found in a slightly altered form in England.

From these facts Mr Seebohm reaches the main position of his work[3], that the English "three-field" manorial community is due to tribal households of Alamannic Germans, settled in South-east Britain by their Roman rulers, and using the aboriginal inhabitants as serfs to till their land. These Alamannic tribal households are supposed to have either usurped the lordship of existing Roman villas, or to have taken the Roman villa in some respects as the type of their settlements. Local investigations in the neighbourhood of Hitchin show many instances of historical continuity between the Roman villa and the modern village, suggesting that the Saxon settlers occupied and tilled the localities they found already under cultivation. The mediaeval serf would then derive his origin from the Roman slave, the Roman *colonus*, and the German tribe-slave or *laet*.

The evidence that these settlements of tribal households

[1] Seebohm, p. 347.

[2] *Ansiedelungen und Wanderungen Deutsche Stämme.* Marburg, 1881, pp.

155 *et seq.* Seebohm, p. 360.

[3] Seebohm, p. 359.

were manors is very slight, though such a state of things would not be impossible. Mr Seebohm, while admitting the "precarious nature" of his suggestion, urges that the evidence to support the theory of settlement by free village communities is equally insufficient. In answer to this it can only be said that the latter is more in accord with what is known of the Teutonic family and its institutions.

Mr Seebohm states as the results of his investigation: a "one-field" system of agriculture, a step more advanced than the simplest form of tillage, existing in South-east Britain when the Romans landed;—a three-field system of rotatory crops, introduced during the Roman occupation, probably by Alamannic settlements under Roman authority;—this system carried out by the settlers by means of a manorial community in which they were the lords, and the conquered population the labourers and serfs;—the adoption by the North German invaders of the three-field manorial system, which they found in use on their landing.

If this hypothesis be well founded, it obviously effects a great change in our views of English institutions. For I understand Mr Seebohm to assert the entire absence of Marks, or settlements by free village communities, except in so far as those cases where tribal households are the lords of a manor come under such a title. The *liberi tenentes* he explains to be those who till the demesne land of the lord, as tenants by *gafol* or rent of *laen land,* but not owing work or servile services.

The chief difficulty in Mr Seebohm's way is the very scanty traces of any such South German settlements, or military colonies of South German race, as he contends for[1]. The *Littus Saxonicum* is undoubtedly the shore exposed to Saxon ravages, and not the shore colonised by Saxons. The remarkable similarity of continental and English place-names and the presence of the marks of Alamannic settlements as investigated by Arnold are facts entitled to some weight. The Bishop of Chester, writing in 1875, before the latest German

---

[1] Stubbs, i. 59, 63, note; Freeman, *Norman Conquest*, i. 11.

investigations, considered the theory "not improbable, but resting on very scanty evidence:" and this evidence has certainly now been strengthened.

Further, there are very slight proofs of the existence of manors on any large scale before A.D. 900: the expressions in the Laws of Ina concerning *ceorls* with a meadow in common, and in the Laws of Ethelbert concerning "the king's *tun*, the *eorl's tun*" are very insufficient; and though proof is certainly difficult, its burden is undoubtedly on Mr Seebohm.

Again, the theory of universal manors, with descent of the *yard-lands* or manorial holdings to one son only, is difficult to reconcile with the undoubted Anglo-Saxon law of succession among all the sons equally, which appears as the rule, and not as an exception. Yet this rule, as applied to manors or hams, would break up the equal holdings or *yard-lands* into varying fragments. In short we may, without underrating the ingenuity of Mr Seebohm's arguments, or the value of a large portion of his reconstruction of the English land system, decline at present to accept his theory of a Roman and South German parentage for the manor.

The English land system is therefore in the main Teutonic, or its Roman origin has not yet been established, even in part. To Mr Coote's theory of simple derivation of the English from the Roman system we may oppose a complete refutation. No Roman system, pure and simple, will explain the curious "three-field" system, which, whether tilled by a free community or as a manorial settlement, covered the greater part of England. Mr Seebohm's more guarded theory of South German and Roman origin we may regard as unproven as yet: its maintenance, together with recent German researches, will compel the advocates of a North German origin for our early land system to restate their case, and to dispel or recognise the new difficulties which new knowledge has brought against them.

CHAPTER IV.

ROMAN influence is not alleged to have seriously affected this branch of the Anglo-Saxon law. In the time of Bracton indeed it acted through ecclesiastical channels to produce changes of importance, but what little is known of the early English law of the family and kindred is purely Teutonic; and the family was, as in the other German tribes, the most important institution of private law, and the foundation of the whole police and criminal systems.

The Family Law of the Anglo-Saxons consists of two distinct parts :—

(1) *The law of the maegth, maegburh, or kindred*[1], which has exercised very slight influence on modern law. It is certainly not Roman, but Teutonic.

(2) *The law of the family*[2], which, in its essential characteristics, remains to the present day the same. This again appears largely Teutonic. Sir Henry Maine indeed says that, "All the Germanic immigrants seem to have recognised a corporate union of the family under the *mund,* or authority of a patriarchal chief, but his powers are obviously only the relics of decayed patria potestas[3]." But the absence of agnation, and the recognition of kinship through the mother, point rather to a tribal household, probably developing from polyandry, than to the Roman *patria potestas* of a patriarchal system.

---

[1] *Anglo-Saxon Law*, p. 123.
[2] Ibid. p. 148.
[3] *Ancient Law*, p. 144.

In the *maeg-lagu*, or law of the kindred[1], admittedly Teutonic, we need only notice one point. Every person had two *maegthe*, his father's kin (*faedren maegth*), and his mother's kin (*médren maegth*), the *maegth* being the whole kindred of some one *propositus*. The wife did not pass into her husband's *maegth*, but remained in her own; and this *médren maegth* could protect the rights of the wife and children against the father. We have here the fact of "men calling themselves relatives of their mother's relatives," which Sir Henry Maine has expressly stated to be incompatible with and fatal to the *patria potestas*[2].

The Teutonic family presents more marked features of difference from Roman law. Agnation and its results are absent, and its system of emancipation is radically different. For though in the early Teutonic family there was a formal emancipation on attaining majority (which was physical maturity), by giving arms in the assembly, or by cutting the hair, this ceremony, while it destroyed the father's rights over the son's person, in no way affected the son's position in the father's kindred or his rights of succession[3]. The slight evidence as to Anglo-Saxon law seems to show a fixed age of majority (at first 10 years, then 12, with a tendency to lengthen to 15[4], the age of majority for non-military tenures under the Normans). During the minority the father is guardian of the child, but his personal control ceases at majority, and there is nothing in Anglo-Saxon law to show that he had any rights in the son's property after that period. The attainment of majority in girls, at the age of 12, freed their persons from the disposal of the father. This system is clearly unlike the Roman *patria potestas*.

The marriage relation, with its effects on property is distinctly Teutonic, and, as such, has affected all later law[5]. The marriage at first was a real contract of sale; the *beweddung*

---

[1] See *Anglo-Saxon Law*, pp. 123—144.

[2] *Ancient Law*, p. 149.

[3] *Anglo-Saxon Law*, pp. 155—161.

[4] 21, the present age of majority, was that fixed by the Normans for military tenures.

[5] *Anglo-Saxon Law*, p. 166. Kenny, on *Effects of Marriage on Property*. London, 1879. pp. 22, 65.

or betrothal, on which the *weotuma* or price of the bride was prepaid, was followed by the *gifta*, the delivery or nuptials. The *weotuma* gradually became a mere earnest, or *wed*, to make the contract binding, while the substantial part of the price was paid to the woman herself after consummation, as the *morgen-gifu*, or her morning-gift. Clerical influence then combined the *wed* or *weotuma* and the *morgen-gifu* as the *dos ad ostium ecclesiae*; and from this we can trace without interruption the descent of the dower of English Common Law, while the Roman *dos* and the French *dôt* have no place in the chain of evidence. No evidence of any gift from the wife's kindred appears before the Conquest[1]. If there were no express morning-gift, the wife would take half of her husband's estate at death if she had children, a third if she was childless. But these shares by express stipulation at the church door might be: (1) restricted; (2) enlarged to half if the widow were childless, or to the whole property if she had children. Mr Kenny is of opinion that the early evidence shows a system of community of joint acquisitions in Saxon times similar to the French and Scotch law[2]. The husband may undoubtedly make gifts to his wife during coverture.

The system of kinship before the Conquest was purely Teutonic: no distinction existed between the whole and the half-blood. A species of adoption is found, which gave no rights of kinship, but only the rights of succession at death[3]. Natural children could not be legitimated; and it is probable that no right of representation in succession existed, though it had become recognized by the time of Bracton.

We have already dealt with the rights of succession to land, and it only remains to mention succession to personalty[4]. It has been argued that Anglo-Saxon law restrained testamentary disposition by dividing the chattels into three parts, one of which went to the wife, one to the children (irrespective

---

[1] *Anglo-Saxon Law*, p. 176. Kenny speaks of the "fatherfee" as such, but cites no authorities (p. 22).

[2] Kenny, p. 25.

[3] *Anglo-Saxon Law*, pp. 126—130.

[4] *Anglo-Saxon Law*, p. 134. Coote, *Neglected Fact*, p. 59. Coote's *Ecclesiastical Practice*, Introd. p. 45 *et seq.* Coote's *Romans in Britain*, p. 287.

of sex), and the third was at the disposal of the testator. This, which is said to resemble the Roman *legitima pars,* is sustained by passages from the Kent Custumal, and from Bede as to the Northumbrian practice. It undoubtedly became the almost universal custom after the Conquest, though in London, at the time of Bracton, the unlimited right of testation was the rule[1]. But there are no traces in Anglo-Saxon law of any distinction between movables and immovables, reality and personalty[2]: the early law also appears not to have recognized any restriction on the right of testation. Customs there may have been, and the later lawyers disputed whether the writ "*de rationabili parte bonorum,*" which enforced the above division, lay at common law or by custom; but any such law appears to have its origin after the Conquest. And though it was maintained and developed by clerical courts and judges learned in the civil law, it is yet unlike the Roman law, both in its widow's share, which is evidently connected with the right of dower where there was no express agreement[3], and in its absence of distinction between emancipated and unemancipated children.

It seems clear therefore that so far as the law of the Family and Household is concerned, Anglo-Saxon law owes nothing to Roman influences. In the Law of Persons outside the family, Mr Coote claims Roman origin for the distinction between *thegns* and *ceorls*[4], whom he alleges to have been distinct castes, and therefore distinct nationalities, the *ceorls* being the Romano-British inhabitants, descendants and representatives of the Roman *coloni*. Mr Finlason makes the same claim[5]. The *colonus* stands or falls with Mr Seebohm's theory, which we have already discussed, but Mr Coote claims in addition the idea of a privileged order as a "striking non-German fact." He neglects to consider the existence of the large number

---

[1] Somner's *Gavelkind*, pp. 92—98.

[2] *Yrfe* means both land and chattels.

[3] *Vide supra,* p. 42, and see *Law of Edmund,* Kenny, p. 26. Coote's *Romans in Britain,* p. 288. Mr Coote notes the curious coincidence in the widow's *luctus* or year of grief, which may

be derived from Roman clerical influence. Blackstone had also noticed this, I. 456.

[4] Coote, *Neglected Fact,* pp. 1, 47—52, 113; *Romans in Britain.*

[5] Finl. Reeves, Pref. p. 51.

of slaves[1], many of whom were undoubtedly British, or the fact, which appears fatal to the idea of caste, that a *ceorl* with the necessary amount of property could become a *thegn*, the *thegn* an *eorl*. The ranks also among the Anglo-Saxons correspond with the ranks in Continental Teutonism[2]. It is true that the institution of the *comitatus*[3] is undeveloped when the invaders leave for England, but it springs up from similar causes in both countries. And Mr Coote's assertion that the *nobiles* of Tacitus, the *eorlas* and *adalings*, whose existence conflicts with his theory, were not a privileged class, seems certainly inaccurate[4].

We may therefore conclude that no part of the Anglo-Saxon Law of Persons can safely be attributed to Roman influence.

---

[1] *Servi, theow, laet, esne.*

[2] Stubbs' *Hist.* I. 81.

[3] *thegn, gesith.*

[4] Coote, *Romans in Britain*, p. 443.

CHAPTER V.

ROMAN LAW IN EARLY PROCEDURE.

THE intricate but interesting subject of Anglo-Saxon procedure need not detain us long, for it is hardly seriously maintained, except by Mr Coote, that it is in any important respects
influenced by Roman law[1]. It shows on the contrary the
common features of all Teutonic systems, and in some respects
is even purer than the continental codes, which frequently bear
marks of Roman influences, while its differences from the well-
known Roman procedure are radical[2]. Mr Finlason however
says confidently:—"As to the general principles of jurisprudence, and the administration of justice, there can be no question
that they were derived from the Roman system, although
doubtless in a very rudimentary form[3]." Condescending to
particulars, he asserts "its fundamental principle of the supremacy of public justice over private law[4]" to be the result of the
revival of Roman influence. Now it is certainly true that
the irregular procedure of the feud did not become finally
suppressed till a strong central authority was found in the
Norman kings, but there is no evidence to connect its gradual
decay with the influence of Roman law ; the growth of a strong
central power furnishes sufficient explanation. Mr Finlason
also claims as Roman,—" the great principle that the duty of
securing that justice should be administered rested with the
sovereign[4];" while he admits that it is scarcely to be found

[1] Coote, *Romans in Britain*, 294—
313.

[2] *Anglo-Saxon Law*, pp. 183—306.
O. W. Holmes on *Common Law*, London,

1882.

[3] Finl. Reeves, Pref. p. 53.

[4] Ibid. Pref. p. 54.

in the earliest Saxon laws, though gradually recognized and developed. The truth is that the extension of the king's power, the tendency to regard offences as "*contra pacem domini regis*," as well as sources of compensation to the person injured, increase with the power of the central authority. The king becomes regarded as the "fountain of justice," and the Court of Chancery springs from the exercise of the royal conscience; but there is no evidence to show any connexion between the Saxon laws bearing on this point and Roman law.

The presence of the bishop in the shiremoot side by side with the *ealdorman*[1] may indeed have led to modifications in procedure, and clerical influence usually favoured the rules of the civil and canon laws: against this may be set the fact that, during the greater part of the period before the Conquest, the English Church was remarkably free from foreign influences. The only traces of clerical influence forthcoming are in the introduction of *books* or charters as witnesses, and probably in the Christian modifications of the ordeal.

Though Mr Finlason admits that the trial by jurors upon evidence was the development of a much later period, he yet claims trial by jury as of Roman origin[2]. He alleges in criminal justice, "a mode of trial by king's judges, and jurors or sworn judges of the facts;" and in civil cases, "a system of trial by sworn witnesses upon whose testimony of their own knowledge the body of men, who acted as judges, determined." This probably refers to the "transaction witnesses," who no doubt did assert facts, but his idea of the procedure in which they took part is curiously inaccurate[3]. He has indeed to confess that his "trial by jurors or witnesses, and whole system of criminal procedure; a system of presentment by grand jurors, of indictment upon their oaths, and of trial by juries[4]," has no countenance from the written laws, but is based entirely upon the apocryphal statements of the "Mirrour of Justice[5]."

---

[1] Stubbs' *Hist.* i. 114.

[2] Finl. Reeves, Pref. pp. 21, 63. Coote, *Romans in Britain*, p. 312.

[3] *V. sub* p. 47.

[4] Finl. Reeves, Pref. p. 65, note.

[5] *e.g.* "Alfred hanged Friburne be-cause he judged Harpen to die, whereas the jury were in doubt in their verdict, for in doubtful cases we ought to save rather than to condemn," cited Finl. Reeves, Pref. p. 64, note.

While the "twelve senior thegns" of Ethelred[1] bear some, though a much criticized, resemblance to the subsequent grand jury, there is nothing to connect them with Roman influence, and the general opinion now refers the origin of trial by jury to the development of the system of inquest by sworn recognitors, introduced in the Norman reigns as an administrative method of gaining information mainly financial[2].

The great difference between Teutonic and Roman procedure may be briefly stated[3]. In the Roman suit, judgment was given after hearing the evidence, and it decided whether the claim of the plaintiff was rightly founded or not. In the German suit judgment was given before the hearing of evidence ; it was based merely on the assertion of the plaintiff, and its confession, denial or a counter-assertion by the defendant. This judgment, when pronounced, only decided on whom the burden of proof was to fall, or which of the two parties was to be called on to prove his case. This judgment given, the party to whom the proof was assigned proceeded to support his case by complying with rules of the strictest formalism. In Anglo-Saxon law three methods of proof were allowed[4]. In the first place, the party might vouch for the truth of his case with *compurgators,* who swore to their belief in their credibility of their principal, and not to their knowledge of the fact he asserted. He might, secondly, confirm his oath by that of the Transaction- or Community-Witnesses[5], who swore to what they had seen, but only if they were called by the party proving. If his oath failed or (to use the expressive Saxon term) "burst," (and the precise quantity of oath he must produce was carefully prescribed by law), he might as a last resort invoke the aid of God, and submit himself to the ordeals of fire, water, or the holy bread, that heaven might testify to his innocence. To these two methods,

---

[1] Ethelred III. § 3. Thorpe. Stubbs' *Hist.* I. 103.

[2] Stubbs, I. 608.

[3] *Anglo-Saxon Law,* p. 288. Mr Coote's account, *Romans in Britain,* p. 300, is curiously inaccurate, and takes no account of this striking difference.

[4] *Anglo-Saxon Law,* p. 186.

[5] Established by the laws of Edgar and Athelstan. Thorpe. *Anglo-Saxon Law,* p. 187.

oath and ordeal, the Church had added the use of documents, which were produced by the party to whom proof was awarded.

In the Criminal Procedure[1], which was essentially an enforcement by the individual of his right to compensation, with sometimes a payment to the Crown or the lord of *wite* for breach of the peace, the proceedings were in form the same. The judgment, after hearing a mere assertion by the prosecutor, and denial or confession by the accused, usually condemned the latter to prove his innocence or pay the fine[2]. This proof was almost always awarded to the accused, the few exceptions being in cases where a flagrant criminal was the prisoner, such as a thief caught in the act or by the hue and cry[3], or in cases where negligence was presumed in the accused[4]. If he either provided the necessary quantity of oath, his neighbours and kinsfolk swearing, "By the Lord the oath is pure and not false that *N.* swore;" or if he satisfied the requirements of the ordeal, he was acquitted. Wager of Battle was of Norman introduction.

It will be seen how unlike the Roman practice this rather clumsy and technical procedure was. Anglo-Saxon criminal law was in an advanced stage of the development observable in Teutonic procedure. This progress was from individual vengeance in the feud, initiated by the State who outlawed the offender; through the substitution for private revenge of a fixed composition to the injured man or his kindred; to the idea of true punishment exacted by the state for offences against itself. Anglo-Saxon criminal law was in an intermediate stage between the second and third of these periods[5].

The line of progress in Teutonic civil procedure is also well-marked[6]. The earliest procedure is purely executive: actions for debt, based on formal contracts, were enforced without any examination of material right in the suit. We find later a contradictory procedure, based on the investigation of material

---

[1] *Anglo-Saxon Law*, p. 262. Coote, *Romans in Britain*, pp. 303—312.

[2] *Anglo-Saxon Law*, p. 290.

[3] Ibid. p. 295.

[4] Ibid. p. 296. Cases of straying cattle or unfenced bounds. In these the prosecutor swore. *Laws of Ina*, 40, 42, § 1.

[5] *Anglo-Saxon Law*, p. 275.

[6] Ibid. pp. 185, 260.

right; and the gap between is bridged by developments of the land procedure. But the procedure throughout is utterly unlike that of the Roman courts.

There is no trace, for instance, in Anglo-Saxon sources of any period of usucapion, or adverse possession giving ownership or protection from actions[1]. The first trace of such an institution is in the Laws of the Conqueror[2]. Again the Anglo-Saxon usufructuary had *seisin;* but the Roman *usufructuarius* had not *possessio*[3]. In the Roman Law the plaintiff must prove his ownership of land; in the German procedure, he merely asserted that the defendant could have no right, and required him to prove his alleged right. For contrary to all Roman precedent, ownership was not usually the basis of German suits[4]. And examples might be multiplied.

Anglo-Saxon procedure, Civil or Criminal, owes then nothing in its origin to the Roman Law, and is but slightly influenced in its development. The introduction of charters and writings as modes of proof is clerical, and probably Roman; and some modifications may have been due to the presence of the bishop in the shire-moots. But in its main features Anglo-Saxon procedure is conspicuously free from Roman influence.

---

[1] *Anglo-Saxon Law*, pp. 226, 253. In one of the charters land is sued for after 34 years' silence. Cod. Dip. CCLVI.

[2] *Laws*, Thorpe, § 6.

[3] *Anglo-Saxon Law*, pp. 233, 234.

[4] Holmes, *Common Law*, pp. 166, 175.

CHAPTER VI.

ROMAN LAW IN THE EARLY CONSTITUTION.

PART I. *Shires and Hundreds.*

WE have now to consider the Roman origin claimed for Anglo-Saxon Local organization; first, with respect to divisions of the country, such as shires and hundreds, and, secondly with regard to municipal institutions and the gilds.

The difficulties of investigation into the origin of shires and hundreds are enormous; the conflicting theories innumerable. The Bishop of Chester has collected the most prominent of them in an elaborate note[1], in which even so great an authority can do no more than offer conjectures. But Mr Finlason is very decided[2]: "the counties and hundreds could not have been of Saxon origin, for the 'shire' is mentioned in the earliest Saxon laws, those of Ina, as already existing; and, on the other hand, hundreds are not mentioned until the Laws of Edgar, later than the British laws." To Mr Finlason, to be mentioned as existing in early times, or not to be mentioned till a late date, alike prove the non-Saxon origin of an institution; and the two arguments are, perhaps, of equal weight. He cites the *centenarius ager*, of the Romans, (which originally meant the land of a hundred citizens), and the Welsh *cantred*[3], and concludes that as "there is no trace in the Saxon laws of the formation of hundreds and counties, it seems that their real

---

[1] Stubbs, *Hist.* I. 97.
[2] Finl. Reeves, Pref. p. 38.
[3] Ibid. Pref. p. 14 ; Text, pp. 7, note, 42, note.

origin is to be found in the Roman usages introduced among the Britons." He adopts also the "Mirrour's" view of shires, that all counties ending in "-shire" are based on the Roman counties or divisions, while the others "belong to the English by conquest[1]."

Mr Coote[2], while he grants "*hundreds*" and "*wapentakes*" as names to be "reminiscences of old Germany and applied from a real or fancied analogy", yet asserts the counties to be the Roman *civitates* with their accustomed *territorium*, the hundreds to be the *pagi* into which they were divided. We have however no information as to the extent of the Roman organization, and it is impossible to compare the two systems and say that the county of Kent is coincident with the *territorium* of Rochester; of Lincoln with the *territorium* of *Lindum*; or to identify this hundred with that *pagus*. On the contrary, an instance quoted by Mr Coote shows that the *territorium* of *Londinium* may have been much larger than the county of Middlesex[3].

On the other hand, while we have definite information as to the formation of the Mercian and some Northern *shires*, the irregularity in size of the hundreds proves that they were not portioned out by any one enactment, but came into existence gradually, the boundaries of each being decided by local conditions[4]. The existing *shires* are of three classes[5]. They are coincident with historic kingdoms, as Kent, Sussex, and Essex: or they are subdivisions of kingdoms, which existed before the absorption of their parent kingdom, as *Hampton scir*, *Defna scir*, and the other shires of Wessex: or lastly they may be subdivisions of kingdoms, made after the absorption of the kingdom, as the *scirs* of Mercia, portioned out by Edward the Elder. The *scir* of the laws of Ina only relates to Wessex. But there is no valid reason to attribute even the earliest divisions to aught else than the settlement of related tribes.

---

[1] Finl. Reeves, p. 42, note. No account is given of the title by which the other shires "belong to the English". Mr Finlason seems to think that Warwickshire and *Euerwic scir*, (*i.e.* Yorkshire), are the same, which is rather startling.

[2] Coote, *Neglected Fact*, pp. 63—71. *Romans in Britain*, pp. 330—342.

[3] And see *Romans in Britain*, p. 342.

[4] Stubbs, *Hist.* I. 98, 99.

[5] Ibid. I. 109.

There is hardly any modern writer who does not accept the hundred as a Teutonic institution, the dispute being as to its original basis. The Bishop of Chester is of opinion that the geographical hundred was the *pagus* or district, in which the hundred warriors settled, of a size varying according to the local necessities and features of the country. He explains the Law of Edgar as recognizing the already existing hundred as a basis for police, while at some time it was also made the basis of taxation[1].

The essay in " Anglo-Saxon Law " on the Courts of Law argues elaborately in favour of the existence of territorial hundreds before the Law of Edgar[2]. The author concludes that just as the " state " of the 7th century became the " shire " of the 10th, (which is not universally true), so the shire, or division of the state, of the 7th century, became the hundred in the 10th; and he instances the " shires " still existing as local divisions in Cornwall and Yorkshire, as compared with the " hundreds " in other countries[3]. But this theory, though probable and interesting, need only be used here to confirm the opposition to any Roman origin for these divisions of Saxon States. The division, originally personal in part, became entirely territorial. But as all the Teutonic constitutions contain some trace of the personal idea, and as the *Lex Salica* shows that in the 5th century the administration of the hundred played an important part in the Frankish system, we need not assume a shadowy and far-fetched Roman origin, when Teutonic sources appear so clear.

[1] Stubbs, i. 98—108.

[2] *Anglo-Saxon Law*, pp. 8—20.

[3] He finds the hundred in the fre- quent use of " *regio* " in charters ; *regio Hohg* = now, the Hundred of Hoo, *regio Eosterge* = the Hundred of Eastry.

PART II. *Towns and Gilds.*

Towns and Gilds furnish the advocates of Roman influence
with some of their most vigorous claims. Mr Pearson[1],
Mr Thomas Wright[2], Mr Coote[3] and Mr Finlason[4] all speak of
Roman origin as here almost undoubted: yet we find the
Bishop of Chester writing that "there is no evidence which
connects the *burhs* of the Anglo-Saxons with the remains of
Roman civilization[5]", and Dr Brentano refuses even to consider
a Roman origin for Gilds[6].

Both Sir Francis Palgrave and the Bishop of Chester agree
that very little indeed can be stated with certainty about the
constitution of the *burh* of early times[7]; and this paucity of
information continues till the treasures of Domesday are
reached. The burden of proof may therefore be thrown on
those who assert a connexion, amounting to historical identity,
between the Anglo-Saxon *burh* and the Roman *civitas* or
municipium. Mr Finlason contents himself with an assertion of
the undoubted connexion, and the citation, as authorities, of
similar assertions by Mackintosh as to England, and by Guizot
as to France. Sir Francis Palgrave while he agrees that the
political existence of Anglo-Saxon *burhs* cannot be deduced from
the Roman era, yet claims a Roman origin for the Gilds, as
corresponding to the *collegia opificum*; he sums up his views in
these words, "with the exception of the trading Gilds which
descend in a direct line from the College of Operatives, only
scanty vestiges of Municipal institutions can be discerned[8]."

---

[1] *History of England in the early
and Middle Ages*, I. pp. 264, 267.

[2] *Archaeologia*, XXXII. pp. 298—311.

[3] *Neglected Fact*, pp. 69—89.
Romans in Britain, pp. 343—413.

[4] Finl. Reeves, Pref. pp. 9, 49.

[5] *Hist.* I. 92.

[6] Brentano on Gilds, c. I., see also
Spence, *Eq. Jurisd.* I. 54.

[7] Stubbs, *Hist.* I. 93. Palgrave, pp.
103, 331, 629.

[8] Palgrave, p. 628.

Mr Wright, whose views Mr Pearson adopts, and Mr Coote are more explicit. Mr Coote assumes all boroughs to be governed by a *port gerefa* appointed by the king[1]; but the evidence of his existence is his mention in four towns only, while *wic-gerefas* and *tun gerefas* exist in others[2]. There was probably an officer called the *gerefa* in most boroughs, but the evidence of his being appointed by the king is very slight, except in London which has in A.D. 680 a "king's wic-reeve[3]". Both Mr Wright and Mr Coote lay stress on the two classes in the borough[4]. In the Roman cities there were the *vulgus*, or people at large, and the *curia*, or governing body, ultimately presided over by one person, (the survivor of two or four *duumviri*), assisted by a committee of *principales*. They find the *duumviri* in the bailiffs or reeves, (of whom there was only one in a Saxon town), the *curia* in the burgesses, a select and aristocratic governing body of the borough; the *principales* in the aldermen. Such briefly is the analogy suggested: we can only reply that there is no evidence to show that the *burh* in Saxon times was so organized. Many *burhs*, such as London, have undoubtedly had a continuous local existence since the Roman occupation, but we have no information as to their constitution in Saxon times. A "reeve" appears, but he is barely more than a name. The Bishop of Chester implies that in London he was nominated by the Crown; Mr Loftie, that he was elected by his fellow-burgesses[5]. Lincoln has a *gerefa* in the 7th century, while in Domesday it is governed by twelve *Lawmen*, as also is Chester[6]. In the scarcity of evidence we may well conclude that, while there is nothing to justify the notion that Gilds were the basis on which the *burh* was organized, yet very little else can be stated with certainty about the early borough. The Roman, as well as any other constitution, must be dismissed as unproven.

The origin and nature of Gilds have been so elaborately

---

[1] Coote, *Neglected Fact*, p. 71. Romans in Britain, p. 369.

[2] Stubbs, I. 93, note.

[3] Thorpe, p. 14. Wright, p. 305.

[4] Coote, *Neglected Fact*, p. 81.

Romans in Britain, p. 363. Wright, p. 299.

[5] Loftie, *History of London*, I. 79.

[6] Stubbs, *Hist.* I. 94.

discussed by Brentano, Stubbs, Wilda and Hartwig that a mere summary of their conclusions will suffice. The materials for the history of Gilds before the Conquest are very slight; though, as England and possibly London is the birthplace of Gilds, their early history is entirely English[1]. But this paucity of evidence tells against the theory of Roman origin, for a view of Craft-gilds which derives them from the *Collegia Opificum* "needs rather to be proved historically by its adherents, than refuted by its opponents." It is true that in the Laws of Ine and Alfred, a class of *gegildan* are mentioned[2], but who they were and how they were connected with the kinless man's *wergeld* is a matter of great obscurity. There is also under Athelstan[3], the code of a London *frithgild*, for mutual defence; and at the beginning of the 11th century, we have three Gild-Statutes, of Abbotsbury, Exeter and Cambridge[4].

Three, if not four classes of Gilds are found to exist: (1) *the religious or social Gild*[5], whose chief purposes are good fellowship and common performance of religious offices. The members hold periodical banquets, and their contributions provide for religious services, festivals and the burial of members with proper solemnities[6]. The Exeter and Abbotsbury Gilds are of this class.

(2) The *Frithgild* added to these religious and social purposes the temporal functions of mutual defence and responsibility. The members of such a gild were protected against criminals, and the Gild was responsible for the sins of its members. The Cambridge Gild and the London one, (*tempore* Athelstan) were of this class[7]. (3) The *Merchants' or Trading Gild* is at least as old as the Conquest; it regulated the trade of its members, and attempted to regulate that of the town. Originally independent of the municipality, it came to be either

---

[1] Brentano, p. 50.

[2] Ine, §§ 16, 21. Alfred, §§, 27, 28. Stubbs, I. 89, 414. Waitz, *D. V. G.* I. 432—438.

[3] Athelstan VI. 1—12; *Judicia Civitatis Lundoniae.* Stubbs, I. 414.

[4] Brentano, c. I. Stubbs, I. 412—415.

[5] Brentano, c. 2, pp. 17—28.

[6] As to the functions of the *Collegia Opificum*, see the authorities quoted in the *Report of the City Guilds Commission*, 1884, p. 8, note. Coote, *Romans in Britain*, pp. 383—396.

[7] Stubbs, I. 416. Brentano, c. 3. pp. 29—49.

identical with, or closely connected with the governing body of the towns. It was usually of a distinctly aristocratic character.

A similar class of bodies, though of different origin is, (4) the *Craft Gilds*[1], composed of the freemen and bondsmen of each trade, who aimed at furthering the livelihood of their members in their respective crafts. They were later in origin than the Merchant Gilds, and usually came into violent collision with them in a battle of rich against poor, privilege against the people. But this struggle was more marked in the Continental than in the English Gilds.

A well-recognized theory refers the origin of the Religious Gilds to the feasts of the Northern Scandinavian tribes, which are expressly called "Gilds[2]." These, originally of a heathen character become Christianized as the Religious Gilds. Wilda[3] admits the Scandinavian origin of the banquets, but ascribes their special character to monastic institutions: this Hartwig[4] rejects, referring their origin to Christianity in the mixed associations of clergy and laity for mutual support. Against them Brentano argues for the essentially pagan character of the original Gilds, which subsequently came under Christian and monastic influences. The development of fellowship he regards as purely English. England is the birthplace of Gilds[5]: the Frith-, Merchant-, and Craft-Gilds come to England from no foreign source, but are indigenous, arising from the needs of the time and based on the development of the mutual regulation and assistance contained in the German family.

This English view is adopted by the Bishop of Chester, and by Mr Freeman in a letter to the City Guilds Commission, in which he says[6]: "the trade of London is as old as it well can be. The gap between the Roman and English periods is hidden by the blackness of darkness, which shrouds our settlement of Britain, and which...teaches much more clearly than any light

---

[1] Brentano, c. 4, pp. 50—100. Stubbs, I. 417.

[2] Brentano, pp. 3—6.

[3] *Das Gildewesen in Mittelalter.* Halle, 1831.

[4] *Unt. über die ersten anfange des Gildewesens.* Göttingen, 1860.

[5] Brentano, Pref. IX.

[6] 1884. *Report*, p 8, note.

could what the nature of that settlement really was. Had there been any continuity between the institutions of the two periods, that blackness of darkness could hardly have been." The Commissioners remark that[1] "the better opinion appears to be that the mediaeval Gilds were not a relic of Roman civilization, but an original institution." We may safely adopt the same view, or at least pronounce that the case of Roman origin has not been proved by its advocates[2].

[1] *Report*, p. 8.
[2] See also Coote's "*Ordinances of the Secular Gilds of London.*" London, 1871. For Mr Freeman's criticism on Mr Coote's general theory, see Macmillan's Magazine, June, 1870. Freeman, *N. C.* v. 887.

CHAPTER VII

THE Norman Conquest effects no sudden or sweeping changes in our institutions and laws: historical continuity of growth may be traced throughout. The "Feudal system", as it is misleadingly called, the chief product of Norman rule, was present in germ before the Conquest, and would probably have developed even if William had never crossed the channel. True it is that English institutions underwent great changes during the 12th and 13th centuries: Ranulf Flambard, the Justiciar of William Rufus, elaborated the details of feudal tenure with oppressive ingenuity: the Henries, with the clerical family of the Le Poors, developed an administrative system far in advance of the Saxon period both in finance and in the judicature. The second Henry did much to modify the law by direct legislation, and paved the way for our English Justinian, the first Edward. But all these changes are rather in the history of institutions than in the history of Law. Our records of cases are scant and difficult[1]: the Year Books do not commence till 1274; the written Law is scanty. The study of the Law of Rome does not revive till the latter half of the 12th century, and not until between 1180 and 1190 is the great work of Ranulf Glanvil, the Justiciar, published.

We have of course three codes extant[2], which, if genuine, would be of great assistance to our task, the so-called Laws of

---

[1] Collected in Bigelow's *Placita Anglo-Normannica*. London, 1879.
[2] Freeman *N. C.* v. 868. Stubbs
S. C. pp. 74, 80, 100. Stubbs, Preface to Roger of Hoveden, II. 22—47. Thorpe, pp. 190—267.

Edward the Confessor, of William I., and of Henry I. But their unofficial and informal character has been so completely established by the Bishop of Chester and Mr Freeman, that a very brief notice will suffice.

The Laws of Edward the Confessor[1] purport to be the result of the inquiries ordered by the Conqueror in 1069 to be made, through 12 wise men from each shire, as to the laws and customs of the realm. But one article distinctly refers to a Danegeld under William II.[2], and the preamble contains historical anachronisms, fatal to its claims as a contemporary record. The version supplied by Hoveden is probably a version prepared by Glanvil about A.D. 1170, and possibly founded on an early report of the inquiry by jurors in A.D. 1070. It contains no evidence of Roman influences.

The so-called Laws of William, his new legislation apart from the confirmation of old law, are extant in two widely different versions[3]; one, the most ancient, contained in the *Textus Roffensis* and Hoveden, and reprinted by the Bishop of Chester[4]; the second and fuller one, in the Red Book of the Exchequer and printed in Thorpe[5]. The latter version has been fully discussed by the Bishop[6], who holds it to date most probably from the reign of Edward I. One of its clauses purports to remit tallages, a boon appropriate in the reign which saw " De Tallagio non Concedendo" presented to the king, and the Confirmatio Cartarum granted. The form of the charter in the 1st person plural is unique at so early a date. The verbose description in the preamble; " *Francos et Britones Walliae et Cornubiae, Pictos et Scotos Albaniae*", is appropriate to the reign of Edward rather than to the time of the Conqueror. All the evidence therefore points to the Bishop's conclusion, in which Mr Freeman concurs, that the longer version dates from the time of Edward I., and is suggested by the controversies of his reign. The shorter form given by Hoveden[7] is probably

[1] Stubbs, Roger de Hoveden, II. 43. Thorpe, pp. 201—212.

[2] § 11.

[3] Stubbs, Roger de Hoveden, Pref. II. 22.

[4] Stubbs, S. C. p. 80.

[5] Thorpe, p. 211.

[6] Roger de Hoveden, Pref. II. 22—43.

[7] Ibid. II. 42.

"a mere collection of distinct enactments made at different times by the Conqueror." It is not one legislative act, nor even an authentic form of the various enactments made, some of which are accessible from other sources in a more ancient version.

According to a story repeated by Hoveden[1], William showed a marked preference for the *Danelagu*, or laws of the Danish part of England. This tale finds no support elsewhere and is probably incorrect. The Laws of William, as preserved in the shorter version, and his confirmation of the older laws afford no special traces of Roman influence.

There only remains the code of the "Laws of Henry I.", purporting to be a collection of his legislative enactments[2]. But this is clearly not authentic. The number it assigns to the English Bishoprics dates it after A.D. 1133; and it refers to the canonization of Edward the Confessor and Gratian's Codification of the Decretals, both which events took place in 1151. On the other hand it alludes to Queen Matilda as alive, who died in 1118, and contains no references to the laws of Henry II., who succeeded in 1154. Most of its clauses appear to be extracted from old English sources, mingled with some genuine ordinances of William I. The Bishop of Chester considers it "a collection of legal memoranda and records of custom, illustrated by reference to the Canon laws, but containing very many vestiges of old English jurisprudence." It is evidently of a later date than the reign of Henry I. "It would appear to give probable, but not authoritative illustrations of the amount of national custom existing in the country in the first half of the 11th century, but cannot be appealed to with any confidence except where it is borne out by other testimony."

Its most interesting feature for us is the evident acquaintance of the compiler with civil and canon law[3]. In dealing with the conduct of a suit he cites[4] the substance of a passage

[1] Freeman, *N. C.* iv. 425, v. 869.
[2] Freeman, *N. C.* v. 872. Thorpe, p. 267. Stubbs, *S. C.* 104.
[3] If compiled after 1150, Vacarius had begun to teach the Civil Law in England.
[4] Laws, 33, 4. Thorpe, p. 232. C. Theod. lib. 2. cap. 9.

from the Theodosian Code as to the time in which a defeated litigant might appeal against an unjust decision. One of the provisions as to the rights of a husband to use violence against an adulterer seems derived from a passage in one of the novels of Justinian[1]. The compiler also cites the Salic Law[2] as to accomplices in murder, and the Decretals[3] on clerical offenders, while one passage on the widow's rights is identical with a passage in the Ripuarian Laws[4]. A number of chapters contain provisions translated literally from the Saxon Laws[5].

While therefore the compilation is not a collection of laws promulgated by Henry I.[6], but a digest of Anglo-Saxon laws and usages made by some private individual, the fact remains that that private individual is acquainted with and even cites as of some authority systems of law, including the Roman, other than his own.

Any detailed examination of English Law after the Conquest we may leave till Glanvil and Bracton afford us materials more ample than the *Placita Anglo-Normannica*. We may however touch shortly on three features of the period; the rise of feudalism, the removal of the bishops from the secular court, and the changes in the law as to married women.

The removal of the bishops was effected by an ordinance of the Conqueror[7], and commences the long record of difficulties between the State and the Church. It is of interest for our subject, because in the presence of the bishops in the popular courts we have found a constant source of Roman influence on popular laws and customs. But this source of influence is much diminished by their removal to deal solely with those matters "*quae ad regimen animarum pertinent.*" Yet the judges were frequently ecclesiastics and thus in another quarter the clerical and Romanizing influence was continued.

Of greater importance is the rise of Feudalism. At the time of the Norman Conquest it is " a complete organization of society through the medium of land-tenure, in which, from the

---

[1] Laws, 82—8. Just. Nov. 117. Stephen, *Hist. Criminal Law*, i. 15; 55.

[2] Laws, 88, 10. Thorpe, p. 259.

[3] Laws, 5, 27. Thorpe, p. 221.

[4] Laws, 70, 22. Thorpe, p. 251.

[5] e.g. cc. 7, 8, 11, 70, 87, etc.

[6] Thorpe, p. 268, note.

[7] Stubbs, *S. C.* p. 81.

king down to the lowest landowner, all are bound together
by obligations of service and defence[1]." These obligations
are based on and regulated by the extent of the land, and
the nature of its tenure.   This Feudalism is distinctly
Frankish: as found in France, and introduced into England,
feudal relations had arisen from two sources, beneficial tenures and commendation. The conquering leaders distributed
the land among their followers as *beneficia,* to be held under
the obligation of assisting their lord by military service : or the
weaker landowners gave up their land to more powerful men,
and received it back, with protection, in return for faithful
service.   Commendation, on the other hand, was personal: it
involved the homage of the vassal and the protection of the
lord, but no alteration in the tenure of the vassal's estate.
Feudalism as combined from these had the two-fold character
of land-tenure and of personal relation.   As thus combined, it
was partly of Roman, and partly of German origin[2], "a compound of archaic barbarian usage with Roman Law." The
Roman jurisprudence gives the idea of the usufruct; the
German institutions that of personal subservience.   But there
is no sufficient ground for suggesting that the Roman *em-
phyteusis,* and relation of *patronus* and *cliens* have also a place
in its development.

English Feudalism differs widely from Feudalism on the
Continent.   This result is largely due to the much misunderstood Gemot of Salisbury, and the oath of fealty which "*all
land sittende men*" took there to William.   "Whereas Continental Feudalism was disruptive in tendency, and the vassal
owed allegiance to the *mesne,* rather than to the superior, lord,
the English system was centralizing and coherent in the higher
allegiance of the vassal to the king.   William's policy weakened
the *mesne* lords, and strengthened the crown ; their vast territorial holdings lost their power when scattered over England ;
their tenants' fealty was deprived of its strength by the rights
of the sovereign ; the king and the people were allied against

---

[1] Stubbs, I. 153, 252. Waitz, *D. V.*   [2] Stubbs, I. 254. Maine, *Ancient*
G. II. pp. 226—258. Maine, *Ancient*   *Law,* p. 365.
Law, p. 107.

the feudal lords. Moreover the Anglo-Saxon and Frankish systems had followed different lines of development. Something resembling Feudalism would have developed in England had the Norman keels never furrowed the sand at Pevensey, but it would have developed from different germs. Frank Feudalism sprang from benefices, and commendation; the English system was growing by the changing of the *comitatus* of the king, the *gesiths* or *thegns* doing personal service to their warrior leader, into a territorial nobility, whose lands had been given as a reward for personal service. Tenure of land from another was present; personal service was present, but they were not yet, as always in later feudalism, inseparably combined. Their origin, the territorial development of the *comitatus*, was peculiar to English history[1], and later English feudalism is largely indebted to the Anglo-Saxon polity.

That system became developed in all its oppressiveness by the ingenuity of Ranulf Flambard, the Justiciar of William Rufus, and was developed not by written legislation, but by the creation of custom by particular precedents. The firm rule of William's successor initiated the English judicial and administrative system. The Curia Regis, with its itinerant judges, is the origin of the Central Judicature, which harmonizes the practice of the popular courts of the shire; while the second Henry by making his sheriffs lawyers continues that unifying influence throughout the Courts of the Hundred. The period "which is called the reign of Stephen", had thrown the whole system into confusion and anarchy, but the genius of Henry II. brings order out of the chaos; the fiscal and judicial circuits are restored; the system of inquest by sworn recognitors is borrowed from the Franks and applied, at first for financial purposes, and then for judicial inquiries, in which sphere it is the precursor and parent of Trial by Jury.

Such are the great changes in the system which administered the law; but one considerable alteration in the law itself claims attention, as preparing the way for those alterations which the influence of the Roman Law effected in the position of married women.

---

[1] Stubbs, I. 152.

We have seen[1] that in later Saxon times the childless widow took one third of her husband's estate, the widow with children one half, in the absence of any express agreement as to the dowry. Such an agreement might either restrict this proportion, or extend it to one half if childless, or to the whole property if she had borne children; and this share was absolutely her own. But under the Norman rule[2] the dowry in the absence of agreement was restricted to a life interest in one third of the lands which the husband possessed at the time of the marriage, a portion which might, by express agreement, be either restricted, superseded by personalty, or enlarged to one third of the lands of which he was seised at any time during coverture. The dower from personalty was in the Saxon proportions, but, when given, it barred any dower from the realty[3]. This only applies to the lands held by military tenure; for in socage, gavelkind, and copyhold lands, the dower is still one half, and in the Borough English towns and in some manors the whole of the lands.

[1] *Vide supra*, p. 42.
[3] Kenny, p. 34.
[2] Kenny, p. 65.

CHAPTER VIII.

WE have now reached the limits of the first period in our inquiry, and have endeavoured to ascertain whether, in the first place, the Roman occupation of Britain left any traces of its influence on the Anglo-Saxon polity, and secondly, whether, from the landing of the Teutonic invaders down to the advent of the Justinianean learning, the Roman Law, as then taught or known on the continent, influenced the growth of English Law and institutions. In both these inquiries our results have been mainly negative.

The early English Law is distinctly Teutonic: Roman influences can only be suggested in the vague applications of principles so comprehensive as to be shadowy, or in minor points where careful manipulation of the evidence exhibits curious coincidences. Mr Seebohm's theory of the origin of manors in mingled South German and Roman sources comes nearest to satisfactory evidence, and even that we have seen to remain in the category of hypotheses which may be true but are as yet unproven. The introduction of written instruments as evidence of the transfer of property, and the adoption of wills, are certainly due to ecclesiastical and probably to Roman influences; and the presence of the bishops in the shiremoots may have affected Teutonic procedure, but the traces of such an influence are very slight. The Land-law apart from the manorial system is Teutonic; the Family Law is unmixed in its origin; the divisions of the country and the organization of the towns cannot be claimed with success as Roman, while civil and criminal procedure is utterly unlike that of the tribunals of Rome.

The Conquest, while at first it makes no great changes, has led to the interweaving of Norman and Frankish institutions with the English polity, but, except in as far as Feudalism is connected with the Roman *beneficia*, the influence of the Roman law is not put forth, or is powerless. From the era of Teutonic development we now turn to a period in which the law and its administrators are affected by an influence too fascinating in its intellectual charm to exert no sway over thoughtful minds, too powerful to leave no mark on English Law. In the train of the Archbishop of Canterbury, an Italian named Vacarius, learned in the Justinianean Law which the newly-born Law School of Bologna was teaching with a young convert's zeal, had landed on English shores; and from his lips Oxford and England heard the laws of Rome.

PART II.

ROMAN INFLUENCES IN ENGLISH LAW AFTER THE COMING OF VACARIUS.

CHAPTER I.

THE INTRODUCTION OF THE ROMAN LAW.

JUSTINIANEAN Law was almost unknown in the Western Empire until the teaching of the Law School at Bologna in the twelfth century brought it into prominence[1]. The tale, adopted by Blackstone, of the finding of a single copy of the Pandects at the siege of Amalfi in 1135, may be dismissed after Savigny's destructive criticism, which shows it to have originated long after the siege and probably in the desire of the Pisans to uphold the superiority of their text, the *Litera Pisana*, over the *Litera Bononiensis* of the rival school, Bologna. This latter was commenced by the lectures of Pepo, but first brought into fame by the teaching of Irnerius and his successors[2]. It illustrated the writings of Justinian by short notes, called *glosses*, and hence its teachers obtained the name of *Glossatores*. By their teaching the Roman Law rapidly spread among those Western nations who had only previously known it by the versions of the Theodosian code contained in the Alarician Breviary and Edict of Theodoric[3]. Both in Italy and France the new study was received with great favour and the Emperor Lotharius

---

[1] Kaufmann's *Mackeldey*, p. 66.
Twiss, *Bracton*, Pref. II. 68.
Selden ad Fletam, c. 6 § 2.
Irving's *Introduction to the Civil Law*, pp. 84—92. London, 1837.
Savigny's *Geschichte des Romischen Rechts im Mittelalter*. Heidelberg, 1815—1831.

[2] Bulgarus d. 1166. Martinus d. 1165. Rogerius d. 1192. Azo d. 1220. Accursius d. 1260.

[3] *Selden ad Fletam*, c. 5 § 4. *Mackeldey*, Kauf. pp. 48, 49.

enacted that causes should be decided according to the one
Roman *corpus* of the Civil Law[1].

Under these circumstances Theobald, Archbishop of Canterbury, in 1143 brought to England in his retinue Vacarius, a
Lombard skilled in the new learning[2]. Selden, aided by a
missing full-stop, has succeeded in most ingeniously confusing
the identity and history of Vacarius, but the tangle has been at
length unravelled by the learned monograph of Wenck. The
Norman Chronicle contains the statement: "*Obiit Bechardus,
VI Abbas Becci, cui successit Rogerius, Magister Vacarius,
gente Longobardus, cum leges Romanas anno* 1149 *in Anglia
discipulos doceret et multi tam divites quam pauperes ad eum
causa discendi confluerent. Suggestione pauperum de Codice
et Digesto exceptos ix libros composuit, qui sufficiunt ad omnes
legum lites quae in scolis frequentari solent decidendas, si quis
eos perfecte noverit.*" The full-stop being omitted between
Rogerius and *Magister*, Selden has first identified Rogerius,
7th Abbot of Bec, who was afterwards offered the see of
Canterbury, with Vacarius, and has then further identified his
composite with Rogerius Beneventanus, an Italian civilian
and author of several legal works. He made this composite
being leave England in 1149 for his abbey, and consequently a
teacher of Roman Law in England before 1149. This confusion
Wenck has succeeded in clearing up by showing that the name
of the seventh abbot was Roger de Bailleul, proving his French
origin; that he was therefore not the same as the Italian Civilian, and that the impossible combination "Rogerius Magister
Vacarius," indicates clearly a dropped full-stop after "Rogerius."

Vacarius undoubtedly lectured at Oxford in the Roman Law,
and that University has ever since been connected with that
study. Its Bachelor of Civil Law takes what are practically
honours in its Law School, its Doctor of Civil Law possesses the

[1] Selden, c. 6 § 2.

[2] *Magister Vacarius, primus Juris
Romani in Anglia Professor.* Wenck,
Leipsic, 1820. Duck, *De usu et authoritate Juris Civilis Romanorum,* London,
1679. Irving, pp. 84—89. Spence, I.
108. *Selden ad Fletam,* c. 7 § 3. Wenck

puts the date of Vacarius' coming between the years 1143—1146. Wenck,
p. 21.

The article on "Vacarius" in the
Penny Encyclopaedia gives the results
of Wenck and Savigny.

most honourable degree the University can confer. Its doctors may be open to the censure of the anonymous pasquinade:

" *In Institutis Comparo vos brutis;*
In Digestis nihil potestis;
In Codice satis modice;
In Novellis, Similes Asellis;
Et vos creamini Doctores! O tempora! O mores! [1]"
but the memory of the ancient studies has survived in the name.

The work of Vacarius, in nine books, consisted in a series of comments on the compilations of Justinian. His lectures appear to have been directed to those parts of the Roman Law which bore upon or illustrated the Law of England. For it was a principle of the Vacarian school that those parts only of the Roman Jurisprudence should be adopted which were in harmony with the development of the English Law. The former statutes of the Chair of Civil Law at Oxford contain the regulation: " *quam libet partem Corporis Juris Civilis exponat, eosque praecipue titulos, qui ad usum et praxim in hoc regno conducunt.*"

But the study of Roman Law in England did not find favour with the Crown. John of Salisbury reports the action of Stephen [2]: " *Tempore Regis Stephani a regno jussae sunt leges Romanas, quas in Britanniam, domus venerabilis patris Theobaldi...asciverat. Ne quis etiam libros retineret edicto regis prohibitum est, et Vacario nostro indictum silentium: sed, Deo favente eo magis virtus legis invaluit, quo eam amplius nitebatur impietas infirmare.*"

Some attribute this prohibition to personal enmity against the Archbishop, the patron of the new learning; others to the fact that Vacarius taught also Canon Law, which conflicted with the laws of the realm. This latter theory seems improbable; for the first authoritative collection of Canon Law, the *Decretorum Collectanea* of Gratian, was only published in 1151, and Wenck is of opinion that Vacarius did no more than borrow from the Canon Law some few illustrations for his Civil Law lectures. Moreover the study of the Civil Law shortly afterwards fell into

---

[1] Cited in Warren, *Law Studies*, II. 1341.   [2] *Selden ad Fletam*, c. 7 § 3.

disfavour with the Papal Court, on account of its tendency to supersede the Canon Law. In 1164[1] Pope Alexander III. decreed that no religious person should teach Physic or Civil Law out of his monastery, and this was confirmed by Pope Honorius III. William of Malmesbury had said *"nullus clerus, nisi causidicus[2]"*; and the church from the earliest times was well skilled in the Roman Law, and apt to extend the knowledge of it. The Schools of Learning of York and Northumbria, before their destruction by the Danes, were skilled in the Roman Law as then known; St Dunstan had books of Roman Law among his library; Archbishop Lanfranc who had been prior of Bec, *"illa famosa schola,"* was learned in the *Jus civile*[3]; and Thomas à Becket had studied Law at Oxford[4]. The household and pupils of Theobald continued the knowledge of the Law of Rome. *Policraticus*, the work of John of Salisbury written some time before 1180, constantly cites the Civil Law, in some cases as being referred to in English Courts[5]. The Ordinary considers a matter referred from the king's court by the aid of *"Legum Principum et Civilium,"* and Rescripts of the Roman Emperors are cited[6]. Petrus Blesensis gives an interesting account of the studies of the Archbishop's household in the reign of Henry II., when *" omnes quaestiones regni nodosae referuntur ad nos,"* and the household exercised themselves *"in causarum decisione*[6]*."*

Before dealing with the legal writings of the period, Glanvil, Bracton, Britton and Fleta, some contemporary references to the *Jus Civile* will show how the air was full of the Law of Rome. Giraldus Cambrensis, writing at the end of the 12th century, cites with approval the Institutes of Justinian. Gervase of Tilbury, a little later, in computing the size of Britain, cites the Pandects as an authority for the measure he adopts[7]. The Vision

---

[1] *Selden ad Fletam*, c. 7 § 7.

[2] *ibid.* The Monks of Abingdon in 1070 were *"legibus patriae optime instituti."*

[3] Selden, *ibid.*

[4] Irving, p. 89. Duck, II. 8. 2. 29 : *inter juris Romani peritos oxonienses enumeratur.*

[5] Selden, c. 8 § 1. Twiss, *Bracton*, II.

Pref. 76.

[6] Selden, *ibid.*

Holcot writing temp. Henry III. says *" Leges et Canones innumerabiliter sunt fecundae, concipiunt divitias, et pariunt dignitates; ad illas confluunt quasi tota multitudo scholarum his diebus."* Duck, *De usu* II. 8. 2. 32.

[7] Selden, c. 8 § 1.

of the Monk of Evesham speaks of a certain monk as the most learned of the Civilians and Canonists of his time; *"peritissimus eorum quos Legistas et Decretistas appellant*[1]*."* The *"Golias"* sarcastic poems of the 12th and 13th centuries, usually attributed to Walter Map, contain traces of the widespread authority of Roman Sources. The poem, *"De Judicio extremo"* in describing the stern justice of the Last Day, proceeds:

> "Judicabit judices judex generalis;
> Ibi nihil proderit dignitas papalis,
> Sive sit episcopus, sive cardinalis,   .
> Reus condemnabitur, nec dicetur: Qualis.
> Ibi nihil proderit quidquam allegare,
> Neque vel *excipere*, neque *replicare*,
> Neque ad apostolicam sedem appellare,
> *Reus condemnabitur*, nec dicetur, quare.
> Cogitate, miseri, qui et quales estis,
> Quid in hoc judicio dicere potestis,
> *Ubi nullus Codici locus aut Digestis*,
> Idem erit dominus, judex, actor, testis[2]."

On the other hand, in 1234[3], for some unknown reason, the teaching of Law was forbidden in the schools of London[4]. But John de Lexington, one of the Justices in Eyre, is described as, *"in utroque jure, Canonico scilicet et civili, peritus*[4]*."* Edward I. endeavoured to officially assist the study by bringing over to England Franciscus Accursius, son of the celebrated Glossator, but he seems never to have got further than Toulouse[4]: *"interea Tolosae jus civile aliquamdiu docuit."* In the Yearbooks for 1312 Inge, Justice, is recorded as saying to the Counsel in a case of cosinage[5]: *"Que respondez vous à la ley empiel donque sur quel ley de terre est fondu, et que veut que heritage soit descendu a plus digne,* quod possessio fratris facit sororem here-

---

[1] Selden, c. 8 § 1.

[2] *Mackeldey*, Kauf. p. 72.

In 1217, the Constitutions of the Bishop of Salisbury ran " *Nec advocati sint clerici, vel sacerdotes in foro seculari, nisi vel proprias causas, vel miserabilium personarum prosequuntur.*" Spelman, *Concilia* II. 140.

[3] And in 1254, Innocent IV. prohibited any Professors or Advocates of the Law assuming Ecclesiastical dignities. Duck, *De usu* II. 8. 2. 33.

Duck states decidedly " *in judiciis quae secundum jus Anglicanum exercentur, juri civili Romanorum authoritatem tribui nunquam passi sunt.*" (II. 8. 3. 4).

[4] *Selden ad Fletam*, c. 8 § 2. Spence *Eq. Jurisd.* I. 131.

[5] Yearbooks: 5 Edw. II. f. 148.

dem?" *Devom*, a counsel, answers: "The imperial law rests on right, but we are in possession, and claim nothing through the brother." And so in the Reports of Richard of Winchedon, and in a MS. preserved in the Inner Temple, and cited by Selden, the Pandects are referred to by Counsel and Commentators on at least three recorded occasions[1].

But during the 14th century the knowledge of Roman Law began to wane. In 1347 Skipwith, whom Selden calls a celebrated lawyer, dealing with a case of *"inhibitionem novi operis"* says: *"in ceux parols* 'contra inhibitionem novi operis' *ny ad pas entendement"*: to which the Judge answers; *"Ce n'est que un restitution en leur ley pourque a cel n'avoums regard[2]."* And there is very little trace of its influence on the pleadings of the time. The Barons at Merton in 1235 had expressly refused to adopt the rule of the Civil and Canon Law as to Legitimation of natural children by subsequent marriage in the celebrated words: *"Nolumus leges Angliae mutare[3]."* In the disputes in 1292 as to the succession of Scotland, the citation of the Imperial Law was expressly rejected[4]. A proclamation of Edward II. contains the phrase: *"eo quod regnum Angliae ab omni subjectione Imperiali sit liberrimum"*; but this, though cited by Selden, seems rather to concern the authority in England of nominees of the Emperor[4]. In the indictments of 1388, the king referred the charges "to the judges, serjeants, and other sages of the law of the realm, *and also to the sages of the civil law*": both classes of sages took the matter into consideration and reported that "the appeal was not made according to the requisitions *of either law."* Upon which the Lords of Parliament resolved that the matter must be decided in Parliament and by the law of Parliament *"pour que ce royaume d'Engleterre n'estait devant ces heures, ne à l'entent du roy...et seignoirs du parlement unque ne serra rulé ne governé par la ley civil[5]."*

These scattered references show a period of popularity almost amounting to enthusiasm, followed as might be expected

---

[1] Selden, c. 8 § 3.

[2] *ibid.*, § 5. Case of the Abbot of Torre. Y. B. Mich. 22 Edw. III. pl. 37.

[3] Selden, c. 9 § 2. Stubbs *Hist.* II. 52.

[4] Selden, c. 9 § 2.

[5] 3 *Rolls of Parl.*, 229—244, 11 Rich. II. Selden, c. 9 § 2. Stephen, *Hist. Crim. L.* I. 152. Coxe's *Güterbock*, p. 13 note.

by a period of decline and neglect. They afford no ground for the remark of Chief Justice Fortescue that some kings of England "*leges civiles ad Angliae regimen inducere et patrias leges repudiare fuisse conatos*[1]." The only king whose actions even suggest such an assertion is Edward I., whose attempted patronage of Accursius might be supposed to have such an aim, and the whole tenor of his legislative history makes the supposition absurd.

But this period of enthusiasm corresponds with that of the production of the first systematic treatises on English Law; and, if those treatises were affected by its popularity, the results of Roman influence might survive through the centuries when Roman law, without disguise, was suspected and even repudiated. To the works of Glanvil and Bracton therefore we now turn.

[1] Fortescue. *De Laudibus* c. 33. *ad Fletam*, c. 9 § 2.
Selden, *Notes on Fortescue* p. 40. *Selden*

CHAPTER II.

THE first systematic Treatise on the Laws of England is a work entitled, " *Tractatus de Legibus et Consuetudinibus Regni Angliae*[1]," and usually attributed to Ranulph de Glanvil, Chief Justiciar during the reign of Henry II., and to a date between the years 1180, and 1190[2]. It has a definite and somewhat limited scope, which its Preface states thus: "*Leges autem et jura regni scripto universaliter concludi nostris temporibus omnino quidem impossibile est, cum propter scribentium ignorantiam tum propter earum multitudinem confusam; verum sunt quaedam in curia generalia et frequentius usitata, quae scripto commendare non mihi videtur praesumtuosum.*" His materials for the treatise are "*Leges regni, et consuetudines de ratione introductae et diu obtentae*"; and he aims at constructing a hand book of procedure in the Curia Regis, "very useful to most persons, and highly necessary to assist the memory[3]." The author is acquainted with the Civil and Canon Laws, and has made some, though not a great, use of them. The Preface, commencing "*Regiam Potestatem*", is modelled on the Procemium, "*Imperatoriam majestatem,*" to the *Institutes* of Justinian, which indeed seems to have been a favourite subject for imitation or

---

[1] Glanvil, translated by Beames, Lond. 1812. *Bracton*, Twiss, i. Pref. 30—32. Güterbock, pp. 31, 44, 48. Spence, i. 119—123. Foss, *Judges of England* i. 180, 376. Reeves, i. 254.

[2] There is no positive evidence for

ascription to him, but tradition and the evidently authoritative position of the writer, point strongly to the chief justiciar, who arrived at that post in 1180, and was killed at Acre in 1190.

[3] Beames' Translation.

plagiarism. The *"Regiam Majestatem"*, that Scottish source of legal controversy[1], has in all probability copied it through Glanvil; Bracton imitates it, probably directly; and Fleta has copied it.

Glanvil in some places expressly points out where the English Law differs from the Civil or Canon Law. Book VII. begins: *"In alia enim acceptione accipitur Dos secundum Leges Romanas,"* and its 15th chapter points out the difference of Law as to Legitimation: *"et quidem licet secundum canones et Leges Romanas talis filius sit legitimus haeres, tamen secundum jus et consuetudinem Regni nullo modo &c."* But such differences are not always noted, either because the writer was not aware of them, or because the competing rule had not been so put forward, as to make a statement of the distinction necessary. For instance, where the rule is laid down that the custody of the person shall never be in those who would succeed to the inheritance, no notice is taken of the contrary Roman rule, *"ubi successionis est emolumentum ibi et onus tutelae esse debet[2]."*

The only part of the work which suggests Roman influence is Book X., which deals with Contract Law. Some terminology is Roman: e.g. *crimen falsi*[3], (I. 2: XIV. 7); *crimen quod in legibus dicitur crimen laesae majestatis* (I. 2): *dominium* (VII. 1); the terminology of Contract Law, *mutuum, commodatum, locatio, conductio, emptio-venditio, arrha,* (III. 1: X. *passim*)[4]. The Tenth Book has however a distinctly Roman appearance, so much so, that Bishop Nicholson has accused Glanvil of "aping the Roman code[5]." It follows the Roman divisions; *"aut enim debetur ei quid ex causa mutui aut ex causa venditionis, aut ex commodato, aut ex locato, aut ex deposito[6]."* *Mutuum* is defined, conformably with Roman law, as dealing with things *"quae consistunt in numero vel pondere vel mensura[7],"* but Glanvil

---

[1] (1) as to whether it is original, or derived from Glanvil.

(2) as to whether it is part of the Scotch law.

[2] Glan. vii. 11. Just. *Inst.* i. 17, pr. and cf. Stephen, *Hist. C. L.* iii. 130, on Glan. x. 13.

[3] in this case there is similarity in substance, Stephen i. 20, iii. 378.

[4] See also Bk. 12. c. 24, for possible influence of the rules as to *pluris petitio.*

[5] Beames, p. 246, note.

[6] Gl. x. 3.

[7] Just., *Inst.* iii. 14 pr.

immediately plunges into the further security of *datio plegiorum,* which shows no traces of the influence of the laws as to *fide jussores.* In c. 6 the author breaks away from his definition of *mutuum,* and speaks of lands and tenements as lent as a *mutuum.* *Commodatum* is defined as *"ut si rem meam tibi gratis commodem ad usum inde percipiendum in servitio tuo,"* but if the thing is lost or destroyed, Glanvil requires the borrower to pay a reasonable price, while the Roman law only did so if the borrower had not used *exacta diligentia,* except in the case of a *mutuum*[1]. So under *Emptio-Venditio*[2], whereas Roman law completed the purchase as soon as the price was fixed, Glanvil required also either delivery or payment in whole or in part, or earnest, *arrha.* Where an earnest had been given, the buyer could recede by forfeiting it, but, as to the seller, *"Quaero",* said Glanvil, *"utrum sine poena id facere possit."* By the time of Bracton the Roman rule of rescission on forfeiture of twice the earnest had been adopted[3]. An express warranty of quality is apparently necessary to support rescission, whereas the Roman law implied such a warranty in all contracts. *Locatio-conductio* is defined : *"ut cum quis locat rem suam alii usque ad certum terminum, certa inveniente mercede*[4]*,"* of which the *certus terminus* has no place in Roman law ; and the remaining chapters are filled with purely English procedure. But Glanvil reminds his readers : *"Praedictos vero contractus qui ex privatorum consensu fiunt, breviter transigimus, quia privatas conventiones non solet Curia domini Regis tueri, et quidem de talibus contractibus, qui quasi private quaedam conventiones censeri possunt, se non intromittit Curia Domini Regis*[5]*."* For all contracts which could not be proved by evidence admissible in the King's Court (i.e. the duel, writing, or transaction witnesses), were matters for the ecclesiastical courts[6]. Hence contracts neither in writing nor involving the transfer of property did not come before the Courts of the King.

---

[1] Gl. x. 13, cf. Just. *Inst.* iii. 14, 2.

[2] Gl. x. 14. Just. *Inst.* iii. 23, pr.

[3] Br. f. 62, a. See *post,* p. 93.

[4] Gl. x. 18.

[5] See also x. 8, *"ideo si privatae conventiones non fuerint servatae, Curia Domini Regis se inde non intromittit."* See *post,* pp. 100, 101.

[7] Holmes, *Common Law,* p. 265.

This Book on Contracts then owes very little except terminology to the Roman law; it exhibits large omissions and frequent variances, and even the terms taken undergo alterations of meaning. Its Roman appearance may have been derived from the clerical judges of the ecclesiastical courts, which punished breaches of contract as "*laesio vel transgressio fidei*[1]."

Our conclusion therefore is that the work of Glanvil, though it bears traces of his acquaintance with the Roman law, and adopts in some few cases its terminology, is otherwise entirely free from Roman influence, and shows the almost complete purity of the English Law at the end of the 12th century from Roman elements.

[1] Güterbock, p. 61, note.

CHAPTER III.

ROMAN LAW IN BRACTON.

THE work of Bracton[1]: "*De Legibus et Consuetudinibus Angliae*", calls for far more careful attention. The writer was evidently well acquainted with the laws of Rome, and in one way or another Roman learning has supplied no small part of his work, but the extent and nature of its influence is a matter of great controversy. While Mr Reeves is of opinion that the Roman law is only used by Bracton as an illustration and ornament, not adduced as an authority, and doubts whether the Roman parts of his work if put together would fill three whole pages of his book[2]; M. Houard[3] has been so struck with his Romanizing tendencies as to omit him entirely from his collection of Anglo-Norman legal sources, as a corrupter of the law of England. Sir Henry Maine speaks of "the plagiarisms of Bracton," and considers it "one of the most hopeless enigmas in the history of jurisprudence that an English writer of the time of Henry III. should have been able to put off on his countrymen as a compendium of pure English law, a treatise of which the entire form and a third of the contents were directly borrowed from the Corpus Juris[4]." Biener holds that Bracton allows no legislative authority to the Roman law[5]; Spence,

---

[1] *Bracton*, ed. Sir T. Twiss. 6 vols. Rolls Series. *Bracton and his relation to the Roman Law* : by Prof. Carl Güterbock, trans. by Coxe, Philadelphia, 1866. Foss, *Judges of England*, II. 249—252. Long's *Discourses*, Lond. 1847, pp. 93—107. *Text of Bracton*, by Prof. Vinogradoff,

Law Quarterly Review, April, 1885.

[2] Finl. Reeves, I. 529.

[3] *Traités sur les Coutumes Anglo-Normandes*. Paris, 1776.

[4] Ancient Law, p. 82.

[5] *Das Englische Geschwornengericht*, cited by Güterbock, p. 56.

that he reproduced Roman incorporations which were good and valid English law[1]; while Prof. Güterbock is of opinion that Bracton has in general reproduced only those Roman elements, which were actually received in England as valid law, though in some instances he has made additions to them[2]. Where authorities differ so widely, a decided answer seems hardly possible.

The work itself professes to deal with "*facta et casus qui quotidie emergunt et eveniunt in regno Angliae, ut sciatur quae competat actio, et quod breve[3]*"; its avowed object is to teach, "*qualiter et quo ordine lites et placita decidantur secundum leges et consuetudines Anglicanas*"; and this task is undertaken "*ad vetera judicia justorum perscrutanda[4],*" by examining diligently the ancient judgments of the wise.

It is now accepted that the author is Henricus de Bracton (or Bratton), who appears constantly as a justiciar between 1246 and 1267. He was an ecclesiastic, Archdeacon of Barnstaple, and afterwards Chancellor of Exeter Cathedral. The date of his work, or of the greater part of it (for, as its second title, *in varios tractatus distincti*, denotes, the several tracts may easily have been composed at different times), is probably between the years 1256-1259[5]. Since Glanvil's time the new procedure had become more settled, and the *eyres* of the justices itinerant had provided ample precedents, of which Bracton avails himself to the full. He cites 378 original writs and 484 decided cases[6], all of the reign of Henry III., with one exception in the reign of John. The cases cited are usually those tried before Martin de Pateshull or William de Ralegh[7]. The former occupied a prominent position among the *justiciarii* at the end of the reign of John, and beginning of the reign of Henry III. One of the justiciars accompanying him on circuit prays the Court at Westminster for relief, " for the said Martin is strong, and in his labours so sedulous and practised that all his

[1] Spence, I. 124.
[2] Güt. p. 57.
[3] Br. f. I. b.
[4] f. I. a.
[5] For a discussion of the date see

Twiss, I. Pref. 16—25, Güterbock, p. 25.
[6] Güt., Coxe's note, p. 45.
[7] Twiss, I. Pref. 28, II. Pref. 40, III. Pref. 27.

associates, especially W. de Ralegh and myself, are overpowered by his labour, for he works every day from sunrise to night[1]." Ralegh was also a prominent ecclesiastic, and a judge from 1229 to 1239 when he became Bishop of Norwich. In 1258[2] Henry de Bracton was ordered to return the Rolls of M. de Pateshull and W. de Radley, which he had in use, probably for this work ; and from these two justiciars Bracton has garnered his store of precedents. He cites a few statutes[3], especially the Statute of Merton. There seem only a few passages in his work, which suggest an immediate use of Glanvil[4], and in some of these Bracton is far more diffuse and detailed.

The work is divided into five books[5] ; the first two divided into chapters and paragraphs, the last three into 15 treatises on procedure. The work thus falls into two parts.

I.—Books I., II. and III. to folio 104*a* ; which contain the substantive law. This part follows the Justinianean division of *jus ad personas*, vel *ad res*, vel *ad actiones pertinens*[6].

II. The remainder of the work is composed of tracts on criminal law and legal procedure, which however leave the treatise unfinished. In this part, owing to the peculiarly English character of the procedure, the Roman division is followed less closely, but we have the fundamental division into *Actiones Reales, Personales, vel Mixtae* and the subdivision of *Actiones Reales* into *Possessoriae vel Petitoriae*.

There is ample evidence of Bracton's intimate acquaintance with the civil and canon law. He expressly cites the *Digest* twelve times, and the *Code* ten times[7]. The Novels are not referred to, and the *Institutes* only once, and then in conjunction with a source with which Bracton was more familiar : " *ut in Institutis plenius inveniri potest et in Summa Azonis*[8]." But a large

---

[1] Twiss, II. Pref. 42.

[2] Madox, *Hist. of Exchequer* II. 257.

[3] Br. ff. 227, 416, etc. Güt. p. 44.

[4] cf. Gl. VII. 5, with Br. II. c. 26. Gl. x. 14, with Br. II. c. 27. Güt. p. 44. I should add to these, the passage on treason. Gl. XIV. 1. Br. f. 118 b : and the definition of murder, Gl. XIV. 3. Br. f. 134, b.

[5] For abstract, see Güt. pp. 35—38. Long, pp. 93—94. Reeves, I. 530.

[6] Thus: *Jus ad Personas*, Lib. I. c. 6—11. *Jus ad Res*, Lib. I. c. 12, Lib. II. *Jus ad actiones*, Lib. III. tract. I, c. 1—4.

[7] Güt. p. 50, 51, note.

[8] Br. f. 10.

number of passages from the Roman law are incorporated in the text, without any acknowledgement of their origin. Most of Bracton's Roman materials are derived indirectly from the *Corpus Juris* through the *Summa Azonis*, the summary of the Roman law compiled by Azo, the celebrated *Glossator* of Bologna, who died about 1230[1]. This work was in such high repute in Italy as to give rise to the popular proverb "*Chi non ha Azo, non vada al Palazzo*," or will not rise to the judicial office. With this *Summa* Bracton was well acquainted, and where in his 1st and 2nd Books he follows the order of the Institutes, he usually transcribes the corresponding passage from Azo. His knowledge of any other legal writers seems doubtful[2].

The Canon Law is cited in two or three places, apparently from the Decretals of Gratian and incorporated in others; Bracton also cites the provisions of the Lateran Council of 1219. The Canon Law has influenced his account of the Criminal Law[3].

A statement by Duck that Bracton taught Civil Law at Oxford, though not improbable has no direct evidence in support of it[4]. At the same time, the formalism of parts of the first three Books, and the closeness with which they follow Azo, suggest that they are founded on lectures or readings on the subject.

Bracton's First Book: On Persons.

Bracton's first book is misnamed "*De Rerum Divisione*." This title only applies to its last chapter, which should in strictness form the first chapter of Book II. A general introduction (cc. 1—5), and chapters "*de personis et earum statu*" (cc. 6—11), compose the rest of the book. I have carefully compared it with the corresponding portions of the *Summa* of Azo[5], and with the Justinianean sources, and I have no hesitation

---

[1] Twiss, Pref. I. 28, 34, Pref. II. 80, Güt. p. 51,—following Eschbach, Mackeldey gives 1220.

[2] Güterbock finds no trace of the influence of *Vacarius*, and only one possible quotation from *Placentinus*; Twiss alleges one citation from *Bulgarus*, but the reading is doubtful. Güt. p. 55. Twiss, VI. Pref. 53.

[3] Güt. p. 64. Twiss, I. Pref. 38, 39. Stephen, *Hist. Crim. Law* III.

[4] *De usu* II. 8, 3, 9, citing Bale, *Scriptor. Britan. cent.* 3.

[5] *Summa Azonis*, Venice, 1596. Bk. I. and II. tit. 1, of Azo's version of the Institutes.

in saying that about two thirds of it are taken all but *verbatim* from Azo. Where the *Institutes* are cited indirectly, which frequently happens, they are quoted in the form given to them by Azo. In only two places does Bracton break away for more than three or four lines of his work from his model[1]. On the other hand, while so much of Bracton is derived from Azo, large portions of Azo, such as the titles on *adoptio, capitis diminutio,* and several on *tutela* and *cura,* have been omitted as inapplicable to English Law.

A careful study of Bracton's variations from the *Summa* suggests his method of procedure. He had to reduce to form a chaotic mass of English Law and custom, "*omne jus de quo tractare proposuimus...secundum leges et consuetudines Anglicanas.*[2]" His object was to reduce this confusion to such order that judgment by precedent or according to rule might be possible:—"*a similibus procedere ad similia*[3]." In the Roman Law he had ready to his hand an admirable form. He followed Azo closely, omitting such parts as were inconsistent with the existing English Law; varying those parts which might by modification be made consistent; and adding illustrations of his own from English sources, where the Roman ones did not strike him as apt. But where there was no English Law on the matter treated of he adopted Azo almost exactly, not from any desire to impose Roman Law on England, but because he thus gave completeness to his exposition, while, as the matter had never arisen in English Law, he perhaps did not consider it of great importance. We can thus explain the constant appearance in the extracts from Azo of Roman terms, having no English counterpart, which Bracton has not apparently thought it worth while to alter[4]. To read the two works side by side is the best

[1] c. 8, on feudal dignities. c. 10, on serfs and serfdom, in the middle of which the Roman mark of tame animals, having "*animum et consuetudinem revertendi,*" is applied to slaves.

[2] Bk. I. c. 6. f. 4, b.

[3] f. 1, b.

[4] *e. g. Praetor enim jus dicitur reddere,* (Azo, p. 1048, Br. f. 3), *usus, ususfructus, patria potestas, manumissio,* *adoptio,* the Roman names of servitudes, *haereditas jacens, emancipatio, res sacrae, religiosae, sanctae, mobiles et immobiles.* But it is difficult to explain his adoption *verbatim* of Azo on the sacred nature of walls, and the capital offences committed by those who get over them. Br. f. 8. Azo, p. 1063. *Sub,* p. 127.

proof of the correctness of this theory of his method and it would be difficult without great tediousness to afford equally forcible evidence; but a few striking examples of each class of variation may be supplied.

I. *Cases where Bracton has omitted passages of Azo as inconsistent with English Law.* Azo defines the seashore as public up to the rise of the highest winter tide : Bracton, following him verbatim before and after this passage, omits it as conflicting with the claim of the Crown to the shore between high and low-water mark[1]. Similarly, Bracton omits the rules as to the rights of the finder of a *thesaurus*, as conflicting with the Crown-rights to Treasure Trove[2]. And these instances are the more striking because immediately before and after the omitted passages Bracton is following Azo very closely[3].

II. *Cases where Bracton has modified passages from Azo into consistence with English Law.* This is especially seen in the application of the maxim *Partus sequitur ventrem*[4]. This was only the English rule in cases of illegitimacy ; as Bracton says, " *sequitur conditionem matris quasi vulgo conceptus.*" If either of lawfully married parents was *constitutus in villenagio*, the child was a serf, but lawfully married parents, not in villeinage, made the child free, though the mother was born a serf[5]. Bracton can hardly fail to have been aware of this difference from the Roman Law, and Littleton, who followed him, certainly was as he writes, " *et c'est contrarie a la ley civille car la est dit, partus sequitur ventrem*[6]." A similar change is seen in Bracton's use of the two terms, *statu liber* and *adscriptitius glebae.* The *statu liber* in Roman Law is a slave "*qui statutam et destinatam in tempus vel conditionem libertatem*

---

[1] Br. f. 8.   Azo, p. 1061.

[2] Br. f. 8.   Azo, p. 1063.

[3] See also Azo, p. 1055. *In potestate aliena sunt servi, item filii.* Bracton (f. 9, b) omits *item filii.* He also omits Azo's passage (p. 1063) as to the sacredness of *legati.*

[4] Br. f. 5.   Azo, p. 1052.

[5] Güterbock's statement (p. 81), that in marriage the offspring followed the

father, is shown to be too wide by Bracton's "*Item dicitur servus natione, de libero genitus, qui se copulavit villanae in villenagio constitutae sive copula maritalis intervenerit.*" f. 4.

[6] Littleton, *Tenures* § 187. As to the genuineness of this passage see the note to this section in Tomlins' edition, Lond. 1841.

habet[1]"; being conditionally freed by will. Bracton, citing the phrase from Azo, uses it of a slave who has deserted his master and whom his master does not claim within a year[2]. So the *adscriptitius glebae* in Roman Law was a *colonus* bound to the land, who passed with its sale, and had no rights of property against his master[3]. But Bracton uses the term of a freeman holding in villeinage who cannot be dispossessed of his land by his lord so long as he pays the customary dues. Again, Azo, speaking of the duration of *patria potestas*, says, "*Item morte civili dissolvatur, ut cum pater damnatur in metallum vel in opus metalli vel deportatur in insulam*," which Bracton corrects into— "*item morte civili ut si pater damnetur propter aliquam feloniam commissam*[4]."

III. *Cases where Bracton illustrates his Roman principles by English examples. Jus possessionis*[5] is explained by a feud, the subject of an *assize mort d'ancester*, and a freehold held for life. Azo's Roman illustrations of the maxim "*conditio feminarum est deterior in multis quam masculorum*[6]" are omitted. His explanation of *emancipatio* is accompanied in Bracton by the remark "*secundum quod antiquitus fieri solet*[7]": and the passage on *tutela* is expanded by references to the wardship of feudal lords[8]. Cemeteries are introduced as an illustration of *res sacrae* and the statement that they cease to be sacred if taken by the enemy is omitted[9]. And there is throughout the work a revision on minor points, which shows that Bracton has copied with intelligence. Thus he only reproduces three of Azo's six meanings of "*jus civile*[10]," omitting references to the Twelve

---

[1] *Dig.* 40, 7, 1.

[2] Br. ff. 4, b, 7, 197, b. *Est enim statu liber qui personam habet standi in judicio quasi liber, licet non sit.* cf. Azo, 1051, 1052. Bracton also introduces a new condition of *statu servi*, analogous to *liber homo bona fide serviens.*

[3] Cod. xi. 47. Br. f. 7. *Dicuntur glebae ascripticii, quia tali gaudent privilegio, quod a gleba amoveri non poterunt, quamdiu solvere possunt debitas pensiones*, cf. Azo, 1051.

[4] Azo, p. 1057. Br. f. 6, b. Cf. also Azo, p. 1077 with Bracton, f. 6, a, on *intolerabilis injuria*, and see Vinogradoff, 197.

[5] f. 3. But see on this passage Vinogradoff, 196. See also on *ingenui* (f. 5).

[6] Azo, p. 1054. Br. f. 5.

[7] Azo, p. 1057. Br. f. 6, b.

[8] f. 6, b.

[9] f. 8. Azo, p. 1062.

[10] f. 4. Azo, p. 1050.

Tables and the *Responsa Prudentum,* and the statement that "*jus civile*" without other words refers to the Law of Rome.

To turn to positive results Bracton has taken the definitions of *justitia, jus, jurisprudentia, aequitas,* and the *tria praecepta juris,* from the *Institutes* as represented in Azo, together with his distinction between human and divine justice and much connecting matter[1]. In his fifth chapter[2] he has the definitions of *jus naturae, jus gentium, jus civile,* and the division into *jus privatum* and *jus publicum,* relating *ad statum reipublicae*[3], and dealing with the subject matter of *sacra, sacerdotes, magistratus.* The sixth chapter[4] contains the Institutional divisions into *jus ad personas, vel ad res, vel ad actiones pertinens,* and of *homines* into *liberi* and *servi*; Azo's difficulties as to *adscriptitii* and *statu liberi*; the definitions of liberty and slavery, taken through Azo, from the *Institutes*; the maxim *partus sequitur ventrem*; and parts of Azo on *ingenui,* especially a passage on the effect of servitude during pregnancy[5]. In his seventh chapter he follows Azo on *libertini* and on monsters, even in his quaint illustrations[6]. The eighth chapter, on the ranks of persons, is of Bracton's own composition. The ninth contains the Institutional division, *homines sui aut alieni juris,* with Azo's addition "*aut dubii*[7]." Azo's account of *postliminium* is taken almost verbatim, with one curious exception[8]. The maxims, "*quidquid per servum juste acquiritur, id domino acquiritur,*" and "*pater est quem nuptiae demonstrant,*" are both adopted. The tenth chapter expands Azo on guardianship with reference to feudal wardship; and the whole of this chapter, which deals with a subject on which English materials

---

[1] Br. I. c. 4. Azo, p. 1047.

[2] Azo, p. 1048.

[3] Azo has *ad statum rei Romanae.*

[4] Azo, p. 1051.

[5] Azo, 1052. Just. *Inst.* I. 4, pr.

[6] Azo, p. 1053, 4.

[7] Azo, p. 1055. *Ins.* I. 8.

[8] Where Azo says (p. 1055) it is *impossible* that a prisoner should have a son *in potestate sua,* Bracton, using the same arguments in the same words, writes it is *possible* (f. 6). This is probably a transcriber's or printer's error, though Sir T. Twiss takes no notice of the incongruity. cf. Br. f. 18, b, *valent,* with *Dig.* 39, 5, 15, *non valent.* Azo (f. 1103) *aestimare poterit* with Br. f. 98, b, *aestimare non poterit.* And see *sub* p. 87, note 8; p. 101, note 4.

are at hand, shows more originality. The twelfth chapter, *De Rerum Divisione*, follows Azo very closely: it adopts the Roman divisions of *Res; in patrimonio nostro vel extra; corporales vel incorporales: mobiles vel immobiles; communes, publicae, universitatis, nullius, singulorum ;* and copies Azo's illustrations all but word for word[1].

In fact no mere recital of similar subjects will show the identity of order and language which proves convincingly that, during the greater part of this first book, Bracton has simply copied the *Summa Azonis.* Whether in doing so he has suppressed any English Law at variance with his text, or has added any new law to that which he found existing, or again whether the matter thus incorporated has survived in English Law are questions we must reserve. And, after the examples cited by Prof. Vinogradoff, we must wait for a trustworthy examination of the MSS. before we can decide whether some of the modifications are not really glosses by English lawyers on Bracton's Roman Text.

Bracton's Second Book.

The first three chapters of Book II. *De acquirendo rerum dominium* are taken almost literally from Azo[2]. They deal with methods of acquisition *jure gentium* on purely Roman lines; but Bracton's treatment shows that he is only applying Roman rules where there is no express English rule on the subject. In speaking of acquisition of wild animals by capture, he adds to the Roman rule the qualification, "*nisi consuetudo vel privilegium se habeat in contrarium,*" and again "*et haec vera sunt nisi aliquando de consuetudine in quibusdam partibus aliud fiat[3].*" Again, as to *insulae in mari natae*[4], Bracton adds "*nisi consuetudo se habeat in contrarium propter fisci privilegium*": and with respect to islands in a public river, he adds to Azo's *conceditur*

---

[1] Azo, Book II. on Institutes, Title 1.
[2] Br. ff. 8, b.—11. Azo, pp. 1063—1072.
[3] Br. ff. 8, b, 9. Azo, p. 1064.
[4] Br. f. 9. Azo, p. 1064.

occupanti, his own English comment "*et per consequens regi propter suum privilegium*[1]."

Occupatio, Alluvio, Accessio, Specificatio and *Confusio* are all treated almost in the words of Azo, though Bracton omits most of the Roman illustrations of his model[2], and adds English ones[3]. On minor points he corrects Azo; thus he omits the rules as to the acquisition of *thesaurus*, as inconsistent with English Law; he changes the *difficilis persecutio* of a hunted animal, which destroys property in the pursuer, to *impossibilis persecutio*[4]; he inserts the Roman provisions as to *agri limitati*, but omits the rule as to their capture by the enemy, as improbable in England[5]. In several places he abridges his models; he gives the rule as to *accessio literarum*, and states frankly *ut in Institutis plenius inveniri potest et in summa Azonis*[6]; Azo, in fact, gives some 50 lines of illustration of the rule, which Bracton omits. In treating of accession of buildings he adopts the maxim "*omne quod inaedificatur solo cedit*," but abbreviates and anglicizes his model. His copying results in two curious slips; he quotes Azo that *confusio* differs from *mixtio* in three respects, but he only gives two of them[7], and by the omission of a negative in an attempt to combine two sentences in one, he entirely misrepresents Azo[8]. His fourth chapter[9], which treats donation as a means of acquisition *jure civili*, instead of *jure naturali*, as in Azo, copies almost word for word Azo's section on *res corporales seu incorporales*, and on servitudes. But with this chapter continuous copying of Azo

---

[1] Br. f. 9, b. Azo, p. 1065. Compare also Azo, 1063, *per occupationem eorum quae non sunt in bonis alicujus, ut sunt ferae bestiae*, with Bracton's insertion after *alicujus* (f. 8, b) of the clause "*et quae nunc sunt ipsius regis de jure civili, et non communia ut olim.*" These extracts look suspiciously like glosses, which have wandered into the text.

[2] *e.g. de glande legenda, tigno injuncto, actio de dolo, doli exceptionem.* Azo, p. 1064.

[3] Br. f. 8, b. He adds *cygni* to Azo's list of tamed wild animals. It would be interesting to know Sir T. Twiss'

authority for translating *pavones*, seafowl, a *genus* not usually supposed to include peacocks. Tw. I. 67.

[4] Azo, p. 1064. *Ins.* II. 1, 12. Br. f. 8, b.

[5] Br. f. 9, b. Azo, p. 1065.

[6] Br. f. 10. Azo, p. 1067.

[7] Br. f. 10, b. Azo, p. 1069. Bracton, or Twiss' version, omits Azo's *item confusa sunt communia omnia etiam sine voluntate dominorum, sed mista demum cum voluntate.*

[8] Ibid. *Si autem (non) separari.* cf. p. 85 *supra*, note 8.

[9] Br. f. 10, b. Azo, 1070—1072.

ceases: and up to this point we infer that, while Bracton has adopted Roman Law bodily, he has yet modified or omitted whatever portions are actually inconsistent with existing English Law.

The 5th chapter shows great variations. The definition of *donatio*...*"quaedam institutio quae ex mera liberalitate et voluntate, nullo jure cogente, procedit ut rem transferat ad alium[1],"* corresponds to Azo's *"quaedam mera liberalitas quae, nullo cogente, conceditur."* But by its interpretation it is made to cover a much wider ground than the Roman *donatio*[2]. The feudal relation was conceived as one of good faith between lord and vassal, and might therefore be said to rest on "pure liberality" on the part of the lord. Hence any donation of land, in return for services or otherwise, by alienation or free gift, by the rules of the feudal system, comes within Bracton's *donatio*. His next 21 chapters[3] treat this subject with a rambling show of precision, and also contain a good deal of Bracton's law as to Possession, with chapters on *usucapio* and servitudes. Though the whole form of the discussion is Roman[4], I cannot trace any sustained following of Roman authorities in these chapters, which undoubtedly contain a great mass of purely English law.

But the general tone of the discussion shows continual Roman influence; the Justinianean sources are expressly cited twice[5]; the triple division of *donationes mortis causa* is taken from Ulpian[6]; while some passages are certainly taken from Azo[7]. The illustrations also are Roman: *"Do tibi digestum ut des mihi codicem[8]"*: *"Do si coelum digito tetigeris[8]—si Titius consul factus fuerit[9]—si navis venerit ex Asia[9]."* The four innominate contracts are set out in full. Bracton also expressly notes the agreement of the English and Roman laws as to the effect of felony on

---

[1] Br. f. 11. Azo, p. 876. Cod. viii. De Donationibus.

[2] Güterbock, p. 109.

[3] Br. ff. 11—60.

[4] *e.g. quid sit donatio, et qualiter dividatur, quis donare possit, et quis non. Item quae res possit donari, et quae non, et cui dari possit, et cui non. Item qualiter acquiratur possessio.* Br. f. 11.

[5] Br. f. 12, b, from Digest *de Donationibus* 39, 5, 15. Cf. also, f. 30, b. Br. f. 16, b, from Codex ii. 3. 13. *De pactis.*

[6] Br. f. 60. *Dig.* 39, 6, 2.

[7] *Quid sit possessio.* Cf. Azo, p. 740. Cod. vii. with Br. f. 38, b, and Azo, p. 1070—1 with Br. f. 41, b.

[8] f. 19.

[9] ff. 19, 47.

donations, in the words "*convenit lex cum consuetudine Angli-cana*[1]". The discussions, "*Per quas personas nobis acquiratur Possessio*[2]" (which treats of a *servus communis, servus alienus, procurator* &c.), and "*Quibus modis amittitur Possessio*[3]*" suggest the influence of the *Digest* and the *Summa*.

Bracton's doctrine of Possession, while curiously un-Roman on some points, has been derived in the main from civilian sources. We need not consider how far it truly represents the law of England till we come to Lord Holt's celebrated judgement in *Coggs v. Bernard*, but may content ourselves with pointing out briefly the salient Roman features in Bracton's exposition[4].

He defines *possessio*, in the words of Azo, as "*corporalis rei detentio, id est corporis et animi cum juris adminiculo con-currente*"; with Azo he divides it into *civilis, quae animo tantum retinetur*, and *naturalis, quae corpore tantum retinetur*[5]. It must be either acquired, or lost, *animo et corpore*. But while Azo does not allow civil and natural possession to exist in the same person at the same time, Bracton speaks of it as possible. Possession, according to him, was not lost unless both elements, *corpus* and *animus*, were gone, a doctrine directly contrary to the Roman rule[6], (which however gave a very lenient interpre-tation to loss of corporal possession). But he adds a curious variation, that possession might be retained "*solo corpore sine animo, ut post mortem alicujus donec corpus efferatur ad sepul-turam*", where possession was by the *dead* body[7].

Animus and *corpus* are both treated on Roman lines[8]; *traditio*, as a means of acquisition *corpore*, is defined as "*in*

---

[1] Bracton misquotes the Roman Law, reading *valent*, for *non valent*. The *Digest* reads "*Post contractum capitale crimen donationes factae non valent nisi condemnatio secuta sit*"; but Mommsen suggests the reading *retro infirmantur enim, si condemnatio secuta sit*, which would agree in sense with Bracton's "*post contractum crimen donationes factae valent nisi condemnatio secuta sit.*" cf. Selden, *Fleta*, III. 1. Br. f. 12 b, 30 b, 129. *Dig.* 39, 5, 15.

Güt. 112.

[2] Br. f. 43, b.

[3] ff. 45 b, 51.

[4] Bracton II. c. 17—22. Güterbock, pp. 90—100, 109—117. Twiss, I. Pref. 42 et seq. Holmes, *Common Law*, 164 —246.

[5] Br. f. 38, b. Azo, f. 740.

[6] *Dig.* 41, 2, 44, 2.

[7] Br. f. 41, b.

[8] Br. f. 38, b. 41, b. 51.

possessionem inductio de re corporali", and Bracton insists on the necessity for *"vacua possessio"*, as a pre-existing requisite. This, though going beyond the Justinianean sources, was at the time the prevalent civilian view[1]. Several passages from the *Digest De acquirenda vel amittenda possessione* are cited on the acquisition of possession[2]. On its loss we have already noticed Bracton's departure from the Roman sources. His views on *Quasi Possessio* of liberties, servitudes, and other incorporeal rights are obscure, but more akin to the opinions of the Canonists than to those of Bologna[3]. A scale of degrees of possession in right is taken in its terminology from Azo[4].

Bracton has borrowed from the Roman law many of his divisions of *donatio*, e.g. *inter vivos, mortis causa, simplex,* vel *conditionalis,* vel *sub modo,* and under the latter head, *conditiones; potestivae, casuales, impossibiles, ex insidiis fortunae, suspensive* and *resolutory.* The *donatio.* requires for its validity, *mutuus consensus et voluntas,* and the hindrances to mutual consent, *error, metus, vis,* are treated by him in accordance with Roman sources[5].

Donatio, as stated by Glanvil[6], was perfected by *traditio,* until which it remained *nuda promissio.* Bracton supports this by the Roman maxim, *"traditionibus et usucapionibus rerum dominia transferuntur."* The nature of this *traditio* is plainly Roman[7]; for symbolical tradition, tradition of lands, *traditio brevi manu,* and the necessity of *justa causa,* are treated in the spirit and nearly in the words of the *Digest.*

A striking case of Roman influence is to be seen in the prohibition of donations from husband to wife during coverture[8]. Such gifts were valid during Saxon times, and Glanvil

---

[1] Güt. p. 94.

[2] cf. Br. f. 44 with *Dig.* 41, 2, 1, 20. Br. f. 43, b, with *Dig.* 41, 2, 1, 10.

[3] Güt. pp. 98, 99.

[4] Br. f. 39, 160. Azo, f. 190. This reference is from Güt. 100, note, but I cannot find the passage in Azo.

[5] *vis,* cf. Br. f. 16, b, with *Dig.* 4, 2, 2. *metus,* Br. f. 16, b, 17, with Azo f. 100—102. *Dig.* 4, 2, 5, 6, and 9. *error,* Br. f. 15 b, 16, with *Dig.* 39, 5,

10; 45, 1, 4; 41, 1, 36.

[6] Gl. VII. 1.

[7] cf. Br. f. 40, *Dig.* 41, 2, 3, 1. Br. f. 44, *Dig.* 41, 2, 1, 20. Br. f. 39, b, 41, b, *Dig.* 41, 1, 31. Br. f. 41. (*assignari*), Azo f. 1070.

[8] Kenny on the *Effects of Marriage on Property,* pp. 45, 75, 110, 111. Güt. p. 110. Twiss, Pref. I. 43. *Fleta,* III. 3, 12.

is silent as to their prohibition. Güterbock indeed suggests they were used to evade the feudal restrictions on the amount of the *dos ad ostium ecclesiae*. But Bracton expressly states "*hujusmodi donationes non valent*[1]", and cites in support three recent cases in which the judges declared all such gifts in excess of the legal dower, whether made in view of or after marriage, void. He gives no reason for the change, though he supports the allowance of any dower at all by instancing the Roman *donatio ante nuptias*. The author of *Fleta* is more explicit, and gives as the reason, *quia prohibetur in lege*. There can be therefore very little doubt that the influence of the Roman law is responsible for this change. Anticipating its future history, this Roman policy was indirectly reversed by the Court of Chancery in 1712, when in *Mitchell v. Mitchell*[2], it held a gift by the husband to the wife without the intervention of a trustee, good in equity. But this is only possible where the husband constitutes himself a trustee for his wife. An instance of failure to make a valid gift is to be found in the recent case of *Breton v. Woolven*[3] (1881), where Hall V. C. said; "It is a monstrous state of the law which prevents effect being given to such a gift."

Treating of possession *per usucaptionem*, Bracton states considerable changes in the law, though they do not appear to have taken deep root[4]. *Usucapio* in the Roman law was the acquisition of ownership by possession; it required a certain length of uninterrupted possession, *bona fides* and a *justus titulus*[5]. But Bracton's *usucaptio* was a means of acquiring *sine titulo et traditione per longam continuam et pacificam possessionem*[6]. The length of possession required was left "*ex justitiarorum discretione*[7]." It was not a means of acquiring *dominium*, but only possession, which gave the possessor the possessory legal remedies, even against the negligent owner, who has still his *jus majus*, only extinguished by the loss of his writ of right. It was in fact more akin to the Roman "*prescriptio*" (which

[1] f. 29.

[2] Bunbury, *Reports*, p. 207, note. Kenny, p. 102.

[3] *L. R.* 17 Ch. D. pp. 416, 419.

[4] Br. f. 52. Güt. p. 118.

[5] *Dig.* 41, 3. Hunter, *Roman Law*, p. 119.

[6] As opposed to *traditio ex titulo et justa causa acquirendi*.

[7] Br. f. 51, b.

protected the possessor against actions, but did not give him ownership), but differed from it in not requiring *bona fides* and *justus titulus*[1]. When Bracton says " *longa enim possessio parit jus possidendi, et tollit actionem vero domino petenti*[2]", his expressions must be interpreted in the light of the foregoing remarks.

Prescription or usucapion were unknown to the early law, and Glanvil only refers to them in connexion with the recognition of Novel Disseisin, which must be brought, "*infra tempus a domino rege de consilio procerum ad hoc constitutum*[3]." But Bracton asserts a general prescription, "*quia omnes actiones in mundo infra certa tempora habent limitationem*"; he names several periods of time[4], though the vagueness of his statements points to imperfect development. The Statute of Merton had dealt specially with the recovery of land; except on this point, however, it seems that the only influence of the Roman law has been in furnishing terms which have been misapplied.

Treating of servitudes and liberties Bracton again borrows from Rome his terminology and some principles[5]; thus of praedial servitudes, which alone have influenced English law, we have *jus eundi, aqua ducendi, pascendi* &c., though their discussion is almost entirely English. On acquisition of servitudes by *quasi-traditio*, he follows Azo with some deviations. The servitude from the point of view of the dominant tenement, which Glanvil has called *aisiamentum* (easement), is called by Bracton, *libertas*[6].

Donationes mortis causa are divided according to Ulpian[7]. They are to be regulated by the lay courts, though *Fleta* identifies them with testaments, which were dealt with by ecclesiastical tribunals. But in treating of them, Bracton

---

[1] It also differed from the Canon Law rule "*quod nulla valeat praescriptio absque bona fide.*" Güt. 119.

[2] Br. ff. 40, 52. Cf. "*longa possessio parit jus*"; "*longa possessio sufficit pro jure.*"

[3] Gl. XIII. 32, 33.

[4] *Longa enim absentia scilicet x. annorum* f. 45, b.; *longum tempus*

scilicet x. xx, xxx, *annos,* f. 422. As to servitudes—*tempus quod excedit memoriam* f. 230. Cf. Azo, "*cujus non exstat memoria*", Güt. 124.

[5] Bk. II. c. 23, 24.

[6] Br. f. 220, b. Gl. XII. 14. Güt. 174.

[7] *Dig.* 39, 6, 2.

mingles distinctively English matter with a free use of the *Digest*[1]. His treatment of wills is scanty, as the Courts Christian had cognizance of them. Wills and executors are the undoubted offspring of the Roman law[2], and executors and administrators furnish the only examples of universal succession in English law[3]. At the time of Bracton the executor had not entirely superseded the heir, but the liabilities of the latter were becoming narrowed, for whereas in Glanvil the heir was bound to warrant the reasonable gifts of his ancestor[4], in Bracton he was only bound to do so to the extent of the property he inherited[5]. This corresponds to the limitations introduced by Justinian. But the chapter on wills, which only applied to movables, contains a certain amount of peculiarly English matter, especially with reference to the Custom of London.

On Sale, Bracton again deviates from Roman law[6]. *Emptio-Venditio* in the Roman system was a consensual contract; but according to Bracton unless at the time of the agreement either an earnest (*arrha*) is given, or the whole or part of the price is paid, or until the contract is reduced to writing, either party can withdraw from the mere agreement[7]. Justinian called the *arrha, argumentum emptionis*, a proof, not a part of the contract, but Bracton quotes the same phrase as proving the *arrha* to be an essential element of a valid contract. Glanvil had doubted whether the vendor could retreat from the contract, without forfeiting the earnest; Bracton decides, in accordance with Justinian, that he forfeits *twice* the earnest[8]. Between the

---

[1] Bracton, f. 60. *Dig.* 39, 6, §§ 2, 26, 27. Güt. 133, 134. *Fleta*, II. 57, 1.

[2] In some places the Canon law is preferred to the Civil, e.g. to the number of witnesses, stated to be *two*, Br. f. 61, though in f. 354 the *seven* witnesses are mentioned.

[3] Holmes, *Common Law*, pp. 340—350.

[4] Gl. VII. 2.

[5] Br. 61.

[6] Br. II. c. 27. Güt. 144. Just. *Inst.* III. 23, pr.

[7] *Inst.* III. 23, pr. Br. 61, b. But

in c. 28, f. 62, apparently following Justinian, Bracton speaks of sale as contracted "*postquam de precio convenerit.*"

[8] Glan. x. 14. Br. f. 62, *supra*, p. 76. The "*Regiam Majestatem*" also forfeits *twice* the earnest. See Moyle, I. 418, note.

The doctrine of forfeiture of earnest still survives; see *Howe v. Smith* (1884), *L. R.* 27 Ch. D. p. 102, where Fry, L. J., expressly refers it to Bracton and the Roman law.

times of agreement for sale and of delivery by the vendor, the Roman law put the thing sold at the buyer's risk, so far as accident was concerned; Bracton, following Glanvil and the old law, puts it at the risk of the seller[1]. His reference to conditional sale is from the *Institutes*[2]. According to Bracton and Justinian the buyer of movables may rescind in case of undisclosed faults; but in the case of land, according to Bracton, the buyer must bring an action to enforce delivery of the land as contracted for. In modern times the development of commerce has led to the adoption of *"Caveat Emptor"*, as the general rule, but subject to many exceptions[3].

Bracton treats *Locatio-Conductio* very briefly[4]; the fixing of the price is its investitive fact. The hirer's liability *qualem diligentissimus paterfamilias* is taken from the *Institutes*, and the liability of the hirer's goods in his hired house for rent is treated on Roman lines.

Succession as a means of acquiring dominion is treated in cc. 29—34[5]; but on this head the influence of the Roman law has been slight. That system either gave universal succession according to the testator's will, or distributed his property by fixed rules, according to nearness of kin to the deceased[6]. But by the English law, a man could not make a will as to lands, *quia solus Deus heredem facere potest;* the descent of his lands was settled either by the form of their donation, or by rules which gave preference to the male sex and to priority of birth, and which forbad ascendants to succeed. These rules, which at this time only applied to lands held by military tenure[7], were feudal innovations, so far as primogeniture is concerned, on the

---

[1] He actually cites the *Institutes*, substituting *qui eam tenet* (i.e *venditor*) for *emptorem*. Br. f. 62. Just. *Inst.* III. 23, 3.

[2] Ibid. III. 23, 4.

[3] Benjamin *On Sale*, 3rd edit. pp. 606—633.

[4] Br. 62, 62, b. Just. III. 24, 5, et. al. Güt. pp. 146, 147.

[5] Br. ff. 62, b—77, b. Twiss, I. Pref. 44—46. Güt. pp. 125—133.

[6] e.g. *tempore Justiniani.*

(1) Descendants, in order of kin.
(2) Ascendants, by proximity.
(3) Collaterals.
No difference between males and females, or by priority of birth. Novels 118, 127.

[7] Br. f. 62 b—64. When Bracton says "*haereditas est successio in universum jus, quod defunctus habuit*" f. 62 b, he is using a Roman maxim without adapting it to English law.

Saxon rules which first called the sons equally, and then the daughters together. There is no evidence of the right in representation in Saxon law[1]. In the time of Glanvil the question as between a grandson and his uncle was still in dispute; and he himself, while stating both views, prefers the grandson's right[2]. But the question soon became of practical importance in the disputed succession of John and Arthur, in which John, the uncle, attained the crown. Bracton states the law as definitely in favour of the grandson[3]; and this recognition of the right of Representation is probably due to Roman and clerical influence.

In personalty, rules, which are not Roman, limit the power of disposing by will, to either one-third or one-half of the personalty, after the payment of debts, funeral expenses, and the wife's quarantine[4]. But this innovation on Saxon procedure is certainly not Roman. The old Saxon rules, dividing the land equally among the sons still existed on all socage and gavel-kind lands though these, as they appeared less frequently in the King's Courts than the great military fiefs, are less noticed by Bracton[5].

Bracton's distinctions as to *haeredes* are tinged with Roman law on several points. He defines the *legitimus haeres* as "*quem nuptiae demonstrant*," and adopts Azo's *liberi legitimi et naturales,* "*qui ex justis nuptiis et legitima uxore procreantur*[6]". Glanvil had forbidden those to inherit "*qui ex legitimo matrimonio non sint nati*[7]", but Bracton admits an exception in the case of those who have ignorantly but publicly contracted an invalid marriage, in the belief of its validity and without the prohibition

---

[1] e.g. a grandson did not take his deceased father's share. *Anglo-Saxon Law*, p. 132.

[2] Glan. vii. 3.

[3] Br. f. 64, b, 267, b. Güt. 132. Twiss, i. Pref. 45.

[4] Br. f. 60, b. *Anglo-Saxon Law*, p. 76.

[5] Br. f. 76.

[6] Br. f. 64. Azo, f. 132, b. Sir T. Twiss here affords another instance of the care with which he has edited Bracton. Tottell's text (f. 63) runs

that those who have contracted an invalid marriage clandestinely seem to have acted *non ex parte sciente* (!), *vel saltem affectatores ignorantiae.* This is in substance a quotation from the Canon Law (X. c. 3, 4, 3), and Twiss notes the reference: yet if he had taken the trouble to turn to his reference he would have found the obvious reading "*expertes scientiae;*" and he even notes that one MS. reads *scientiae.*

[7] Glan. vii. 13.

of the Church; following the Canon law, which he expressly cites, he states their children to be legitimate[1]. Here there was no English custom to the contrary, but in the case of *legitimatio per subsequens matrimonium* such a custom did exist, and the attempt of the Church to introduce the Roman rule was successfully resisted. Glanvil had noticed the opposition[2], and Bracton recognizes the legitimacy of such children "*ad ea quae pertinent ad sacerdotium*," but not "*ad ea quae pertinent ad regnum propter consuetudinem regni, quod se habet in contrarium*." At the Parliament of Merton in 1236 the clergy had made an attempt to change the law, to which the barons returned their well-known answer, "*Nolumus leges Angliae mutare, quae usque ad illud tempus usitatae fuerunt et approbatae*." The compromise effected required the spiritual courts only to decide the fact of birth before or after marriage, by which means they escaped from giving a decision on the legitimacy of children previously born[3].

Brothers of the half-blood can, according to Bracton, succeed as heirs to each other[4]. He also notes at length two forms of procedure, which appear to be of Roman origin. When the inheritance was to be divided among daughters as co-parceners, or sons of a tenant in socage, a method of partition was adopted, apparently copied from the Roman *judicium familiae herciscundae*[5]. So also, when the wife of a deceased tenant declared herself pregnant, and her child-bearing would affect the descent of the inheritance, the truth of her allegation was inquired into by a procedure, closely resembling the Praetorian edict "*De ventre inspiciendo*," and probably derived therefrom[6].

We may remark on the phrase "*quasi-succedit*" that it supports the theory of the development of the doctrine of

[1] Br. f. 63. Güt. 127.

[2] Glan. VII. 15. Br. f. 63—63, b.

[3] No definite rule as to the case in which the child of a married woman born after the cessation of the marriage was her former husband's, was laid down, as in the Roman law, but each case was left on its own merits. Some other particulars as to Bastardy appear however of Roman origin, Güt.

130.

[4] Br. f. 65, b, but cf. f. 267, see *sub* p. 115. Maine, *Ancient Law*, 151.

[5] This phrase has an unfortunate history. *Herciscunda* appears as a lady, in Britton (III. 7, 1), and as a tenure, in Coke.

[6] Cf. *Dig.* 25, 4, with Br. ff. 69—71. Güt. 131.

transmission of rights and liabilities to assigns *inter vivos,* from an application of the Roman doctrine of universal succession, treating assignment *inter vivos* as quasi-succession[1].

Bracton's treatment of homage, relief, and the custody and maritage of heirs is almost entirely English[2]. Roman influence may be traced in the suggestion as to females attaining their majority at 12 years of age, with the reason given, though this age is rejected in military fiefs for 15[3]. The rule as to the guardianship of blood relatives, excluding any who could be suspected of a claim to the inheritance, is directly contrary to the Roman rule *" ubi spes successionis, ibi et onus tutelae debet esse*[4].*"*

The last two chapters of Bracton's 2nd book deal with the question of *dos*[5]. The early *morgen-gifu,* or gift from the husband to the wife, had become transformed under clerical influences into the *Dos ad ostium ecclesiae,* and in lands held by military tenure this had been cut down under feudal influences to a life-interest in one-third of the husband's lands, where no lesser sum was agreed on. This is entirely unlike the Roman *dos,* which was a limited gift from the wife's family to the husband. Bracton treats the *dos ad ostium ecclesiae* as a *donatio propter nuptias,* and introduces the Roman *dos,* in a woman's *maritagium*[6], which he divides into *profectitia* and *adventitia,* terms taken from the Roman law, but with changed meanings[7]. The Roman *dos profectitia* was the contribution made by the wife's father or male ascendant; the *dos adventitia,* the contribution made by the wife, or any other relation of hers. But in Bracton, the *dos profectitia* is given by father, mother,

---

[1] Holmes *On Common Law,* Lect. XI. Br. f. 68, b.

[2] Br. ff. 78 —91.

[3] f. 86, b. One would not have thought it a great strain on Sir T. Twiss' ingenuity to conjecture that when Tottell printed that a socage tenant came of age at 25 years (!) he was printing from a MS., which had XXV., as a slip for XV., and to correct his reprint accordingly, to agree with Glanvil, VII. 9.

[4] f. 87, b. *Vide supra,* p. 75.

[5] Kenny, *Effects of Marriage on Property.* Bracton, ff. 92—98. Twiss, II. Pref. 16, 17. Güterbock, pp. 135 —137. Long, pp. 99—104; misleading owing to Mr Long's ignorance of Teutonic law.

[6] f. 92.

[7] *Dig.* 23, 3, 5. Neither has Sir T. Twiss' critical insight enabled him to correct "*lecto mortali*" into *lecto maritali,* on f. 92.

vel alio parente; the *dos adventitia* by other than the father and mother, *sive parens sit, sive extraneus.* Thus, besides disagreeing with the Roman law, the definitions clash with each other, as a dowry given by an uncle would fall under both heads. But they seem of no practical importance, though repeated by *Fleta*[1]. Bracton also refers to a *dos parapherna*[2], a phrase evidently derived from the Roman *paraphernalia,* or parts of the *dos* which the wife retained as her absolute property; in Saxon times the wife besides her share of the property was entitled to retain her bed and apparel on the death of her husband, and in the time of Bracton she had probably the right of disposing of her jewels and dress by will. But feudal theory cut down her power over her *paraphernalia* to her apparel *"pur ceo que necessaire que el ne alera naked mes d'estre conserve del shame et del cold*[3]*."* A Roman name has been applied to a Saxon institution cut down by feudal principles[4].

Dower, exceeding the *dos rationabilis,* which was one-third of military lands, was revoked. But though Bracton mentions it only casually[5], large portions of the land of the country were still held on the old rules of dower.

A curious incident of the marital relation, probably derived from the Roman law, is the life-tenancy of the husband in his wife's lands of inheritance, if issue has been born alive, a tenure known as *"per legem Angliae,"* or "by the curtesy of England[6]." It is prominent in English, Scotch[7], and Norman law, though the general feudal law expressly forbids it[8]; it is contrary to the

[1] *Fleta* v. 23. 4, who calls *profectitia, perfectiva* (!).

[2] παρὰ φερνήν.

[3] Rolle, I. 911.

[4] *Parapherna* also existed in the custom of Normandy, Güt. 136. Pannier, *Ruines de la Coutume de Normandie,* pp. 80, 81.

[5] f. 93, 94, "*nisi aliter observetur de aliqua consuetudine speciali, vel nisi terra teneatur in socagio, ubi diversi mode fit dotis constitutio, vel in gavelkind, vel si socagium adjungatur feodo militari.*"

[6] Br. f. 89, b, Kenny, pp. 73—82. The term " *Courtesy* " first occurs in the Yearbook of 1302; it does not relate to the "courtesy" of the law, but to the fact that the husband, being tenant of the *whole* fief, on the birth of issue, can sit as tenant in the Lord's Court, (*curia*), whereas the widow, holding only a *part*, is so tenant to the heir. Kenny, pp. 74, 79.

[7] Derived through the *Regia Majestas* from Glanvil.

[8] Feud. I. 15. *Si femina habens beneficium et maritum moriatur, nullo modo succedit in beneficium maritus, nisi specialiter investitus sit.* (Wright, *Tenures,* p. 195, 2nd edit. 1734.)

rules of succession of the Roman law, and unknown in Saxon times. Sir M. Wright, following Sir T. Craig, suggests that it is an application of Constantine's rule as to the *peculium adventitium*[1], which gave the father a life interest in all property coming to the son, through the mother. This would account for the necessity of issue born alive, and also for the fact that the husband had no such right in a life-estate of his wife's, or in property to which his son succeeded not in right of his mother, but as remainder man[2]. The curious limitation that the child must have cried within four walls may have resulted from the rules of evidence which, following the Canon law, prohibited females from taking part in a sworn inquest. Thus the birth of a live child could not be proved by the attendant women, and men could not testify from sight, "*quia non est permissum quod masculi intersint hujusmodi secretis:*[3]" but they could witness from hearing, and the cry was an evidence of life. The "*infra quatuor parietes*" may either be derived from a similar German law, or, according to Caspar, from Ante-Justineanean sources.

In the prohibition of conjugal donations and the introduction of curtesy we have substantial effects of Roman influence, but on other points the English law as to dowry seems unaffected by Rome.

Bracton's Third Book.

Bracton's Third Book is divided into two treatises, "*De Actionibus*" and "*De Corona*," which deals with Criminal law. The treatise on Actions[4] deals also with obligations, and completes Bracton's consideration of contracts, which had begun with the chapters on *Emptio-Venditio* and *Locatio-Conductio*[5] in the 2nd Book. In the first half[6] of the treatise the influence of

---

[1] *Cod.* 6, 60, 2. Wright, p. 196.

[2] This however was contrary to the amending constitution of Arcadius and Honorius, which gave the father such an interest in property coming from maternal ancestors. *Cod.* 6, 60, 2.

[3] *Abbreviatio Placitorum*, p. 267. Kenny, p. 80.

[4] Twiss, II. Pref. p. 25—32. Güterbock, pp. 138—158. Pollock on *Contracts* (3rd edit. 1881). Introd. pp. 7—20. Text. pp. 145—157. Holmes, *Common Law*, pp. 247—307. Long, pp. 104, 105.

[5] *Supra*, pp. 93, 94.

[6] ff. 98 b—104 b.

the Roman Law is very marked: much of the text is taken word for word from the *Institutes,* and parts are derived from the *Digest* and from Azo[1]. The scantiness of Bracton's exposition of the law of contracts is explained, on the one hand by the slight importance of personal property, on the other by the jurisdiction of the ecclesiastical courts over all promises not susceptible of proof by the strict rules of the Common Law, as *laesiones fidei,* breaches of faith[2].

By English law contracts could only be sued upon in the Curia Regis, if either partly performed, or embodied in a sealed writing. All other "*stipulationes conventionales*" were called by Bracton *nuda pacta,* and subject to the Roman doctrine "*ex nudo pacto non oritur actio*". The term thus appropriated underwent considerable changes of meaning. At Roman Law, it had been, not an agreement made without consideration, but an informal agreement, which did not come within some one of the privileged classes which were actionable, or which had no *causa,* or mark assigning it to one of the privileged classes. But in Bracton it means an agreement which cannot be proved by one of the recognized methods of proof in the King's Court[3]. Two hundred years later it had come to mean, "a promise where nothing is assigned why it should be made," an agreement without consideration[4]. Prof. Pollock had suggested that the Court of Chancery introduced the doctrine of Consideration into Contracts from its development in the Law of Uses[5]. But

---

[1] Sir T. Twiss' references here are both very inadequate and very misleading. In 12 pages of text (II. 108—130), I have counted 20 wrong references, and 23 references to parallel passages omitted. The translation is equally careless; e.g. *pavones* = seafowl, *nepos* = nephew, when "*grandson*" is the obvious translation; *actio negotiorum gestorum* translated "action on the case", in a book written 30 years before such a term was introduced; so *usufructuarius,* followed by *usurarius,* which Twiss reprints from Tottell, and translates *usurer* (!) instead of correcting the obvious slip to *usuarius.* Pro-

fessor Pollock's severe criticism (*Contracts,* 3rd edit. Introd. pp. 7, 8,) is in my opinion entirely justified.

[2] Glan. x. c. 8, 18. Bracton, f. 100. *de quibus omnibus* (*i.e. conventionales stipulationes*) *omnino curia regis se non intromittit nisi aliquando de gratia.* Pollock, p. 151. Güt. p. 139. *Vide supra,* p. 76.

[3] i.e. witnesses, writing, or the duel, [which in debt was practically obsolete].

[4] Pollock, 182, 184. Holmes, 253. Doctor and Student, (1530). Dial. 2, c. 24.

[5] 2nd Edit. *Contracts,* p. 56.

in his third edition, he doubts whether this opinion is tenable, and considers Mr Holmes' theory, though not proved, as of great weight[1].

Mr Holmes had traced the origin of " Consideration," as essential to an agreement not evidenced by deed, to the fact that such an agreement, to be enforceable at all, must be proved by witnesses, whom he traces to the " transaction witnesses " before the Conquest, the *secta* after it[2]. These witnesses would swear to what they had seen and heard, which, in an action of debt, would be the actual transfer of property, or money; and they were in Saxon times only required to be present when there was such a transfer. He therefore suggested that originally a debt not arising from a deed or covenant could only be proved where witnesses had seen a *quid pro quo*, or consideration actually pass; and that this rule of procedure developed into a rule of substantive law that no contract was actionable where consideration had not passed, unless it was in writing; and in that case it was suggested that every deed importeth a consideration. This seems the more probable origin of the English doctrine of consideration and *nuda pacta*; and if true it shows the Roman Law to have done little more than supply the terms " *nudum pactum* " and " *causa*," which acquired a distinctively English meaning.

The first four chapters of the 3rd book are composed almost entirely of Roman material[3]. Indeed the form, which is Institutional and Academic, lends countenance to the supposition that Bracton lectured on the Civil Law at Oxford. " *Actio* " is defined, following the *Institutes* and Azo, as " *jus prosequendi in judicio quod sibi debetur*[4]," and the subsequent explanations are taken from Azo. The *Actio* is said to arise from preceding obligations as a daughter from a mother, the comparison being

---

[1] Int. p. 14.

[2] Holmes, *C. L.* p. 253 *et seq.* v. *supra*, p. 47.

[3] ff. 98, b—104, b.

[4] *Prosequendi* printed by the 1569 edition, and Twiss, is probably a printer's error. Azo and the *Institutes* have *persequendi*. Azo, 1118 ; *Ins.* iv. 6, pr. Azo's *aestimare poterit* (f. 1103) has been altered in the printed editions (f. 98, b) to *aestimare* NON *poterit*, which makes nonsense. Both these obvious misprints appear to have been copied from Tottell's edition.

Azo's[1]. The division of obligations; *orientes ex contractu, vel quasi, sive ex maleficio vel quasi;* is taken from Justinian, and the subsequent doctrine of *vestimenta pacti* is also civilian[2].

Obligations are defined in the words of Azo, following the *Institutes*, as "*juris vinculum, quo necessitate adstringimur ad aliquid dandum vel faciendum*[3]"; they are divided, *re, verbis, scripto, consensu*; and real obligations, (*mutuum, commodatum, depositum* and *pignus*), are dealt with in the words of Justinian, omitting the technical terms of the Roman *actiones*[4]. This passage is not filtered through Azo, but taken direct from the *Institutes*, neither does Bracton appear to have followed Glanvil in this, the most Roman part of Glanvil's work. The passage as to liability for accidental loss is obscure[5], but the printed version appears to contradict Glanvil's statement of the English Law[6], which following an older law made the *commodatarius* liable for *casus*, while Bracton, in accordance with the *Institutes*, relieves him, if he has acted as "*diligentissimus paterfamilias*[7]".

While the general treatment of obligations *verbis, per stipulationem* is Institutional, Bracton makes an important adaptation to English procedure[8]. A simple stipulation, as we have seen, could not be sued on in the King's Courts, as being incapable of proof. After suggesting that a deaf man might make a stipulation by nods, or writing, he adds "*et quod per scripturam fieri possit, stipulatio et obligatio videtur, quia si scriptum fuerit in instrumento aliquem promisisse, perinde habetur ac si interrogatione praecedente responsum sit*[9]," and, though Bracton is silent, *Fleta* expressly says that a writing without seal will not suffice[10]. Again: "*Per scripturam vero*

---

[1] Br. f. 99. Azo, 1103.

[2] Just. *Ins.* III. 13, 2. Güt. 140.

[3] Br. f. 99. Azo, 304. *Ins.* III. 13, pr.

[4] *Ins.* III. 14.

[5] Owing to probable corruption of the text. Lord Holt quotes a different version.

[6] Gl. x. 13.

[7] Güt. 141, n. Br. f. 99, b. *Ins.* III. 14, 2. *Fleta*, II. 56 § 5, follows Bracton.

[8] Br. ff. 99, b, 100. *Ins.* III. 15 and 19.

[9] Br. f. 100, at the end of a passage taken from *Dig.* 44, 7, 1, 15.

[10] Pollock, 150. Br. f. 100, b. Holmes, 272. *Fleta*, II. 60, 25. Güt. 144. cf. Br. f. 101, *obligatio tollitur, si dicatur ......et responditur, vel scribatur.*

obligatur quis, ut si quis scripserit alicui se debere, sive pecunia numerata sit, sive non, obligatur ex scriptura, nec habebit exceptionem pecuniae non numeratae contra scripturam quia scripsit se debere." This was contrary to Roman Law which allowed such an exception to be used within 2 years[1]. In this practical adaptation of the Roman Law, by merger of the obligations *verbis* et *litteris*, Bracton found a connecting link between his Roman principles and the English Law: with a similar object he omits the rule "*alteri stipulari nemo potest*[2]," and makes such a stipulation possible even *sine poenâ*. Apart from these differences the minor distinctions of the Roman Law are faithfully reproduced, even to the extent of speaking of a judicial stipulation as "*quod fit jussu praetoris*[3]." But it may well be doubted whether these extracts have had any substantial influence upon English law.

Bracton just mentions obligations *ex consensu*[4], but as he has already dealt with sale and hiring, and as purely consensual contracts could have no place in the King's Courts, he does no more than mention them. Similarly with obligations *quasi ex contractu* he merely mentions the heads contained in the *Institutes*, using the technical Roman terms and says no more[5]. The persons through whom an obligation is acquired, the means by which an obligation is dissolved, and the general rule, "*obligatio dissolvitur eisdem modis quibus contrahitur*[6]", with several technical terms[7], are taken from the *Institutes*.

Delicts and quasi-delicts are also treated very shortly, the examples of a quasi-delict being the Institutional one of a judge knowingly giving a wrong judgment[8]. *Injuria* is defined, after Justinian, as *quod Jure non fit*[9], and the Roman

---

[1] *Ins.* III. 21, pr. (before Justinian 5 years).

[2] cf. Just. *Inst.* III. 19 : 19 and 21. Br. f. 100, b.

[3] *e.g. Stipulationes pure vel modo, sub conditione; facta et loca in stipulationibus, judiciales et conventionales stipulationes; stipulatio praepostera.*

[4] f. 100, b.

[5] cf. Br. f. 100, b, with *Ins.* III. 27.

[6] Br. ff. 100, b, 101. *Ins.* III. 28 and

29.

[7] *Exceptionem doli; pactum de non petendo; exceptionem metus; exceptionem jurisjurandi; exceptionem rei judicatae; acceptilatio, novatio; quasi traditio;* and the subject matter of the *stipulatio Aquiliana,* though the name is not used.

[8] Br. f. 101. *Inst.* IV. 5, pr.

[9] *Inst.* IV. 4, pr.; cf. Br. f. 101, b.

rule of non-liability of heirs for their ancestor's delicts is followed.

Bracton identifies actions with *placita* or pleas[1]: he adopts both Glanvil's division of *civilia-criminalia*, and Azo's of *realia, personalia, mixta*, which seems a combination of the Institutional divisions *in rem, in personam*, and *rei* vel *poenae persequendae* vel *mixtae*[2]. The term *crimina capitalia* is from the *Institutes*[3], though the illustration is changed. Personal Actions are defined in the words of Azo, and Bracton adds that the heir is bound "*nisi fuit poenalis*[4]." Personal Actions *ex maleficio*[5] are again divided into "*quae persequuntur poenam, vel ipsam rem et poenam*": while actions *in rem* are divided as in Glanvil, into *petitory, super proprietate rei*, and *possessory, super possessione*[6]. The *actio mixta* is defined in Azo's words "*tam in rem quam in personam, quia mixtae habent causam ad utrumque*[7]," and a number of the following divisions are taken from the Roman Law[8].

The Institutional division of Interdicts; *causâ recuperandae, adipiscendae, retinendae possessionis;* is applied by Bracton to actions, and identified with the leading Assizes[9]. Under *actiones recuperandae possessionis causâ* he places the Assize of *Novel Disseisin*, and identifies it with the "*actio unde vi*" (*sic*). *Actiones adipiscendae possessionis causâ* include the Assize *Mort d'ancester*,

---

[1] Gl. I. 1. Br. f. 101, b.

[2] Br. f. 101, b. Azo, f. 1119. *Inst.* IV.; 6; 1, 18—20. Coke, *Inst.* II. 21, 285.

[3] *Inst.* IV. 18, 2.

[4] Br. f. 102: *Inst.* IV. 6, 1. cf. Azo, f. 1119, *quae competunt contra aliquem ex contractu, vel quasi, ex maleficio, vel quasi, cumquis teneatur ad aliquid dandum vel faciendum.* The phrase *nativae, ex contractibus*, as applied to them is Azo's, who contrasts it with *dativae ex legibus.* Azo, 1131.

[5] cf. *Inst.* IV. 6, 18 : Azo, p. 1126.

[6] Glan. I. 3. Azo, f. 1119. *Inst.* IV. 6, 1. Br. f. 103. Güt. 151.

[7] Azo, 1126. Br. f. 102, b.

[8] e.g. *simplices, duplices; perpetuae, temporales,* Br. f. 102, b; Azo, 1129,

1130; *Ins.* IV. 12, pr. *transitoriae;* Azo, 308; Br. f. 103. *in simplum, duplum, triplum, quadruplum,* Azo, 1127; Br. f. 103 ; *Inst.* IV. 6, 21—24. *directa-contraria,* Br. f. 103, to which Bracton adds *indirecta. confessoria-negatoria,* Azo, 218; *Dig.* 8, 5, 2, pr., though Bracton makes *actio confessoria* "*cum dicat quis aliquem rem corporalem suam,*" instead of limiting it to servitudes, as in the Roman Law. He also uses the term "*praejudicialis*" of an *actio,* instead of a *formula,* Br. f. 103, and introduces several terms not otherwise used in English law, e.g. *Actio legis Aquiliae, vi bonorum raptorum. v. sub.* p. 105.

[9] Br. f. 103; *Inst.* IV. 15, 2.

identified with the "*actio quorum bonorum.*" An instance of *actiones retinendae possessionis* is found in "*interdicta ne quis alteri vim fiat.*"

In treating of "*quibus competant actiones*", Bracton appears to vary from Roman Law. The Roman *actio furti* was open to anyone *cujus interest rem salvam fore*, but not to the owner, if he had an action against the person in possession before the theft. Bracton allows the owner an *actio furti sive condictio*, against the thief or his successor. Now the bailee at English law had an action against the thief, and for that reason was liable over to the owner[1], who according to Roman law would therefore have had no *actio furti*. Probably Bracton means by "*actio furti sive condictio*" no more than *condictio*, in which case he accords with the Roman law which gave the *dominus* a *vindicatio, actio ad exhibendum* or *condictio,* for the thing itself though the *actio furti* was not open to him[2]. The *Actio legis Aquiliae* is thus adapted to English law, "*Actio legis Aquiliae de hominibus per feloniam occisis vel vulneratis dabitur propinquioribus parentibus, vel extraneis homagio vel servitio obligatis, ita quod eorum intersit agere*[3]", which appears to refer to the *wergeld* while anticipating Lord Campbell's Act.

Other Roman actions, *actio injuriarum*[4], *quod metus causa*[5], *de dolo,* are briefly dealt with. The *Actio de vi* is described as *duplex, "scilicet rei restitutoria et poenalis",* whereas the Institutional meaning of the term is "*quia par utriusque litigatoris in his condicio est nec quisquam praecipue reus vel actor intelligitur, sed unusquisque tam rei quam actoris partem sustinet*[6]." In dealing with the "*Actio quod vi aut clam*" Bracton follows the *Digest* closely, except that so far as the Interdict is penal, or for compensation, it could not be brought against the heirs according to Bracton, whereas the *Digest* gave it to and against heirs "*in id quod ad eos pervenit*[7]". The *Actio sive Interdictum de*

[1] Holmes *C. L.* 175.

[2] cf. *Inst.* IV. 1, 19.

[3] Br. f. 103, b, the rule as to *actio vi bonorum raptorum* is taken from *Inst.* IV. 2, 2.

[4] Br. f. 103, b. *Ins.* IV. 6.

[5] Ibid. *Ins.* IV. 6, 27. *Dig.* 4, 2.

14, 3.

[6] *Ins.* IV. 15, 7.

[7] Br. f. 104. *Dig.* 43, 24, 15, 3. Bracton's clause "*sed datur in eo* [*sic.* Twiss], *quae sunt restitutoria*," may be meant to cover this.

itinere actuque privato is cited *verbatim* with the prefix, *Ait enim praetor*[1].

At this point, Bracton's close following of the *Institutes* ceases, though the influence of the Civil and Canon Laws is still noticeable[2]. Frequent Roman citations are found, especially towards the end of the Treatise, on the question of the order in which actions should be tried, where in two folios there are found eleven quotations from the *Digest* and *Code*, and one from the Canon Law[3]. Bracton cites the well-known Roman maxim, "*quod principi placuit legis habet vigorem*", with the addition of a quotation apparently from the *Lex Regia* which is expressly referred to: the distinction between ordinary and delegated judges is also derived from the Canon Law[4]. In short, the whole treatise shows considerable study of the Roman Law, and is largely made up of Roman material, though it may be doubted whether it practically affected the English courts in any marked degree.

Bracton on Criminal Law.

The second Treatise of the third book deals with Criminal Law[5], which had been touched upon in the preceding Treatise. Thus the general principles as to punishment are taken word for word from the *Digest De Poenis*, although Bracton modifies them wherever any contrary English law exists[6]; *e.g.* where the *Digest* in illustrating the effect of the *causa* on the punishment to be awarded, says; "*ut in verberibus quae impunita sunt a magistro allata vel parente*," Bracton adds "*nisi modum excedant*," as English law did not recognize the unrestrained right of correction of servants or children[7]. The definitions of crimes show some marks of Roman influence, but the English procedure is of native growth, and the English law differed from the Roman

---

[1] Br. f. 104. *Dig.* 43, 19. 1, pr.

[2] cf. *actio praejudicialis*, f. 104, *crimen falsi*, f. 104, b, the passage on *judicium*, f. 106, taken from Azo 158, and on *munus*, f. 106, b, from the Canon Law and Code, which is expressly cited (*Cod.* 9, 27. 3), Güt. 154.

[3] ff. 114, 114, b.

[4] Br. f. 107, 108; Güt. p. 155.

[5] ff. 115—119, b.

[6] cf. Br. f. 104, b, 105 with *Dig.* 48, 19, 16 ; 7, 8, 11, 16.

[7] *Dig.* 48, 19, 16, 2; Br. f. 105.

in this cardinal respect that it treated as *pleas of the crown* offences which at Rome were the subjects of civil actions[1]. The influence of Canon law and ecclesiastical procedure is more marked than that of the Civilians[2].

Bracton's *crimen laesae majestatis* appears to derive hardly anything but its name from Roman law[3]. Güterbock indeed claims its definition as taken from the Roman law[4], and Sir T. Twiss says "Bracton adopts the whole doctrine of the Roman law, as well as the collateral penalties attached to the crime[5]"; but neither writer gives any references in support of his assertion. I have carefully compared the *Digest* with Bracton, and can find no likeness which justifies such a conclusion : indeed on several points there is direct opposition. In Roman law, "*famosi qui jus accusandi non habent sine ulla dubitatione admittuntur ad hanc accusationem*": in Bracton the accuser is required to be "*integer famae et non criminosus*[6]." The Roman criminal might be tried after his death that the exchequer might obtain his estate[7]; the English traitor escaped by death. The only instances I can trace of Roman influence appear in the provisions as to confiscation of goods, and perpetual disinherison of heirs, which, and especially the latter, suggest a free use of the *Code*[8]. But *majestas* is wider than Bracton's Treason, the one being *contra rem publicam*, the other *contra dominum regem*. Bracton seems rather to expand the English law as given in Glanvil[9]; both treat of the same three heads, *mortem domini regis, seditionem regni, vel exercitus,* but Bracton adds a clause concerning accessories. Sir J. F. Stephen says "this account of the crime of treason has some resemblance to the *Majestas* of the Roman law, though it cannot be said to be expressly taken from it[10]"; and I am not sure that even this does not overstate the resemblance.

Bracton includes under *majestas* the *crimen falsi*[11], which covers forgery and coining ; in this he has substantially followed

---

[1] *e.g. furtum, injuria,* robbery.

[2] Güterbock, p. 167.

[3] cf. *Dig.* 48, 4, with Br. f. 118, b.

[4] Güt. p. 168.

[5] II. Pref. p. 57.

[6] cf. *Dig.* 48, 4, 7, pr. with Br. f. 118, b.

[7] *Cod.* 9, 8, 5, pr.

[8] *Cod.* 9, 8, 5. Br. f. 118, b.

[9] Gl. XIV. 1.

[10] II. 244 *Hist. Crim. Law*: again II. 245. "The whole chapter recalls, *though it does not quote or directly imitate*, the Roman law."

[11] Br. f. 118, b; 119, b. Gl. I. 2; XIV. 7.

Glanvil, and the earlier Saxon laws contain provisions against coining. There is here no clear trace of Roman influence, though as to forgery it is not improbable, writing being almost an ecclesiastical monopoly.

Treasure trove (*thesaurus*) is defined in the words of the *Digest*[1], but Bracton adds that the finder only has it, *jure naturali*, for, he says, "*Cum igitur thesaurus in nullius bonis sit, et antiquitus de jure naturali esset inventoris, nunc de jure gentium efficitur ipsius domini regis,*" thus adapting the Roman law to the English by a very curious method.

Bracton's definitions of homicide and murder follow Glanvil[2], but the divisions of homicide with their accompanying illustrations are to be found in the *Breviarium Extravagantium* compiled by Bernhard of Pavia between the times of Glanvil and of Bracton, and studied together with the *Decretum* of Gratian in the Law School of Bologna[3]. This part of Bracton's work formed the basis of subsequent writings[4] until Lambard's book in 1610, but the progress of the law brought into prominence other questions than those raised by Bracton, and his classification became superseded. Thus the distinctions between murder and manslaughter, and between voluntary and involuntary homicide, came to the front, and the question of provocation was introduced. On some points, *e.g.* that in the case of those engaged at or helping in a fight, the blow of one is the blow of all, the law stated by Bracton is still the law of England[5], and this rule is directly derived from the Canon law, which follows the Digest[6]. On other points derived from the Civilians, as in the statement that to procure abortion, "*si puerperium jam formatum vel animatum fuerit,*" was homicide, the law of England is now to the contrary effect[7].

---

[1] *Dig.* 41, 1, 31, 1. Br. f. 119, b.

[2] Br. f. 134, b. Glan. xiv. 3.

[3] Twiss, ii. Pref. pp. 59, 60. Güterbock, pp. 169, 170. These divisions are set out and criticised from a legal point of view by Sir J. F. Stephen, *Hist. C. L.* iii. 29.

[4] Fleta, Britton, *The Mirrour*, Staunford, *vide* Stephen, *Crim. L.* iii. 33, 34.

[5] Br. f. 121. Stephen, iii. 31.

[6] Decretal of Alexander to Beckett. Twiss, ii. Pref. 60. Güt. 170. *Dig.* 48, 8, 17.

[7] Br. f. 121. *Dig.* 48, 8, 8. Coke cites this (*Inst.* iii. 50), erroneously, as an authority in favour of the proposition that killing a child delivered alive is murder, but killing a live child in the womb is not.

Mr Holmes has suggested a parallelism between the English law of *deodands, res quae sunt causa mortis alicujus,* which were forfeited to the king, and the Roman law as to *noxae deditio*[1]. On the question of outlawry, Bracton cites several passages from the *Code* and *Digest*[2], and places the outlaw on the footing of one who has suffered *maxima capitis deminutio*; but though he avails himself of the Roman phrase "*caput lupinum,*" the conception of the outlawed man is certainly Teutonic; as is also the appeal *de pace et plagis*[3]. In this latter case Bracton has introduced a passage as to castration, abortion, circumcision and slaying thieves by night, taken word for word from the *Digest*[4].

The chapter on Robbery shows a trace of Roman law in the requirement that one complaining of the robbery of another's goods in his charge must show "*quod sua intersit appellare*[5]"; though probably this only means that he must show that the goods were in his custody, which supported an action at Common law.

The chapter on Arson agrees with the *Digest* in that only a civil action could be brought for negligent or accidental burning[6]. There is no trace of Roman influence in the account of Rape. As to the classes of suicides Bracton follows the *Digest*[7], but while the suicide *per taedium vitae* did not forfeit his property by Roman law, Bracton allows him only to transmit his lands to his heirs, and writes that he forfeits his movables.

Bracton's account of Theft affords a good example of his "intelligent copying" from the Roman law. Paulus, whose definition is cited in the *Digest* and the *Institutes*, had said[8]: "*Furtum est contrectatio rei fraudulosa (lucri faciendi gratia*[9])

---

[1] Holmes, *C. L.* c. 1; Br. f. 122.

[2] Br. ff. 125—129. *Cod.* 9, 39, 1. 9, 40, 2. *Dig.* 48, 8, 3, 6: 47, 16: 48, 17.

[3] Bigelow on Torts, p. 222.

[4] *Dig.* 48: 8, 3, 8, 9, 11. Br. f. 144, b. Cf. also a passage on infants and madmen: Br. f. 136, b. *Dig.* 48, 8, 12.

[5] Br. f. 146. Cf. Just. *Inst.* IV. 1, 13.

This appears not in accord with the Saxon law; v. Holmes, *C. L.* 168, et Br. ff. 150, b: 151.

[6] Br. f. 146, b. *Dig.* 48, 19, 28, 12.

[7] *Dig.* 48, 21, 3, 4. Br. f. 150.

[8] *Ins.* IV. 1, 1. *Dig.* 47, 2, 1, 3. *Paulus ad Edictum.*

[9] So in *Digest*; the MSS of the *Institutes* disagree as to inserting these words. Sandars, 400.

vel ipsius rei vel etiam usus ejus possessionisve." Bracton words
his definition *"Furtum est secundum leges contrectatio rei alienae
fraudulenta cum animo furandi, invito illo domino cujus res illa
fuerit*[1]*".* He thus makes two important omissions from, and two
additions of less importance to, the Roman definition. He omits
(1) *lucri faciendi gratia,* (2) *usus possessionisve :* he adds (1) *invito domino ;* (2) *cum animo furandi.*

To deal first with his additions. That the unwillingness of
the owner of the thing stolen was an essential element in theft,
was clearly laid down by the Roman writers: *"Furtum fit
generaliter cum quis alienam rem invito domino contrectat*[2]*" ;*
even the use of a thing, believed to be contrary to the will of
the owner but in fact not so, was at first not theft, till it was
made so in the case of slaves who were enticed to steal, in
order to detect the enticer[3]. Theft must be *invito domino,* and
that unwillingness must be known to the thief: Sir J. F.
Stephen's doubt as to whether it was an essential element
seems over-cautious[4]. Similarly the addition *" cum animo
furandi "* is contained in Roman law, *" quia furtum sine affectu
furandi non committitur*[5]*."* But there was a difference as to
the time when the *animus furandi* must exist: according to
English law, if the first taking was lawful, no subsequent taking,
with some exceptions, could amount to theft[6]; and so Glanvil
had said: *" a furto enim omnimodo excusatur per hoc quod
initium habuit suae detentionis per dominum illius rei."* This
doctrine indeed finds some countenance in Roman law[7], but the
weight of authority is opposed to it[8].

Bracton's omissions are more important. So long as there
is a fraudulent taking, it is immaterial in English law whether
it be *" lucri faciendi gratia,"* or from any other motive[9], and
Bracton therefore omits the phrase. Similarly the English law

---

[1] Br. f. 150, b. *Quaere:* whether
"secundum leges" here refers to the
Roman Law.

[2] *Inst.* iv. 1, 6.

[3] Ibid. 8.

[4] Hunter, *Roman Law,* pp. 87, 88.
Stephen, *C. L.* iii. 131.

[5] *Ins.* iv. 1, 7.

[6] Stephen, i. 31, iii. 130. Glan. x.
13.

[7] *Dig.* 47, 2, 68, pr.

[8] *Ins.* iv. 1, 6. *Dig.* 47, 2, 54, 1.
Dig. 47, 2, 48, 4; which Stephen cites
seems rather to relate to the *actio locati*
than *actio furti.*

[9] Stephen, *C. L.* iii. 132.

has always required an intent to deprive the owner of his property; a temporary deprival of possession is not theft; the definition therefore omits "*usus possessionisve ejus.*" Bracton thus appears merely to have adopted the Roman phraseology, with such a revision as was necessary to make it accord with English law. The same procedure is observed in his appropriation of the Roman distinction of *furta manifesta vel nec manifesta*, which in the Roman law, is a distinction of substance, involving a difference of crime and punishment, while in Bracton it relates mainly to the procedure against the thief and the evidence of his crime. Thus *furtum nec manifestum* is "*ubi quis suspectus est de latrocinio per famam patriae, per indictamentum et rectum, et ubi graves praesumptiones faciunt contra ipsum*[1]." *Furtum manifestum* is "*ubi latro deprehensus est seisitus de aliquo latrocinio, scilicet 'hondhabende et bacberende,'*" which exposed him to the summary procedure of *infangentheof*, no other proof being necessary. Bracton's account of theft indeed deals almost entirely with procedure, and the later subtleties of the English law find no anticipation in him.

His account of the relation of husband and wife shows very slight traces of Roman influence, though he cites the *Digest* as to respite of sentence on a pregnant woman[2]. He cites the Roman definition of *injuria, quod non jure fit*, and its application to oral or written defamation as well as blows[3]: he follows the Roman law in allowing a lord to bring an action for injuries to his serfs, but goes beyond it, in allowing the serf also to bring an action[4]. The distinctions as to *injuria levis vel atrox*[5], and as to the character of the injury[6], the rule as to an action against the procurer of the injury[7], and the cessation of the action *dissimulatione*[8] are all taken directly from the *Institutes*.

But the greater part of the treatise is occupied with procedure which appears free from any Roman influences, though Güterbock points out traces of the Canon law[9]. As to the

[1] Br. f. 150, b.

[2] Br. f. 151, b. *Dig.* 48, 19, 3.

[3] *Ins.* IV. 4, pr. 1, Br. f. 155, b.

[4] Bigelow on Torts: Boston, 1875. pp. 224, 225. Br. ff. 115, 155, b.

[5] *Ins.* IV. 4, 9. Br. f. 155, b.

[6] Cf. ibid. *loco*, veluti si in conspectu praetoris, with Br. f. 155, b, *loco*, si in curia domini regis.

[7] *Ins.* IV. 4, 11. Br. f. 155, b.

[8] Ibid. 12. Ibid.

[9] Güt. pp. 168—171.

definitions of crimes, Sir J. F. Stephen says that "the influence of the Roman law is clearly traceable in all the definitions, though it was in all cases adopted with modifications peculiar to England[1]." The result of our examination shows this to be too wide. Roman law is only clearly visible in Bracton's account of theft and *injuria*; there are very slight traces of it in Homicide, *Laesa Majestas, Crimen Falsi,* and *Occultatio Thesauri*; but in Wounding, Maim, False Imprisonment, Robbery, Arson and Rape, there is, I think, nothing to show any use of the Roman law. And as to those crimes which do show traces of Roman influence, the last part of Stephen's remark is emphatically true. It is clear that where the law of England is contrary to the law of Rome in Criminal Law, Bracton has followed the law of England.

Remainder of Bracton.

Bracton's Fourth Book is composed of Treatises on the different Assizes or forms of real action. The word *"assize"* denotes, (1) a legislative act, as the Assize of Northampton; (2) the form of trial established by a particular legislative act, as the Assize of Novel Disseisin; and (3), its modern sense, the court which holds such trials, the Assizes[2]. Its development is of interest in the history of Trial by Jury and the progress of the *Curia Regis,* but shows no traces of Roman influence. At the time of Glanvil the *assize* was a jury to determine by sworn inquest the right to seisin, while preliminary questions which did not involve that right were decided *per juratam.* " Trial by jury " thus meant the method of determining issues not tried by an assize[3]. In the time of Bracton, the assize might be turned into a jury to try preliminary questions. Assizes however gradually gave way before the superior advantages of the action of ejectment.

The Assize of *Novel Disseisin* shows marked traces of Roman

---

[1] *C. L.* ii. 202.

[2] Stubbs, i. 573.

[3] Bigelow, *L. C.* on Torts, p. 346. See also on the relations of the *jurata*

and the Assize Mr L. O. Pike's learned Preface to the Yearbooks, 12 and 13 Edw. III. in the *Rolls Series,* Lond. 1885.

influence. It is first mentioned in 1176 in the Assize of North-ampton: "*Item justitiae domini regis faciant fieri recognitionem de dissaisinis factis super Assisam*[1]," but the actual Assize introducing this form is probably lost. Glanvil alludes to it thus "*de libero tenemento suo disseisito hujus constitutionis beneficio subvenitur*[2]," and Bracton says, "*de beneficio principis succurritur ei per recognitionem assisae novae disseysinae, multis vigiliis excogitatam et inventam*[3]." A measure introduced at a time when the influence of the Roman law was at its height was likely to, and does bear strong traces of Roman influence.

A man turned out of possession of land might, according to Bracton, use force to reinstate himself *sine aliquo intervallo,* for he had only lost *possessio naturalis,* not *civilis*[4]. But if he had not re-ejected his disseisor while the disseisin was "flagrant," his only remedy was the Assize of Novel Disseisin, the results of which might be corporal punishment for the "Spoliation" against the peace of the realm, pecuniary damages for the unjust detention, and the recovery of the land and of its mesne profits[5]. Now this Assize in its leading features shows strong similarity to the Interdict *Unde vi,* and also to the *Remedium Spoliationis* of the Canon Law[6].

Both applied only to immovables, and Bracton has so far identified them as to quote the *Digest* that ejectment from a ship did not give such a remedy[7]. Both implied a previous disseisin, and in each something turned on the character of the disseisin. The Roman remedies were different according as the disseisin had been unarmed or by *vis armata,* and Bracton has adopted the same distinction, and quotes largely from the *Digest* to illustrate it[8], though it does not lead to any practical results. The Assize could only be brought by those "*qui*

---

[1] Stubbs *S. C.* p. 145 § 5, Twiss, III. Pref. p. 12.

[2] Gl. XIII. c. 32: cf. c. 38, *poena hujusmodi constitutionis; ex beneficio constitutionis regiae.*

[3] Br. f. 164, b.

[4] Br. f. 162, b: 163, Twiss, III. Pref. 24. Güterbock, pp. 159—165, Williams, p. 219.

[5] Br. f. 161, b., 164, b. Bigelow, 347.

[6] Güt. p. 161. Bracton frequently uses the term: e.g. *spoliationem contra pacem.* Br. f. 161, b.

[7] Br. f. 168. *Dig.* 43, 16, 1, 7.

[8] cf. Br. f. 162, b. *Dig.* 43, 16, 3; 5—11.

nomine suo proprio tenementum tenent et non alieno[1]*."* For, as the *Digest* said, "*possessor alieno nomine non possidet licet in possessione fuerit*[2]," and possession, not property, is the basis of both the Assize and the Interdict[3]. The Interdict was available for a mere possessor, whether *dominus* or not, unless he had originally obtained possession from his disseisor *vi clam aut precario*[4]. Both English and Roman Law forbade the ejected person from taking the law into his own hands unless immediately on the disseisin, when the force used might be considered as self-defence[5].

But while the main outlines of Assize and Interdict are the same, the details of the Assize are purely English, and the numerous intricacies of feudal law are carefully explained in their bearing on the Assize. Though this material is non-Roman, the form of the discussion shows the Roman tone of Bracton's mind. He cites the Civil and Canon Laws to show that the claimant must succeed on the strength of his own title, not the weakness of the possessor's[6], and quotes the "*jus gentium*" in a curious way to prove that "*agris sunt termini positi*[7]." The maxim *nemini res sua servit* is adopted under the form " *nemini servire potest suus fundus proprius*[8];" the *Digest De vi* is laid under constant contribution, while Roman phrases are plentiful[9].

It seems probable, therefore, that the Assize of Novel Disseisin, introduced by direct legislation when the Roman law

[1] Br. f. 165.

[2] *Dig*. 41, 2, 10, 1. Br. f. 167, b.

[3] Br. 166, b, *item competit cuilibet, quis proprio nomine fuerit in seisina juste vel injuste,...non competit alieni assisa nisi ei qui possidet.*

f. 195, b. (of a person possessing unjustly against the true lord),—*quia si ab illis disseisitus fuit qui jus non habent, recuperabit incontinenti per assisam; sed quantum ad verum dominum, si recenter ejectus fuerit, non recuperabit.*

[4] Hunter, *R. L.* p. 105.

[5] Br. f. 163, b. cf. *Dig*. 43, 16, 17, 9. Güt., p. 163.

[6] Br. f. 183, b.

[7] Br. f. 211.

[8] f. 220, b.

[9] e.g. *scintilla juris, haereditas jacens, res sacrae et sanctae*, with quotations from the *Institutes* as to walls (II. 1, 10, Br. 207, b, cf. Br. f. 8): *familia*, with quotations from the *Digest* as to the use of *vis* by a *familia*, (Br. f. 171, b, *Dig*. 43. 16. 1. 12—17): *infamia* as a punishment of perjured jurors (f. 181, b) *peremptoriae et dilatoriae exceptiones, actio directa, replicatio, justa possessio praetore auctore, possessor malae fidei*, etc.

was of great authority, derived at any rate its leading features from that source. It was unlike the Saxon procedure for the recovery of land, in which the mere assertion of a right to the possession of the land by the claimant was enough to compel the possessor to answer, and the possessor's answer on oath that he had such a right was sufficient to end the suit in his favour[1]. In the Assize of Novel Disseisin, the claimant must prove a right superior to the possessor's, who in turn need only prove a right better than that of the claimant.

The Assize *Mort D'ancester*[2], by which the seisin of a tenant deceased was acquired for the next heirs, is expressly compared by Bracton to the Interdict *Quorum Bonorum* by which the Roman *bonorum possessor* acquired the property of the inherit-ance. But this only lay for corporeal property, while Bracton expressly states that the Assize could recover all things of which the ancestor was seised, *sive consistunt in corpore, sive in jure*[3]. On the other hand both the Interdict and the Assize were only available to the *propinquior heres*[4]; it was not sufficient that he was nearer in title than the possessor, he must be the nearest in title. In this the Assize has broken away from the Teutonic procedure, in which the claimant simply declared that he had a better right to the inherited property than the defendant[5].

The position of the doctrine of Representation has already been noted, and Bracton here refers to the *Casum Regis*, by which an uncle in seisin is preferred to his elder brother's son out of seisin[6]. The rule, which certainly prevailed later, as to the half-blood[7], that neither uterine brothers, nor brothers by the same father, could succeed to each other, probably resulted from an injudicious application of the custom of Normandy, which only forbids the succession of uterine half-brothers, and which is attributed by Maine to the survival of agnation ; for under this system such persons would not be related, though the same reason would not exclude half-brothers by the same

---

[1] *Anglo-Saxon Law*, pp. 242, 327, 365.
[2] Br. ff. 252—280, b.
[3] f. 252.
[4] Moyle on *Institutes*, i. 594, note. Br. f. 252, b, 255 b. *Cod.* 8, 2, 1.

[5] *Anglo-Saxon Law*, p. 258.
[6] *Supra*, p. 45. Br. f. 267, b.
[7] Br. f. 267: but *cf.* f. 65, b. and *supra*, p. 96. Maine, *Ancient Law*, p. 151.

father. The great bulk of this Treatise is English, though Roman influences are perceptible in some passages on possession[1], and in the presumption of paternity[2].

The *Writ de Ingressu*[3] is brought by the heir of a deceased landlord against his ancestor's tenants; and Sir T. Twiss refers this, in its descent from Anglo-Saxon *laenland*, to the Roman *locatio-conductio*[4]. As the introduction of books is clerical, this may be so as to *bookland*, but it is doubtful whether any *bookland* was *laenland*, and the suggestion hardly seems to touch the "unbooked *laens*" universal in manors[5]. In the *Writ de Recto* Sir T. Twiss states that two of the rules of procedure are "heirlooms of the early Roman settlers in Britain[6]." The one requires the service of a summons at the principal domicil in a county[7], the other an interval of 15 days between the service of a summons and the appearance of the party served in court[8]. He gives no authorities for these assertions and I am not aware of any; the latter seems contrary to fact. The Roman procedure of a written summons, *libellus conventionis*, was hardly fully established till the time of Justinian; and the period between service and appearance was, at first 5, then 10, under Justinian 20, but never 15 days, while the summons in Bracton appears to be oral[9].

The long treatise on Essoins seems purely English. That on defaults of appearance, *De Defaltis*, is noticeable for the number of Roman phrases used[10], but otherwise is English.

In the Treatise on Warranties[11] Sir T. Twiss is of opinion that the principle of implied warranty of title by the vendor, or liability to make compensation for cases of failure to warrant, was not Teutonic, (for it is not, he says, found in any Teutonic codes, though he recognizes similar provisions in the laws of

---

[1] f. 262: et cf. f. 264 "*justum titulum et justam causam possidendi.*"

[2] f. 278.

[3] The treatises on the *Writ of cosinage*, *Assisa utrum*, and the *Writ of dower*, show no further traces of Roman influence. As to the last see *supra*, pp. 97, 98.

[4] Br. f. 318. Twiss, v. Pref. p. ix.

[5] *V. supra*, p. 23. Pollock, *Land Laws*, p. 194.

[6] Br. f. 327, b. Twiss, v. Pref. p. 44.

[7] f. 333, b.

[8] f. 334.

[9] Hunter, *R. L.* 810.

[10] e.g. *litis contestatio, scilicet quousque fuerit praecise responsum intentioni petentis* (f. 373).: *actio quod metus causa* (f. 373. b.): *jus accrescendi*, f. 374: *actio mixta*, f. 369. b.

[11] f. 380, b. Twiss, VI. Pref. pp. 9–11.

the Bavarians and Visigoths), but Roman. Yet the authors of
" Anglo-Saxon Law " expressly cite provisions as to warranty
both in immovables and movables[1];—both as to the liability of the
auctor or vendor to be substituted for his vendee in a suit brought
against the latter, and his liability to compensate the vendee
in case of his failure to warrant; and these provisions were
radically different from the Roman procedure. As the Lombard
Law says:—" *Langobardus semper dat auctorem et nunquam
stat loco auctoris; Romanus semper stat loco auctoris et nunquam dat auctorem*[4]." It is true that by Roman practice
the buyer could immediately after eviction give notice to the
seller who might if he chose prosecute the action, but the
buyer could not bring an action against the seller, till sentence
had been pronounced; and this sentence was in form against
the buyer, and not, as in English Law, against the warrantor[2].
The procedure by vouching to warranty appears to follow
Teutonic models, and to have no connexion with Roman
procedure. Twiss' assertion[3] that Glanvil's third book on
Warranties shows a Roman hand is only justified by the
use of the phrases *commodatum, locatio* &c., in its first few lines;
for the subsequent statements that the warrantor appearing
becomes the principal in the suit which is carried on in his
name, and that, failing to warrant he must compensate the
tenant, with the procedure stated, are purely Teutonic and
not Roman[4].

Considering that the idea of Exceptions is entirely Roman,
the long treatise on Exceptions which concludes Bracton's work
contains very little Roman material. The division into *exceptiones peremptoriae et dilatoriae* is Institutional[5], while the
subsequent *replicatio, triplicatio*, appear in the *Digest*[6]. The
last chapter in the work deals very briefly and on Institutional
lines, with the *actiones communi dividundo, familiae herciscundae,
finium regundorum*. The *exceptio rei judicatae* is just mentioned,

[1] *Anglo-Saxon Law*, pp. 219, 254.
[2] Domat., i. 2. 10. Hargreaves' note 315 on *Co. Lit.* i. 365, *a*.
[3] Twiss, vi. Pref. 12. Glan., iii. 1.
[4] *Anglo-Saxon Law*, pp. 219, 254.
[5] *Ins.* iv. 13. *Dig.* 44, 1, 3. Br. f. 399, b.
[6] *Dig.* 44, 1, 2: the *Institutes* have *duplicatio*, which Bracton omits, but adds *quadruplicatio*. The explanation of *replicatio* is from *Inst.* iv. 14. pr. Br. f. 400, b.

but the other exceptions cited in a previous part of the work are
not even referred to[1]; the Roman principle *actor sequitur forum
rei* is quoted[2], but otherwise all the Roman matter introduced is
from previous parts of the work[3].

Nor does it seem that the influence of Roman Law upon
pleading was ever very large, though the contrary opinion is
widely held[4]. It is true that the *formula* bears some resemblance to the assize or writ, in that both were drawn up before
the parties proceeded to the trial of fact, and formed the basis
on which the trial of fact continued, but there are marked
differences in procedure. The *formula* contained in its *exceptiones* a number of defences, which in the Assize were raised
as pleas when the parties came to trial. When the Praetor had
settled the *formula* his work was done, and the issues of fact
went to a *judex* with power to pronounce sentence; but, while
the assize was in a settled form, all the defences to it were
raised orally before judge and jury in open court, and the jury
considered their verdict under the direction of the judge, who
gave judgment on their findings of fact. The record, as drawn
up when pleadings became written, bears some resemblance to
the *formula* in that the case of the two parties is contained in
one written document. But the important point in the English
suit is the issuing of the writ, and not the joinder of issue,
which answers best to the *litis contestatio*. The Roman and
English procedures are so different, that the identification of
judex and jury made by Finlason and other writers is truly
astonishing.

Neither has Bracton's phraseology had much effect on the
English Law; Exceptions have gone out of use, for the "Bill of
Exceptions" of old procedure has no analogy to them. Indeed
Bracton's "*exceptiones*" were not Roman; they were direct
traverses of fact, while the Roman ones were "confessions and
avoidances" similar to the old "equitable pleas." The Replica-

---

[1] *Supra*, p. 103, note 7.

[2] f. 401.

[3] e.g. on *monsters*, f. 438, b , on *actio
mixta*, f. 443, b., *Ins.* iv. 6, 20, *furiosi,
surdi et muti*, f. 420, b.

[4] Story, *Eq. Pl.* § 14. Spence, i. 206.
Starkie, *Ev.* i. 4. Stephen on *Pleading*,
Appendix, Notes, 2, 29. Williams on
Institutes, 208.

tion which survived till the Judicature Acts, and still exists in the Mayor's Court, was not used in the same sense as in the Roman Law. But "peremptory and dilatory pleas" existed before the Judicature Acts in the same sense as the corresponding Roman exceptions.

Results.

This inquiry, perhaps tediously minute, enables us to attempt to answer the questions with which we started.

Bracton's work can be divided into three parts :—

I. The part in which he has copied with almost verbal accuracy, Azo, the *Institutes* or the *Digest*. This consists of perhaps 25 folios out of the 450 or so of which his work is composed,—to be found in Bk. I. (except cc. 8. v. 10); Bk. II. c. 1—4; Book III. ffs. 98 b—104 b. The First Book, which treats of the Law of Persons, is derived from Azo's summary of the First Book of the *Institutes* :—the last chapter of the First Book and the four chapters of Book II., which state the means of acquiring things *jure gentium*, from Azo's summary of the *Institutes:* the 6 folios in Book III. which deal with contracts, from the Third Book of the *Institutes* and the *Digest*. The matter taken is in several places modified to represent the Law of England, and frequent omissions of unsuitable parts show an intelligent copying.

II. A part in which Roman principles appear to be the framework, though large masses of English matter are moulded on them. This consists of the rest of the second and the first treatise of the 3rd book, and the treatise on the Assize of Novel Disseisin ; it deals with donation, possession, inheritance, and the outline of the theory of actions and obligations, and perhaps comprises from a third to a quarter of the work. Embedded in the English matter are some unacknowledged citations from the *Institutes, Digest* and Azo ; but they are not very frequent or of great importance. The influence of Roman principles is clearly seen here, especially in the treatment of possession, though sometimes their only effect is to give a form to English matter.

III. The remainder, and greater part, of the work shows in my opinion, very slight, if any, traces of Roman influences.

Roman terms are occasionally used, as was natural with a writer well acquainted with Roman law, and dealing with a system till then lacking in form and precision. The few citations from Roman sources have usually done duty already in other parts of his work, and make no important additions to the matter in hand. About two-thirds of the work is of this character, English in its matter with some slight traces of scholastic form.

As to the Roman law which Bracton actually incorporated, did he, as Spence and Güterbock hold[1], only reproduce what was already held as valid law in England, being thus a trustworthy source of law and not a plagiarist; or, as Sir Henry Maine suggests[2], did he actually introduce new Roman matter as English law. There seem to me to be no materials in existence for a positive answer to this question; but I myself should incline to agree with Sir H. Maine, (though I think his estimate of Bracton's indebtedness is as excessive as that of Mr Reeves is under the mark[3]), that as regards the first part of Bracton's work, it was new matter to the English Law, directly copied from Roman sources, to fill up a framework of his first three books which he had adopted from the *Institutes*. As to the second part, I think that Bracton has both introduced new Roman matter, and reproduced English law, derived from the Roman by the decisions of other clerical judges, and then recognized as the Law of the Land.

In considering Bracton's 1st Book, a conjecture was offered as to his method of writing[4], and we have found no reason to depart from the opinion there expressed. English Law was reduced to order on a Roman framework, furnished with many Roman terms, its gaps filled up with actual Roman matter, so long as this was not inconsistent with English Law. At the same time Roman influences, acting on the judges, vary some existing English rules, such as those as to nuptial donations, curtesy, and forfeiture of earnest. But I know of no case where Bracton has cited Roman law, the previous English rules being to a contrary effect, unless indeed some recent decisions give him warrant. On the contrary we have seen many examples of his "intelligent

[1] Spence, I. 123, 124. Güt. p. 57.

[2] Maine, *Ancient Law*, p. 82.

[3] Maine, one-third of matter, and whole of form, *Anc. Law*, p. 82. Reeves, not three pages; I. 529.

[4] *V. supra*, p. 82.

copying", as in the adaptation of the definition of theft, the conception of *donatio*, and the account of treasure-trove : and this "intelligent copying" contrasts strongly with the unintelligent plagiarism of his followers, which converted the *actio familiae herciscundae* into "*accioun mixte, que est appelé en la ley le Emperour accioun de la mesnee dame de Herciscunde*[1]." To him English law is undoubtedly indebted for an extensive Roman terminology which survives to the present day; the Roman form of his first three books has been less fortunate, though Blackstone's Commentaries show some traces of its influences. But I do not think that Bracton himself is responsible for many material alterations based on the Roman law, though he records some important ones which have been made by his predecessors and contemporaries under civilian influences; and certainly M. Houard's charge against him of Romanizing the law of England cannot to any serious extent be justified.

[1] *Britton*, III. 7, 1. *V. post*, p. 124.

CHAPTER IV.

ROMAN LAW IN BRITTON AND FLETA.

THE work of Bracton attained great repute[1], while its size and cost prevented its being easily consulted. Several abstracts or epitomes were therefore compiled with more or less fidelity, which served to make known the law as contained in Bracton. These were the treatises known as *Fleta* and *Britton*, and a *Summa* by Gilbert de Thornton.

This latter may be briefly dealt with as no copy of it is at present known to exist[2]. Selden had a MS. in his library, of which he has left us some account. The abridgment was made about the year 1292, and its title expressly states that it is "*Summa de legibus...Angliae a Magistro Henrico de Bryctona composita...quam Ds. Gilbertus de Thornton abbreviavit sub compendio.*" The order of the work is slightly different from that of Bracton: Selden says: " He, as is usual with Epitomisers, passes by a great many things, neither does he always follow Bracton's method, but sometimes another and makes a different distribution." We have very little information as to the Roman or English character of the work[3].

---

[1] See the letter of R. de Scardeburgh borrowing a MS. of Bracton from the Bishop of Bath, and promising to return it in 6 months. Selden *ad Fletam*, II. 2.

[2] Güterbock, p. 68. Selden *ad Fletam*, II. 4. Mr Kenny's censure on English illiberality for not printing Thornton would be more applicable if he would tell us where to find a copy of Thornton to print. See Nicholl's

Britton, I. Pref. 25.

[3] Selden says "He is sometimes an excellent interpreter and expositor of Bracton...though he passes by almost all the quotations of the places cited out of the books of the Imperial Law by Bracton, *and which are basely handled by his Editors*"—(was this prophetic of the Rolls' Edition?): "but he has not omitted them all": and in the following chapters (III. 1, 2) he

"FLETA, *seu Commentarius Juris Anglicani*[1]," is so called from its composition in the Fleet Prison, and is believed to have been written about 1292[2]. It is in Latin, and it abridges Bracton carefully, though the arrangement differs, and the work is about half the size of the original. But besides omissions the author adds new matter which is sometimes of a Roman character. He mentions the *Corpus Juris*, as where, in speaking of accession by *ferruminatio*, he says "*Secundum quod Institutis legitur, ubi dicitur quae pars alteri accrescere debet*[3]." Except in this case he does not expressly quote Roman sources, though Bracton's incorporations are reproduced, in many cases word for word, and in some cases strengthened. Thus *Fleta* expressly gives as a reason for the prohibition of donations *inter conjuges*[4], "*quia omnino hoc prohibetur in lege:...verba autem legis sunt hujusmodi.*" Bracton's citation as to the effect of felony is reproduced with the heading *et ad hoc facit Lex imperatoria*[5], which also serves to introduce the citation as to the respite of pregnant women[6]. New Roman matter, not found in Bracton is introduced in the chapter "*De dotis constitutione*": and some Canonical authorities are cited[7]. Bracton's arrangement is followed except that the subject of criminal law and a book on personal actions are introduced between Books I. and II. of Bracton.

The work called "*Britton*[8]," probably because it was considered as an abbreviation of Bracton, is written in Law French, between 1290 and 1300[9]. During this period the

refers to passages where Thornton has followed Bracton's Roman incorporations.

[1] Güt. p. 69: Nicholl's *Britton*, I. Int. 25. Twiss' Bracton, VI. Pref. 18. Selden *ad Fletam. Fleta*, ed. 1647.

[2] *Nicholls*, " in course of preparation in 1290." *Güterbock*: "composed after 1292." *Twiss*, " shortly after 1292, if not in that year."

[3] *Fleta*, III. 2, 12. Bracton in the corresponding chapter also refers to the *Institutes*, but on a different point, the accession of pictures. Br. f. 10.

[4] III. 3, 12, 15.

[5] III. 10, 3; cf. *Britton*, III. 7, 1; on another subject "*en la ley le Emperour.*"

[6] I. 38. 15.

[7] V. 23: Güt. p. 70: On the other hand, *dos profectitia* appears in *Fleta* (v. 23, 4), as *dos perfectiva*.

[8] Nicholl's *Britton*, 2 vols. Clarendon Press, 1865. Güterbock, p. 72. Twiss, VI. Pref. 18, 62. Selden *ad Fletam*, II. 3.

[9] Güterbock, 1297; Nicholls: "1291 —1292 is the approximate date for the origin of this book." Int. p. xviii.

influence of Edward I.'s legislative ability was very great, and the three short treatises we have spoken of show the interest taken in the law. *Britton* especially bears marks of royal instigation; its form, in the first person plural, *"nous voulums"*, and its constant references to " our writ ", strongly suggest that it is a work undertaken by royal command. Mr Nicholls is of opinion "that *Fleta* was first written, and, together with Bracton was in the hands of the author of *Britton*, who appears to have more frequently made use of the compendium of *Fleta*, than of the larger work[1]." The work, as a whole, is far more practical and modern than that of Bracton, and though it reproduces some of his Roman incorporations, it is distinctly less civilian in character[2]. I have only been able to find one express reference to the Roman Law, and that, a most ludicrous misunderstanding. *Britton* following Bracton on *actiones mixtae* comes to the " *actio familiae herciscundae*," which appears in all the MSS in a form implying that " *Herciscunda* " is a female proper name[3]: Nicholls' reading is *"que est appelé en la ley le Emperour[4], accioun de la mesnee dame de Herciscunde."* This may be called unintelligent plagiarism, as compared with Bracton's intelligent copying. But the Roman matter in Bracton is much abbreviated and reduced, and thus the tendency of the use of *Britton* would certainly be to weaken Roman influences.

---

[1] Nich. Int. p. 27.

[2] Cf. Bracton *De acquirendo Rerum dominio*, Bk II. c. 1—4 : with *Britton*, II. 2, which is Roman, but much abbreviated and modified.

[3] *Britton*, III. 7, 1 : this phrase is unfortunate : Coke speaks of *familia herciscunda* as a tenure ! *Sub*, p. 130.

[4] Cf. *Fleta, Lex Imperatoria.*

CHAPTER V.

ROMAN LAW FROM FLETA TO COKE.

As in *Britton,* so in later writers, though Bracton is quoted constantly, we find his Roman form gone and his Roman matter seldom reproduced; and the preface to Staunford's Pleas of the Crown expressly states: *"Citavi non pauca e Bractono et Brittono, vetustis legum scriptoribus, hoc consilio ut cum leges Coronae magna ex parte jure statuario constant, ponatur ante legentis oculos commune jus quod fuit ante ea statuta condita[1]."* Staunford's work cites Bracton at great length, and includes the whole of his canonical division of homicide[2], and his semi-Roman definition of theft[3]. He also quotes the passage on justice, which Bracton had taken from Azo[4].

There is a curious book, described by Butler as "an ingenious but neglected work," which, had its author fully carried out his plan, might have been of great interest in this essay. It is entitled: "A Parallel or Conference of the Civil Law, the Canon Law, and the Common Law of this realm of England, wherein the agreement, and disagreement of these three Lawes, and the causes and reasons of the said agreement and disagreement are opened and discussed[5]." The author, William Fulbeck, dedicates his work to the Archbishop of Canterbury, "to whom his Majesty hath

---

[1] Ed. 1607. With this cf. similar statement in the *Proœmium* to Coke's 2nd Institute.

[2] Staunford, Part I. c. 4.

[3] *Ibid.* Part I. c. 15.

[4] *Ibid.* II. c. 1.

[5] London, 1601.

committed the executing and maintenance of the Civil and Canon Laws," I suppose in the Ecclesiastical Courts. The form is that of a dialogue in which Nomomathes, a wealthy patron of learning, inquires of Codicignostes, Canonologus, and Anglonomophylax, as to the provisions in various points of their respective laws. Unfortunately Fulbeck's historical faculty is not very keen, and he does not fulfil his promise to "discuss the causes and reasons of agreement and disagreement." The book consists of questions by the patron, and short statements of the Civil and English laws by their respective advocates, the professor of Canon Law being unexpectedly quiet. That the result is not of very great value may be seen from the fact that, though Codicignostes cites Paulus' definition of theft, the English lawyer does not note the omissions which Bracton had thought necessary, and which were still required, to make it English Law. The most interesting passage I have found is one as to the crime of procuring abortion[1]; the Civil lawyer states it to be homicide to kill an infant in its mother's womb, to which Anglonomophylax answers "In Bracton's time it seemeth that our Law did in this point somewhat nearly agree with yours, for he hath these words" (citing Bracton) "but now the law is altered."

Fulbeck is of opinion that the Canon Law is "more ancient than the other two and of greater continuance": while as to the Civil Law he is curiously doubtful. "I do not think that which may properly be called Civil Law, and was so-called at the first is any other than *jus Romanum*, or comments or additions to it." While a fuller work would have been interesting, the book is of value as showing that at that time the idea of any parentage or authority of the civil law, as related to the common law, was at any rate not widely spread. They were compared as unrelated systems of separate growth.

But advocates of Roman origin were not wanting. Dr Cowell, Reader on Civil Law at Cambridge, (best known as the author of the "Interpreter," which the Commons attacked for undue exaltation of the Prerogative, and the king disowned as

---

[1] Fulbeck, p. 100, b, and see *supra*, p. 108, note 7.

"writ only by a civilian by profession, and meddling in matters beyond his reach,") had endeavoured to maintain the unity of the Civil and Common Law, in a book published in 1605 and entitled "*Institutiones Juris Anglicani ad methodum et seriem Institutionum imperalium compositae et digestae.*" Its object was to show that the two laws had "*eadem utriusque fundamenta, easdem rerum definitiones divisionesque, consentaneas plane regulas, similia fere scita sola idiomatis atque methodi varietate disparata......et redigere largiora illa legum nostrarum volumina putidi idiomatis squalore expurgata ad Pandectarum Justinianearum ordinem*"; and he concludes that "*illam jus et legem nostram communem...quod hactenus linguae obscuritate involutum barbarismi notam apud exteros vix evasit... nihil aliud esse quam Romani et feudalis mistionem[1].*" He transfers the old authorities, Bracton, *Britton,* and *Fleta* into the framework of the *Institutes,* which Bracton's borrowings from the *Corpus Juris* and from Azo enable him in some places to do with great accuracy: as for instance in Book I. on Persons, the commencement of Book II. on the Acquisition of things *Jure Gentium,* parts of Book III. on Obligations, and Book IV. on Actions. Where a Roman title has no corresponding feature in English law he mentions it, e.g. "*unde constat hunc Romanorum adoptandi morem aut a nobis nunquam receptum, aut jam pridem, quemadmodum et apud Gallos evanuisse[2];*" and "*ut tam arctus non est apud nos patriae potestatis nexus quam apud Romanos fuit: sic neque est tam solennis ejusdem per emancipationem solutio[3]:*"..."*illam tutelam fiduciariam, quam Romani...imposuerunt, majores nostri penitus neglexisse videntur[4].*"

He accepts the Roman parts of Bracton at any rate as law at the time when they were written, though the curious passage in Bracton as to the sanctity of walls seems to have been almost too much for his faith, for he introduces it with the remark, "*si veteribus juris nostri scriptoribus credimus*", and concludes "*Sed haec poena videtur hodie arbitraria[5].*" It is

---

[1] Pref.
[2] p. 26.
[3] p. 27.

[4] p. 37.
[5] p. 51, *et supra,* p. 82, note 4.

noteworthy that Dr Cowell does not suggest any authority for the Civil Law in the Common Law Courts.

Another discussion of the matter is found about the same date in the Posthumous works of Sir H. Spelman[1], the well known antiquarian, who says " Great portion of our Common Law is derived from the Civil, (unless we will say that the Civil Law is derived from ours), which Bracton also, above 300 years before, right well understanding not only citeth the Digests and Books of Civil Law in many places for warrant of our Common Law, but in handling our Law pursueth the method phrases and matter of Justinian's *Institutes* of Civil Law...I think the foundation of our Laws to be laid by our German ancestors, but built upon and polished by material taken from the Canon and Civil laws...When and how these several parts were brought into our Common Law is neither easily nor definitively to be expressed ...Those no doubt of Canon Law by the prevalency of the clergy in their several ages......those of Civil Law by such of our reverend judges and sages of ancient time, as for justice and knowledge's sake sought instruction therein when they found no rule at home to guide the judgment by. For I suppose they in those days judged many things *ex aequo et bono* and that their judgments after, (as *Responsa Prudentium* among the Romans, and the *Codex Theodosianus*), became precedents of Law unto Posterity."

[1] *On the Law Terms*, last chapter, pp. 99, 101: published in 1723, written before 1641 (? 1614).

CHAPTER VI.

SIR E. COKE in his *Institutes*, (themselves Roman in name), takes a decided position as to the authority of the Civil law. He says: "Our common laws are aptly and properly called the laws of England, because they are appropriated to this kingdom of England...and have no dependency upon any forreine law whatever, no, not upon the Civil or Canon law other than in cases allowed by the Laws of England...therefore foreign precedents are not to be objected against us, because we are not subject to foreign laws[1]"—and again "it is worthy of consideration how the laws of England are not derived from any foreign law, either canon or civil or other, but a special law appropriated to this kingdom[2]." And in a side-note he remarks: "*Nota differentiam...inter malum in se* against the Common law, and *malum prohibitum* by the Civil or Canon law, *whereof the judges of the Common law in these cases take no notice[3].*" Sir Edward Coke indeed had not a high opinion of the Civil law. In his *Prœmium* to the Second *Institute*, he observes: "Upon the text of the Civil law there be so many glosses and interpretations, and again upon those so many commentaries, and all these written by doctors of equal degree and authority, and therein so many diversities of opinion as they do rather increase than resolve doubts and uncertainties, and the professors of that noble science say that it is like a sea of waves"; and with this he contrasts the certainty of the Common law; "*Statio bene fida peritis.*"

---

[1] Coke, II. 98.

[2] III. 100.

[3] III. 153.

This opinion does not hinder him from occasionally referring to the Civil law, though not with great accuracy. He comments with approval on Littleton's statement that the English law is contrary to the Civil law in which *partus sequitur ventrem*, saying, "true it is, for by that law" (stating the law), "both of which cases are contrarie to the Law of England[1]." He makes the curious assertion that, "in prohibiting the lineal ascent in inheritance, the Common law is assisted with the law of the Twelve Tables[2]," which seems entirely inaccurate. He notes the differences in the laws as to guardianship, already alluded to[3], and says that the law of England is contrary to the Civil law, which *"est quasi agnum lupo committere ad devorandum"*; yet he cites the very rule of the Civil law, *"qui sentit commodum debet et onus sentire,"* in support of the position that the owners of private chapels should repair them[4]. Lord Macclesfield strongly disapproved of the English rule, deeming it "to have prevailed in barbarous times, and a cruel and barbarous presumption[5]."

Coke cites very largely from Bracton, and some of the passages are those directly derived from Roman sources[6]; as far as I can find, he only expressly refers to the *Corpus Juris* twice[7]. The rule as to the half-blood, which has been attributed to a misunderstanding of the Civil law, he treats as settled[8]. He states rather curiously and inaccurately that coparcenery was called in the ancient books of law *"familia herciscunda[9],"* which was a tenure ; and compares the Common Civil and Canon laws on kinship, saying, "thus much of the Civil and Canon laws is

---

[1] I. 122, b, 123. *Supra*, p. 83.

[2] I. 11, a.

[3] I. 88, b. Blackstone, I. 461. *Supra*, pp. 75, 97.

[4] Coke, II. 489.

[5] 2 P. Wms. 264, 9 Mod. 142. Hargreaves' notes, 63.

[6] e.g. Bracton's Roman def. of *actio* (Coke, II. 39, Br. 98, b); the division of actions into real, personal, mixed (C. II. 21, 286; Br. f. 101, b); on monsters (C. I. 7, b; Br. f. 5); *de ventro inspiciendo* (C. I. 8, b; Br. ff. 69—71); on treasure trove (C. III. 132; Br. f. 10, 119, b); also cf. C. I. 36, a. with Br. ff.

33, b, 34.

[7] C. II. 658: *Dig.* 48, 19, 18, where he misquotes *meretur* for *patitur* : the quotation is characteristically used to resist a claim of jurisdiction by the Ecclesiastical Courts. Coke also says of the *Regiam Majestatem*, "so called because it beginneth *as Justinian's Institutes do*, with these words," which is incorrect, as the words are *Imperatoriam Majestatem.*

[8] C. I. 14, a, 191, a. note. *Supra*, pp. 96, 115.

[9] C. I. 164, b.

necessary to the knowledge of the Common law on this point." He of course notices the discrepancy between the Common law and the "laws of Holy Church, or Canon law," as to legitimation by subsequent marriage. Speaking of banishment he remarks, "if the husband by act of Parliament have judgment to be exiled for a time, *which some call a relegation,* that is no civil death[1]": this is clearly the Roman "*relegatio*" or exile, which involved no loss of *status.* He refers to the agreement of the Civil and Common laws in forbidding distress on beasts of the plough[2], and cites Seneca as to their agreement in the punishment of rape. He uses the phraseology of peremptory and dilatory exceptions[3], though bargain and sale, (in the *Institutes* a *consensual* contract), is described as a *real* one[4]. The respite of a pregnant woman under sentence till she is delivered, for which Bracton had cited Roman law, is restated[5], but some of Bracton's Roman incorporations are not so fortunate, as where Coke says " We remember not that we have read in any book of the legitimation or adoption of an heir, but only in Bracton[6], and that to little purpose." Coke ascribes the introduction of the rack to the Civil law[7], as "the rack or brake allowed in many cases by the Civil law, whereas all tortures and torments of parties accused were directly against the Common law of England[8]."

In his Fourth *Institute* Coke states to what extent the Civil and Canon law had force in England. It is the *lex et consuetudo parliamenti,* he says, that all weighty matters in Parliament be determined by the course of the Parliament, and " not by the Civil law, nor yet by the Common laws of this realm[9]." The Court of Admiralty is always spoken of as "proceeding according to

---

[1] C. i. 133, a.

[2] C. ii. 132.

[3] C. ii. 426.

[4] C. ii. 672.

[5] C. iii. 17.

[6] Br. f. 63, b.

[7] C. iii. 35, cf. Step. *Hist. C. L.* i. 222.

[8] Cf. also, C. i. 41, a; Br. f. 311. C. i. 47, b. on *traditio.* C. i. 55, a. on *possessio precaria.* C. ii. 198, 441,

on liability of heirs. C. ii. 591, on *ultimum supplicium,* cf. *Dig.* 48, 19. C. ii. 391; *melior est conditio possidentis.* C. ii. 360, 573, et Br. *passim* "*nihil est tam conveniens naturali aequitati unumquodque dissolvi eo ligamine, quo ligatum est.*" C. iii. 2, *Crimen laesae majestatis.* C. iii. 168, *Crimen falsi.* Coke also cites Bracton's definition of theft.

[9] C. iv. 14.

the Civil Law[1]," though Coke gives no reasons for such a procedure. The Court of Chivalry before the Constable and Marshal "proceeds according to the customs and usages of that Court, and, in cases omitted, according to the Civil law, *secundum leges armorum*[2]." In a case as to ambassadors, the Committee of the Privy Council heard the "counsel learned in the Civil and Common laws[3]"; and Coke says of one of their decisions "and this also agreeth with the Civil law[3]." As to the Ecclesiastical Courts, "which proceed not by the rules of the Common Law," Coke writes with some acerbity, "that the King's laws of this realm do bound the jurisdiction of Ecclesiastical Courts[4]." The Convocation proceed according to "*legem divinam et canones sanctae ecclesiae*," the ecclesiastical courts generally by "the laws of Christ[5]." As to the authority of this law in England, Coke is very decided: "all canons and constitutions made against the laws of the realm are made void": "all canons which are against the prerogative of the king, the Common law, or custom of the realm are of no force[6]."

I have only noticed two cases in which the English Common law, as stated by Coke, appears to have been modified by the Civil law otherwise than through Bracton. These are, first, the law as to discontinuance[7], or the alienation made by *tenant en autre droit*, by which the remainderman is driven to an action; the rules as to this bear some analogy to the civilian doctrines of *usurpatio possessionis*, and Coke himself in one place uses the term "usurpations" in connexion with discontinuances[8]. Secondly, the Roman law as to *collatio bonorum*[9], by which emancipated children, wishing to share in intestacy, must bring their property into the stock to be divided, seems to have suggested the custom of London as to "*hotchpot*," and part of

---

[1] C. IV. 134: Duck, II. 8, 3, 24.

[2] C. IV. 125: Hargreaves' note to I. 74, a, b. Duck, II. 8, 3, 12—22. "*Causas ex Jure Civili Romanorum et consuetudinibus armorum et non ex Jure Municipali Anglorum esse dijudicandas.*"

[3] C. IV. 153.

[4] C. IV. 321, 322.

[5] C. II. 487: cf. Duck, II. 8, 3, 26, *et seq. De his omnibus in hoc foro jus dicitur ex Jure Civili, cui porro accessit Jus Canonicum. Ex quibus omnibus constituitur Lex quam nostrates appellant Ecclesiasticum...Lex Civile in hoc foro Lex terrae appellatur.*

[6] C. II. 647, 652.

[7] C. I. 325, a; II. 272.

[8] C. II. 272.

[9] *Dig.* 37, 6. *Cod.* 6, 20. Hunter, *R. L.* p. 663.

the subsequent Statute of Distributions[1], and Coke expressly says, "this is that in effect which the civilians call *collatio bonorum*[2]."

A study of Coke's *Institutes* suggests that the Common lawyers of the time expressly repudiated the Civil law as an authority in the King's courts, or even as the parent of the existing Common law. Coke occasionally notes the agreement or disagreement of the two laws, but with such inaccuracy as to show that his own knowledge of the Civil law was slight. The working out of an Equitable Jurisdiction, and the decisions of the Ecclesiastical and Admiralty Courts were building up systems largely of Civilian origin; but in the Common law, the influence of Roman law has rather retrograded than advanced since the time of Bracton.

[1] 22 and 23 Car. II. c. 10 § 5.   [2] C. I. 177, a.

CHAPTER VII.

THE publication of Coke's work lessened the influence of the earlier writers. His mass of quotations and precedents obviated the necessity for search in Yearbooks, Abridgments, and early writers on the law[1]; and as a result they were mainly known through Coke, whose connexion with the laws of Rome is, as we have seen, slight. But both before and after the publication of the *Institutes,* a controversy existed as to whether Bracton and the old writers were or were not good authorities on English law, in which the reason given for their untrustworthiness was that Bracton had introduced the Civil law. Thus Fitzherbert notes a case which he abridges as follows : *"Bracton dise que l'age le male et female fuit tout un, et tout le Court dise que Bracton ne fuit unques tenu pour auctor en nostre ley[2]."* In *Stowell v. Lord Zouch[3]* (1564—1569), Saunders, C. B., cited Bracton "not as an author in the law, for he said that Bracton and Glanvil were not authors in our law, but as an ornament to discourse where he agrees with the law," and Catline, C. J. of England, cited Bracton "not for an author in our law, but for consonancy and order, where he agrees with better authorities."

Coke cites Bracton constantly without questioning his authority, and Lord Hale, though he says that "Bracton's work

---

[1] Butler's Pref. to *Coke on Lit.* 13th Edit. p. xxii.

[2] *Grand Abridgment,* Title Gard. 71. He refers to Hil. 35 Hen. VI. (1457), which I think is a wrong refer-ence. Neither Case 2 nor Case 17 in that term seems to be the case referred to though they deal with the same subjects.

[3] Plowden's *Reports,* pp. 357, 358.

in the beginning seems to borrow its method from the Civil law," yet speaks of it as a "great evidence of the growth of our laws between the times of Henry II. and III.," and says that "the greater part of its substance is either of the course of proceedings in the law known to the author or of resolutions and decisions in the English Courts[1]." In 1701, counsel arguing in *R. v. Berchet*[2], cites Fitzherbert and Stowell's Case in support of his allegation that Glanvil and *Fleta* were of no authority, but the judges do not notice the point. In the next year (1702), Lord Holt, giving judgment in *Lane v. Cotton*[3], an action against the Post-office for the loss of a letter, says, "and this is the reason of the Civil law in this case, which I am loathe to quote, yet, inasmuch as the laws of all nations are doubtless raised out of the ruins of the Civil law, *it must be owned that the principles of our law are derived from the Civil law,* and therefore grounded upon the same reason in many places." And this expression of opinion took effect two years later (1704) in Lord Holt's celebrated judgment in *Coggs v. Bernard*[4] where, after citing at length Bracton and the Civil law, he says: " This Bracton I have cited is, I confess, an old author, but in this his doctrine is agreeable to reason, and to what the law is in other countries : the Civil law is so[5]."—" I cite this author (Bracton), though I confess he is an old one, because his opinion is reasonable, and very much to my present purpose, and there is no authority in the law to the contrary[6]"...... " I do not find the word '*mandatum*' in any other in our law, besides in this place in Bracton, which is a full authority, if it be not thought too old[7]."

In the *Grand Opinion*[8], a decision of the Judges in 1717, on the Sovereign's right of disposing of the education and marriage of his grandchildren, the counsel for the Prince of Wales expressly objected to the authority of Bracton, saying[9]: "now as to Bracton, *that is transcribed from Justinian,* therefore the

---

[1] *Hist. of Common Law*, published 1713, written before 1676, p. 189.

[2] Showers' *Rep.* 121.

[3] 12 *Mod. R.* 482.

[4] Ld. Raymond, 909. Smith's *Leading Cases*, I. 199 (8th Edit. 1879).

[5] *Ibid.* pp. 208, 209.

[6] *Ibid.* p. 210.

[7] *Ibid.* p. 215.

[8] Fortescue's *Reports*, pp. 401—440.

[9] *Ibid.* p. 406.

Book and instance ought not to be regarded, *for he deviates from the Common law, and is nothing but Civil law.*" The judges gave their opinions separately, and five of them dealt with this objection, three supporting the authority of Bracton, and two denying it. Of the latter, Eyre, J. said[1]: "What is cited out of Bracton and *Fleta* is not law, nor accounted so; there is not any such term in our law as *emancipatio* or *foris familiatio*"; and Price, B. remarked[2]: "It was an article of impeachment to endeavour to introduce the Civil law; Bracton and *Fleta* are old Civil Law Books; they may fetch out of these books Ship money and the dispensing power, they were all fetched out of these old books." On the other hand Parker, C. J. said[3]: "As to the authority of Bracton, to be sure many things are now altered, but there is no colour to say it was not law at any time, for there are many things that have never been altered and are law now." Fortescue, B. said[4]: "The law-books of Bracton and *Fleta* are the ancient Law of the Land extending to all cases; it remains law to this day as to the Royal family because as to them this Law has had no alteration by any Law or Statute whatever, and the Usage has gone accordingly. These law-books are so strong that there has been no way thought of to evade them, but by denying the authority of them, and calling it 'Civil Law.' But I own I am not a little surprised that these books should be denied for law when in my little experience I have known them quoted almost in every argument where pains have been taken if anything could be found in those books to the matter in hand; and I have never known them denied for law, but when some statute or usage time out of mind has altered them." Montagu, B. also supported their authority, and said: "It is objected indeed that this is Civil law; that may be, and yet it may be and is the Law of the Land also, and these books are often quoted by the greatest judges and lawyers heretofore in England and allowed as Law[5]."

Blackstone[6], who speaks of "Glanvil's excellent treatise,

---

[1] Fortescue, *Rep.* p. 427.
[2] *Ibid.* p. 429.
[3] *Ibid.* p. 408.
[4] *Ibid.* p. 419.

[5] *Ibid.* p. 424, he cites Lord Holt in *Coggs v. Bernard.*
[6] *Commentaries*, pub. 1765, IV. pp. 421, 425, 427.

though some of it now be antiquated and altered," includes Glanvil and Bracton in his list of venerated authors, " whose treatises are cited as authority, and are evidence that cases have formerly happened in which such and such points were determined, which have now become settled and first principles." He says that Bracton's treatise "shows still further improvement in the method and regularity of the Common law," and in treating of the doctrines of *acquisitio dominii juris gentium,* he says[1]: "and these (Roman) doctrines are implicitly copied and adopted by our Bracton, and have since been confirmed by many resolutions of the Courts." " The legal treatises written in Edward I.'s reign, as *Britton, Fleta,* Hengham and the rest, are for the most part law at this day, or at least were so, till the alteration of tenures took place."

In *Ball v. Herbert*[2] (1789), counsel in citing Institutional passages from Bracton on the rights in public rivers, questioned the passage in Fitzherbert, and cited Fortescue and Staunford in support of Bracton's authority, but Buller, J. said[3]: "another authority cited is the passage from Bracton...that plainly appears to have been taken from Justinian, and is only part of the Civil law; and whether or not that has been adopted by the Common law is to be seen by looking into our books; and there it is not to be found." Curiously enough, the same passage of Bracton came under discussion in *Blundell v. Catterall*[4] (1821) before Best, C. J., a vigorous supporter of Bracton's authority. While counsel on one hand argued "that the authority of Bracton cannot have much weight, for it is only copied from the Civil law, and was overruled in *Ball v. Herbert*": on the other hand it was said that " Lord Hale mentions Bracton as a good authority: he was Chief Justice of England in the reign of Henry III.[5] (!), and from his station must be taken to be no mean authority of what the Common law was in his day. It is no objection to the passage that Bracton has availed himself of the very words of Justinian. It is impossible that he should not

[1] II. 404.
[2] 3 *T. R.* 257.
[3] p. 263.
[4] 5 B. and Ald. 268, 270, 272, 279,

282.
[5] Best, C. J. repeats this mistake in his judgment, p. 282, and again in *Gifford v. Lord Yarborough,* 5 Bing. 167.

have found the principles there laid down, in the Civil law or in any other well-digested code, for they are directly derived from the law of nature." Best, C. J., in his judgment, cited Bracton, and Buller, J.'s disapproval of his authority, and said: "I admit that Bracton agrees with the Civil law, and I must add with the law of all civilized nations...This, I think, proves that the doctrine is reasonable, and ought to be adopted into our law, unless there is something in our particular situation to exclude it... Bracton's books show that this passage has been adopted into our law...Bracton has not stated this as Civil law, he has made it part of his book...*I do not say that the whole of the passage in Bracton is good law; it was all good law at the time he wrote, and all of it that is adapted to the present state of things is good law now.*"

The same judge delivering the opinion of the judges in the House of Lords in *Gifford v. Lord Yarborough*[1] (1828), where Bracton had been cited as to acquisition by alluvion, said: "It is true that Bracton follows the Civil law, but by inserting this passage in his book, he presents it to us as part of the law and customs of England. Lord Hale says it was much improved in the time of Bracton. This improvement was made by incorporating much of the Civil law with the Common law...We know that many of the maxims of the Common law are borrowed from the Civil law, and are still quoted in the language of the Civil law...To form a system of law sufficient for the state of society in the times of Henry III., both Courts of Justice and law writers were obliged to adopt such of the rules of the *Digest* as were not inconsistent with our principles of jurisprudence. Wherever Bracton got his law from...his authority has been confirmed by modern writers and by all the decided cases." And the present Master of the Rolls, in deciding the well-known case of *Nugent v. Smith*[2] (1875) on carriers' liability, said, "It is obvious therefore that Bracton, or English judges before him, adopted into the English the Roman Law," of bailments.

The result of these authorities seems to be :—(1). In passages where Bracton has copied the Roman Law, he will be

---

[1] 5 Bing. 163, 167.   [2] *L. R.* 1, C. P. D. 18, 29.

accepted as an authority, if confirmed by subsequent cases. (2). Even if such confirmation has not taken place, the passage may be relied on as authority, and its Roman origin will be no objection to it, provided that no later statutes, decisions or customs contrary to it exist.

Such passages therefore form part of the English law, and are not merely used as suggestions for a right decision, as is the case with the Roman law.

CHAPTER VIII.

ROMAN LAW; ITS AUTHORITY IN HALE AND BLACKSTONE.

CONTINUING our survey of the views of the "sages of the Common law," Sir M. Hale enlarges and defines the views of Coke on the position and authority of the Civil law, and is followed in this by Blackstone.

Hale[1] divides the Law of England into Statute Law, and *Leges non scriptae*; and the latter again into (1) the Common law, (2) those particular laws, which are applicable to particular subjects, matters, and courts, explained to be "the Ecclesiastical and Civil laws, so far forth as they are admitted in certain courts, and in certain matters allowed to the decision of those courts. But," says Hale, "it is most plain that neither the Canon law nor the Civil law have any obligation as laws within the kingdom... for no laws of the Pope or Emperor, as they are such, bind here. But all the strength that either the papal or imperial laws have obtained in this kingdom is only because they have been received and admitted...by us, which alone gives them their authoritative essence, and qualifies their obligation...The authority and force they have here is not founded on, or derived from themselves... and hence it is that even in those courts where the use of those laws is indulged, according to the reception which has been allowed them, if they exceed the bounds of that reception, by extending themselves to other matters than have been allowed them, or if those courts proceed according to that law, when it is controlled by the Common law of the kingdom, the Common

---

[1] *History of Common Law.* Written before 1676. pp. 22—26.

law does, and may, prohibit and punish them; and it will not be a sufficient answer for them to tell the King's courts that Justinian, or Pope Gregory have decreed otherwise. For we are not bound by their decrees further or otherwise than as the kingdom here has, as it were, transposed the same into the Common and municipal laws of this realm; either by admission of, or by enacting the same, which is that alone, which can make them of any force in England."

And these particular courts, Hale states to be (1) the Ecclesiastical courts, (2) the Admiralty court, (3) the *curia militaris* or court of the constable and marshal, (4) the courts of the Universities[1]. The Ecclesiastical and Admiralty Courts we may treat hereafter. The Court of the Constable and Marshal is of course of small importance. Hale says of it, "Here the Civil law has been used and allowed in such things as belong to their jurisdiction, as the rule and direction of their proceedings and decisions, so far forth as the same is not controlled by the laws of this kingdom, and those customs and usages which have obtained in England; which, even in points of honour, are in some points derogatory to the Civil law[2]."

As to the Courts of the Universities, in 1407 a judgment of the Chancellor of Oxford, proceeding according to the Civil law in a case of debt, was reversed by the King's Bench, the principal error assigned being that they proceeded "*per Legem Civilem ubi quilibet ligeus Regis Regni sui Angliae in quibuscunque placitis et querelis infra hoc regnum factis et emergentibus de Jure tractari debet per Communem Legem Angliae.*" But a charter of Henry VIII., confirmed by a statute of Elizabeth, allowed their procedure; "and," says Hale, "'tis thereby that at this day they have a kind of Civil law procedure, even in matters that are of themselves of Common law cognizance, where either of the parties to the suit are privileged[3]."

But while the Law of England has admitted the rules of the Civil and Canon law into these Courts, it yet has retained the "*signa superioritatis*[4], the preference and superintendence of

---

[1] *Ibid.* p. 26.

[2] *Ibid.* p. 43, *vide supra*, p. 132, *sub.* p. 152. Duck, ii. 8, 3, 12—22.

[3] Mich. 8 H. 4, Rot. 72. Hale, p. 30.

[4] Hale, pp. 44, 45.

these courts," in that the Common law courts interpret the extent of their jurisdiction and can prohibit them from exceeding it.

And this view of the position of the Civil and Canon laws in the kingdom, and their relation to the Common law is adopted by Blackstone, writing a century later, and is the accepted view at the present day. Blackstone says[1]: "For the Civil and Canon laws, considered in respect to any intrinsic obligation, have no force and authority in this kingdom; they are no more binding in England than our laws are binding at Rome. But as far as these foreign laws, on account of some peculiar propriety, have in some particular cases and in some particular courts been introduced and allowed by our laws, so far they oblige and no further, their authority being wholly founded on that permission and adoption." And he asserts the right of the Courts of Common law to prohibit and annul their proceedings, if they apply the Civil or Canon laws in cases where they have not been received and which are governed by the Common law. He states that he will not consider "what hath been claimed or pretended to belong to their jurisdiction, by the officers and judges of those respective courts; but what the Common law allows and permits to be so. For these *eccentrical tribunals* (which are principally guided by the rules of the imperial and Canon laws), as they subsist and are admitted in England, not by any right of their own, but upon bare sufferance and toleration from the municipal laws, must have recourse to the laws of that country, wherein they are thus adopted, to be informed how far their jurisdiction extends, or what causes are permitted, and what forbidden to be discussed before them...In short the Common law of England is the one uniform rule to determine the jurisdiction of our courts[2]."

---

[1] Bl. i. 14, 15.　　　　　　　[2] Bl. iii. 87; cf. i. 83.

CHAPTER IX.

THOUGH Blackstone is thus decided as to the position of the Civil law in this country, he makes considerable use of it in his *Commentaries* as a standard of comparison, and sometimes attributes to it the origin of an English rule. Another source of influence, indirectly Roman, which was at this time acting on our law, is seen in the citations from Grotius[1], Puffendorf, and those Dutch and German publicists, whose ethico-legal works had exercised and were still exercising great influence in England, especially in the Court of Chancery, and whose writings were much coloured by, where they were not entirely composed of, Roman doctrines and conceptions[2].

Blackstone includes among the "originals of our law,"—"the rules of the Roman Law either left here in the days of Papinian, or imported by Vacarius and his followers." On Bracton's Roman passage as to abortion, he says[3]: "this, though not murder, was by the ancient law homicide, but the modern law does not look upon this offence in quite so atrocious a light." In duress, *metus* and *vis*[4], he follows Bracton and the Civil law, which latter he expressly cites from the *Digest.* On the relation of the prince to his laws, he says[5]: "it may be some satisfaction to remark how widely the Civil law differs from ours." On pirates, he cites the *Digest,* "according to that rule of the Civil law[6]." On Treasure Trove he follows Bracton,

---

[1] e.g. from Grotius, on Equity, Bl. I. 61; cf. I. 259, 447, where Montesquieu and Puffendorf are cited.

[2] Cf. Maine, *Cambridge Essays,* 1856. No. I. *Ancient Law,* p. 97.

[3] Bl. I. 129; cf. IV. 197, *supra,* p. 108.

[4] I. 130; cf. IV. 30.

[5] I. 238.

[6] I. 257.

noting that he uses "the words of the civilians[1]," and says, "Formerly all treasure trove belonged to the finder; as was also the rule of the Civil law." On *bona vacantia* he also cites Bracton, but attributes their assignment to the finder to the law of nature;—"and so continued under the. imperial law[2]." Again, "in this case of idiots and lunatics the Civil law agrees with ours, but in another instance the Roman Law goes much beyond the English," and he instances the *curator* to a *prodigus*[3]. On marriage he expressly says that "the common lawyers have borrowed especially in ancient times almost all their notion of the legitimacy of marriage from the Canon or Civil laws[4]," but notes the different conceptions of marriage, husband and wife being two distinct persons in the Civil law, whilst the English Law considers them in general as one[5]. On legitimacy[6], though he remarks that the rule of the Civil law as to subsequent marriage "is narrowed with us in England," he mentions a case in which the Civil law *has* been recognized, in that where a bastard whose parents are subsequently married, enters upon his ancestor's land and dies seised and the inheritance descends to his issue, any legitimate children of his parent's are barred; and that this is due to the Civil law is shown by the fact that if the parents have never been married, the bastard's issue will have no such rights[7]. He notes the writ "*de ventre inspiciendo*, which is entirely conformable to the Civil law," and suggests that the Civil law prohibition of a widow's remarriage *infra annum luctus* "may account for the early Saxon rule to that effect[8]." He recognizes that the guardian fulfils the offices of both *tutor* and *curator*[9]. He remarks that our spiritual corporations are derived from the Civil through the Canon law, but that[10] "our laws have considerably refined and improved upon the invention, according to the usual genius of the English realm," and he instances the

---

[1] I. 295.

[2] I. 298.

[3] I. 306; see also on *trinoda neces-sitas*, I. 357, and on the Institutional division of slavery, I. 423.

[4] I. 434: cf. 436, 437, 438, 444.

[5] I. 444.

[6] I. 446, 447, 451.

[7] II. 247.

[8] I. 456.

[9] I. 460.

[10] I. 469.

introduction of corporations sole, while he also notes that whereas the consent of the members founded a Roman corporation, the king's sanction was required for an English one[1].

On Rights of ways, Blackstone says, "the law of England seems to correspond with the Roman", and he compares incorporeal hereditaments to servitudes[2]. He remarks on the English dower[3], "to which the civil law in its original state had nothing that bore a resemblance; nor indeed is there anything in general more different than the regulation of landed property according to the English and Roman Laws." He cites from Coke a Roman definition of title, and his outline of the scale of possession follows Bracton, and through him Azo and the *Digest*[4]. On Inheritance he observes that the English Law of descent of real estate reckons nearness of kin by canonical rules, and in granting administration of personal estate, by civil rules[5]. He defends the English exclusion of the half-blood, but notices that the custom of Normandy only excludes uterine brothers, and not brothers by the same father[6]. On monsters, he reproduces Bracton with the remark that "the Roman Law agrees with our own", but notices that the Roman Law allowed a monster to reckon as a child to secure the husband the *jus trium liberorum*, while our law does not consider it a child to give the husband an estate by curtesy[7].

Occupancy, the subject of Bracton's chief plagiarism, Blackstone considers "to be the true ground of all property... according to that rule of the law of nature, recognized by the law of Rome[8]"; and he notes a number of instances from Bracton[9], whom he curiously cites as an authority to show that a new island in the sea is the king's, rather than the occupier's as in the civil law, when the text of Bracton, who copies from Azo, assigns the island to the occupier[10]. On "things personal"

---

[1] I. 472, see also p. 484.

[2] II. 36, 106.

[3] II. 129.

[4] II. 195. Co. *Ins.* I. 345.

[5] II. 504.

[6] II. 227, 228. Maine, *Ancient Law*, p. 151. *V. supra*, pp. 96, 115, 130.

[7] II. 246. *V. supra*, p. 85, 130. Azo's passage on monsters has descended through all the text-writers.

[8] II. 258, 261.

[9] e.g. on alluvion and islands in rivers.

[10] Bl. II. 261. Br. f. 9, b. He cites as the rule Bracton's exception to the rule.

says Blackstone[1], the little that is found in Glanvil, Bracton, and *Fleta*, seems principally "borrowed from the Civilians"... "our courts have adopted a more enlarged and less technical mode of considering things personal than things real, frequently drawn from the rules, which they found already established by the Roman Law, whenever those rules appeared to be well-grounded and apposite to the case in question, but principally from reason and convenience, adapted to the circumstances of the time..." And thus we find most of Bracton's rules as to animals repeated[2]; "the English Law agreeing with the civil that *partus sequitur ventrem* in the brute creation, though for the most part in the human species it disallows that maxim." On *accessions*, he says "these (Roman) doctrines are implicitly copied and adopted by our Bracton, and have since been confirmed by many resolutions of the Courts": on *confusio*, "the English Law partly agrees with and partly differs from the Civil[3]."

For the doctrine of consideration Blackstone suggests a Roman origin, and quotes the civilian division of innominate contracts; he also asserts, as we have seen erroneously, that "our law has adopted the maxim of the civil law, *ex nudo pacto non oritur actio,*" whereas the two laws give *nudum pactum* a different meaning[4]. He incorporates from Bracton the civilian doctrine of *arrha* as *argumentum emptionis*, and notes the agreement of the two laws as to implied warranty of title in contract[5]. Bankruptcy proceedings, he suggests, follow the analogy of *cessio bonorum*[6].

While he notes the Roman and clerical character of the testamentary jurisdiction, he points out differences, as that prisoners are not absolutely incapable of making a will as in the Roman Law; that married women cannot devise lands, or even chattels without their husband's licence; and the absence of any *querela inofficiosi testamenti*[7]. *Donatio mortis causa*, he thinks, seems to have been handed to us from the civil

---

[1] Bl. II. 385.

[2] II. 390, 402, 412.

[3] II. 404, cf. also *animum revertendi*; and his remark that the term *paraphernalia* is borrowed from the *Civil Law*,

II. 435.

[4] II. 445. *V. supra*, p. 100.

[5] II. 447, 451.

[6] II. 473.

[7] II. 494, 497, 498, 503.

lawyers[1]. The Statute of Distributions, he says[2], "also bears some resemblance to the Roman Law of succession *ab intestato*, which, and because this act was also penned by an eminent civilian[3], has occasioned a notion that the Parliament copied it from the Roman Law; though indeed it is little more than a restoration of our old constitutional law......This just and equitable provision," (hotch-pot), "has also been said to be derived from the *collatio bonorum* of the Roman Law; which it certainly resembles in some points though it differs widely in others...and I must acknowledge that the doctrine and limits of representation as laid down in the Statute of Distributions seem to have been principally borrowed from the civil law."

He gives the definition of an action, " as Bracton and Fleta express it in the words of Justinian," and adopts their division into actions real, personal, and mixed[4]. He notes the agreement of the two laws as to the maxim, " *culpae adnumeratur imperitia*"; and as to justification as a defence of a slander[5]; and suggests that some of the rules as to actions by informers, are "borrowed from the rules of the Roman Law[6]." He remarks that Roman Law required trespass to be preceded by direct prohibition by the owner, while English law does not. In procedure he compares the summons to the *jus in vocando*[7]; the doctrine that an Englishman's house is his castle to the Roman refusal to allow even a summons to be served on a man in his own house[8]; bails to the *satisdatio*, (which however was from party to party, while bail was given by third parties to the Court)[9]; defence, to the *litis contestatio*, (which rather corresponds to our joinder of issue)[10]; set-off to *compensatio*, and *exceptiones* to replications and pleas, in which case he uses the division of

---

[1] II. 514.

[2] II. 516.

[3] Sir W. Walker, Lord Raymond's *Rep.* 574.

[4] III. 116. *cf.* attorney and *procurator*, III. 25; *advocatus fisci* and king's counsel, III. 27; right of possession and of property, III. 190; reasonable day's journey, III. 218. The burden of proof in both laws, III. 366.

[5] III. 121, 125.

[6] III. 162.

[7] III. 279: IV. 283.

[8] III. 288, cf. *Dig.* 2, 4, 18, (Blackstone's reference is wrong)—*quia domus tutissimum cuique refugium atque receptaculum sit.*

[9] Bl. III. 201.

[10] III.296. Identification seems carried too far when Blackstone gravely asserts that the scripture precept: "agree with thine adversary quickly while thou art

pleas dilatory, and to the action[1]. He notes that the Civil
Law always requires two witnesses, while the Common Law
may be satisfied with one[2]; and that the Civil Law does not
examine witnesses in public, as does the Common Law[3]; while
on costs, in both laws "*victus victori condemnandus est in
expensis*[4]."

On Crimes, he contrasts the Roman Law "*per vinum delap-
sis capitalis poena remittitur*" with the English law, "which
will not suffer any man thus to privilege one crime by another[5]."
"*Ignorantia juris, quod quisque tenetur scire, neminem excusat,*"
he says, incorrectly, "is as well the maxim of our own law as it
was of the Roman[6]." High Treason he considers as "equivalent
to the *Crimen laesae majestatis* of the Romans[7]," while counter-
feiting the royal seal "seems better denominated by the later
civilians a branch of the *crimen falsi* or forgery, in which
they are followed by Glanvil, Bracton and *Fleta*[8]." In both
Maintenance and Champerty he cites corresponding Roman
enactments[9], and in Libel suggests that our law "corresponds in
this as in many other respects with the middle age of Roman
jurisprudence." He does not use Bracton's Roman definition of
theft[10], though he refers incorrectly to some of its elements; e.g.
"This taking and carrying away must be felonious, or done
animo furandi, or as the civil law expresses it, *lucri causa,*"
where he mixes up two of the elements, and wrongly makes
lucri causa an essential of the English law of theft. He refers
to the old practice, abolished in the reign of Mary, of neither
allowing to prisoners counsel nor witnesses, and states that it
was "derived from the civil law[11]," as also was the respite of
pregnant women till delivery, taken, through Bracton, from the
civil law[12].

in the way with him," *has a plain reference* (!) to the Roman Law of the
twelve tables, *in via rem uti pacunt
orato,* III. 299.

[1] Bl. III. 301, 304. From Bracton's
exceptiones dilatoriae et peremptoriae.

[2] III. 370.

[3] III. 373.

[4] III. 399.

[5] IV. 25.

[6] IV. 26.

[7] IV. 75.

[8] IV. 88, 247.

[9] IV. 135, *cf.* on *Perjury,* IV. 139.
Homicide, 181, 183, 185, 202. *Rape,*
210, 212. *Arson,* 222. *Robbery,* 242.

[10] IV. 229, 232. *V. supra,* p. 110.

[11] IV. 358.

[12] IV. 395. *Vide supra,* p. 111.

While Blackstone therefore utterly repudiates any authority of the civil laws *in themselves* in this kingdom, except in particular courts ; and only allows them in those, so far as they have been adopted by the English courts and have derived their authority from the English Crown, he yet recognizes that large portions of the Roman Law have been incorporated by Bracton and later authorities into the Law of England. But he bases the authority of these parts, not on their incorporation by text writers, but on their recognition by the judges of the realm.

CHAPTER X.

WE have thus dealt with the position with regard to the Roman Law occupied by leading text-writers and authorities from the time of Bracton. Glanvil is comparatively free from any Roman influence. Bracton has incorporated into his book substantial portions of Roman matter, which are reproduced by *Fleta*, and in a less intelligent way by *Britton*. These Roman incorporations are cited without comment by Staunford, and are used by Cowell to show the similarity of the two laws. Coke also cites them, without any allusion to their Roman character, while he claims no authority in the realm for the Roman Law and is indeed a vigorous advocate of the supremacy of the Courts of Common Law. Hale clearly states the relative position of Common, Civil, and Canon Laws, defining the limits of the two latter, and the source of their authority. Lastly Blackstone, following Hale, recognizes the Roman origin of parts of our Law, including the passages in Bracton, and while he recognizes it, adopts them.

Perception of the Roman elements in Bracton leads to a discussion as to his authority in the law, which results in his being generally accepted as binding, if no contrary decisions or customs can be produced. And while the English Courts recognize no authority in the Roman Law, as such, they are yet ready to listen to citations from it in all cases where English authorities cannot be found in point, or where the principles of the English and Roman Laws appear to be similar. Thus in

Acton v. Blundell (1843)[1], where the question was as to rights in a subterranean water course, the *Digest* was fully cited and commented on by counsel, Maule, J. intervening with the remark, "it appears to me that what Marcellus says is against you." Tindall, C. J., in delivering judgment, said "The Roman Law forms no rule binding in itself upon the subjects of these realms; but in deciding a case upon principle, where no direct authority can be cited from our books, it affords no small evidence of the soundness of the conclusion to which we have come, if it proves to be supported by that law, the fruit of the researches of the most learned men, the collective wisdom of ages, and the groundwork of the municipal law of most of the countries in Europe. The authority of one at least of the learned Roman lawyers appears decisive upon the point in favour of the defendants."

The authority of Roman Law in the Common Law Courts cannot be put higher than this, or be better expressed than in these words.

---

[1] 12 M. and W. 324, 353; see Warren's *Law Studies*, 732, note, for an account of the inner history of the case by one of the counsel engaged.

CHAPTER XI.

ROMAN LAW IN THE CHANCERY.

WHILE the judges of the Common Law Courts after the fourteenth century recognized no authority in the Civil Law, and the English people were led by the financial exactions of the Papal Court, and the controversies of the Reformation, to regard with suspicion and dislike everything savouring of Rome, three important courts in the kingdom were largely influenced by the Civil Law, if their procedure was not entirely derived from it. These were the Court of Chancery, the Court of Admiralty, and the Ecclesiastical Courts[1]. The Court of the Constable and Marshal also proceeded according to the Civil Law[2]: "*causas ex jure civili Romanorum et consuetudinibus armorum, et non ex jure municipali Anglorum esse dijudicandas,*" and Duck also states that the Universities of Oxford and Cambridge proceeded according to the civil law: "*dijudicant per jus civile et secundum juris civilis formam*[3]." But these latter are of small importance.

The Court of Chancery originates in the position of the king as the fountain of justice[4]. To him petitions were addressed by suppliants who conceived themselves wronged by the Common Law, or who found no remedy for the injury they complained of. Difficult and novel points arising in the Common Law Courts were also reserved by the judges for the consideration of the king in Council. As the Chancellor was always in attendance on the king, the petitions for royal grace

[1] *Sub.* C. XII. Eccl. Courts; C. XIII. Admiralty Courts.

[2] Duck, II. 8, 3, 12, 22. *V. supra,* pp. 132, 141.

[3] Duck, II. 8, 3, 30. *V. supra,* p. 141.

[4] Stubbs, I. 603, 604 note. II. 268.

and favour were entrusted to him, first for custody, and ultimately for hearing. Under Edward III. the Chancellor's tribunal assumed a definite and separate character, and petitions for grace began to be directly addressed to him instead of coming indirectly into his hands. From 1358, such transactions were recognized as his proper province, and the powerful and complicated machinery of his Equitable Jurisdiction began to grow.

There were reasons why its growth should be on Roman lines. Several lay Chancellors had been appointed in the reign of Edward III., probably in consequence of the petition of the Parliament that, as ecclesiastics were not amenable to the laws, only lay persons might in future be appointed Chancellor[1]. But every Chancellor from 1380 to 1488 was a clerk ; until the end of Wolsey's Chancellorship in 1530 only a few lay holders of the office are found, and up to that year 160 Ecclesiastics had held the office[2]. In this clerical preponderance, the advantages of the Civil law, familiar to the Chancellors by their early training, and as the system in use in the ecclesiastical Courts, are obvious.

But the laws of Rome had a further foothold in the Chancery. There were 12, afterwards 6, Clerks de prima forma[3] and Masters of the Chancery, who " are assistants in the Court to show what is the Equity of the Civil law, and what is Conscience[4]." Down to the time of Lord Bacon some of the Masters learned in the Civil law sat upon the Bench with the Chancellor to advise him, if necessary. The author of the " Treatise on the Masters[3]" states that "the greater part have always been chosen men skilful in the Civil and Canon laws", in order that the decisions of the Chancellor may accord with "Equity, jus gentium, and the laws of other nations," seeing that

---

[1] Spence, I. 340. R. Parning, 1341. Thorpe, Knivet, 1372.

[2] Spence, I. 340—7, 356 note.

[3] Apparently a term of Roman origin. (Hargreaves, Law Tracts (1787), p. 296.) The conferring of the office by placing a cap on the head is compared by the author of this Tract, (probably a master in Chancery, writing about 1600,) to the conferring of the freedom of a Roman city by putting on a cap, or to "capping" a doctor at the Universities (p. 294). But the custom is not traced to these sources, as Spence says, I. 360.

[4] Sir T. Smith, Commonwealth of England, ed. 1663, p. 121. Spence, I. 360, note.

a number of matters came before the Chancellor "which were to be expedited not in course of common law, but in course of civil or canon law[1]." And though the Chancellors became laymen and decided without reference to the Masters, their system was still largely clerical and Roman. Under Charles I. it was ordered that half the masters in Chancery should always be Civil lawyers, and that no others should serve the king as Masters of Request. Duck[2], writing in 1678 says: "*Judicia apud Anglos, in Curiis quae non ex mero jure Anglicano, sed ex aequo et bono exercentur, cum jure civili Romanorum plurimum conveniunt; quarum suprema Cancellaria prima est...Cancellarii autem feres omnes fuerunt Episcopi aut Clerici, plerumque legum Romanarum periti usque ad Henricum VIII. quo D. Richius primus juris Municipalis Apprenticius Cancellarii munus obtinuit: post quem etiam alios episcopos juris Romani peritos, sed plerosque juris municipalis consultos, reges nostri ad hoc munus admoverunt. In hac etiam curia assessores seu Magistri plerumque fuerunt juris Civilis Doctores, et Clericos hujus Curiae antiquitus habuisse eximiam juris civilis scientiam, clarissimum est ex libro Registri Brevium Originalium...In Curia etiam... fere omnes fuerunt antiquitus Episcopi Praelative, in legibus Romanis vel utroque juri versati, Magistri...plerumque Juris Civilis Professores, quibus ex jurisdictione ejus Curiae potestas judicandi ex aequo et bono demandata est. Ad omnes enim curias in quibus non merum et Consuetudinarium jus, sed aequitas spectanda est, nullius gentis leges tam accommodatae sunt, quam jus Civile Romanorum, quod amplissimas continet regulas de Contractibus, Testamentis, Delictis, Judiciis et omnibus humanis actionibus.*"

The general character of the Jurisdiction of the Court of Chancery may be gathered from a speech of James I. in the Star Chamber in which he said : " Where the rigour of the law in many cases will undo a subject, there the Chancery tempers the law with equity, and so mixes mercy with justice[3]": and the "Doctor and Student" of the reign of Henry VIII., reads: "Conscience never resisteth the law nor addeth to it, but

---

[1] Hargreaves, pp. 309, 313.   [3] Cited Spence, I. 409 note.
[2] II. 8, 3 ; 10—11.

only when the law is directly in itself against the Law of God or of reason...in other things *Aequitas sequitur legem*[1]."

This Equitable Jurisdiction has been compared with the Jurisdiction of the *Praetors*, both being used as a means of alleviating the rigour of the older law[2]. Both Equity and the *Jus Praetorium* tend to become as rigid as the systems they originally modified; both are supported by fictions, in the one case of a pre-existing state of nature or Golden age, of whose laws fragments survive and are embodied in the *Praetor's* Edict, in the other of a King, whose Conscience supplied the inade-quacies of his laws. The systems admit of comparison, but there is no trace of causal connexion. It is true that the *Praetor* framed the *formula*, and the Chancellor and Clerks of the Chancery issued the writs. But the *Praetor* administered both his own edict and the *Jus Civile*, and could thus enforce his own innovations, while the Common law judges could and did reject new writs, which seemed to them not in accordance with the Common law. And further, while the *Praetor* by embodying *exceptiones* in his *Formula* could influence the defence to actions, the Chancellor had no control over the defences raised in the Common Law Courts to the writs he issued. The tribunals were separate; the judges different. The influence of the Chancery on the Common law was there-fore far slower in operation and weaker than the Praetorian changes in the *Jus Civile*; while the clerical character of the Chancery, and its innovations on the Common law, raised a spirit of hostility which hindered its influence.

English Equity however, invented and administered by Clerical Chancellors, derived much of its form and matter from Roman sources. I have neither the time nor the knowledge to enable me to give at all an adequate account of this Roman element, but the question has been discussed by Spence[3], and I avail myself of his results. Sir H. Maine[4], without going at length into the subject, thinks that the earlier Chancery judges

---

[1] Probably derived from "*Jus prae-torium jus civile subsequitur*." Spence, i. 409.

[2] Maine, *Ancient Law*, p. 68.

[3] *Equitable Jurisdiction of Court of Chancery*, Vol. i.

[4] *Ancient Law*, p. 44, 45.

followed the Canon law, a later generation the Civil law, and that the Chancellors of the eighteenth century availed themselves largely of the Romano-Dutch Treatises on ethics and jurisprudence, compiled by the publicists of the Low Countries.

One of the most important branches of Equitable Jurisdiction related to Uses and Trusts[1]. *Fideicommissa* had been introduced by the Romans to evade the strict rules as to legacies and successions : the person, to whose good faith the fulfilment of the testator's wishes was entrusted, was at first only bound in honour. Augustus took the first steps towards enforcing trusts by law, and finally created a *Praetor Fideicommissarius* to whom the duty was assigned of giving legal effect to *fideicommissa.*

The English system in its origin only applied to trusts created during life ; for lands were not devisable, and personal estate was not of sufficient importance to call for any special legislation. Conveyances of lands to *A*, that he might pay their fruits to *B*, were introduced, probably to allow the clergy to avoid the Statute of Mortmain, and this device was adopted by the laity, especially during the wars of the Roses to avoid forfeiture for treason, and for other purposes. These " Uses " the Chancery would enforce as binding on the conscience, and the bequests of uses of land which it supported, and which enabled testators to evade the feudal rule of the indevisability of land, were akin to the Roman *fideicommissa.* Both systems were thus introduced to evade the strict law. The jurisdiction of Chancery over Uses dates from the reign of Henry V. ; and when in the reign of Henry VIII., the Statute of Uses gave the legal ownership to the man who already had the Use, the Chancellors regained their jurisdiction and created Trusts by the device of enforcing " a use of an use," which was not affected by the Statute. In this however there was no trace of Roman influence and, as Mr Spence acknowledges, the details of the system of Uses and Trusts were entirely constructed by the Clerical Chancellors without help from the Roman system[2]. We can only say that probably the general conception of Uses

[1] Spence, I. 435—517.   to Co. *Lit.* I. 290 b.

[2] Spence, I. 460 note ; Butler's note

and Trusts and the assumption of Jurisdiction over them were assisted by the acquaintance of the Clerical Chancellors with the Roman *fideicommissa*.

The system of Mortgages[1] was much affected by the doctrines of the Civil law, acting through the Court of Chancery, and a mortgage now is "a security founded on the common law, and perfected by a judicious and wise application of the principles of redemption of the Civil law[2]." The strictness of the Common law viewed the Mortgage in the light of a conditional grant of land by the mortgagor to the mortgagee, the condition being that the land should revert to the grantor on payment by a certain day of the money lent. If not, the land was discharged from the condition and became absolutely vested in the mortgagee. But the Civil law regarded the debt intended to be secured, and not the land, as the principal; payment of the principal debt at any time would therefore release the accessory security on the land: the creditor, if not in possession of the land, could only sell it under a decree from the *Praetor*, and tender of the amount due before the decree of sale released the land. This construction, more lenient to mortgagors, was, under Charles I., adopted by the Chancery, who allowed an "equity of redemption" to the mortgagee within a reasonable time, though after the day on which, according to the Common law, the land would be forfeited for non-payment. To maintain their jurisdiction against both the Common law judges and the debtors themselves, the Chancellors held void any conditions in the loan by which the borrower lost his "equity of redemption." And this is similar to if not derived from a constitution of the Emperor Constantine, which expressly rendered such stipulations void[3]. We can thus trace the altered view of Mortgages, the necessity for foreclosure, and the protection of the equity of redemption, as established in the Court of Chancery, to the Civil law.

In the construction of legacies and documents, the Chancellors have availed themselves freely of Roman rules[4]. The

---

[1] Butler's notes to Co. *Lit.* I. 205 a., 290 b. Spence, I. 601. Coote on *Mortgages*, 4th edit. pp. 1, 14. Warren, *Law Studies*, p. 521.

[2] Coote, p. 1.

[3] *Cod.* 8, 34, 3.

[4] Spence, I. 518, 523, 566.

Chancery had no original jurisdiction in testamentary matters, and therefore felt bound to adopt the rules of the Ecclesiastical Courts, which were those of the Civil law. In *Hurst v. Beach*[1] the Vice-Chancellor directed the opinion of civilians to be taken as to the admissibility of evidence in a case as to legacies, and on the practice of the Ecclesiastical Courts. In *Hooley v. Hatton*[2], where the question was whether two legacies to the same person in a will and codicil were cumulative or sub-stitutive, the case was argued with citations from the Civil law ; and Lord Thurlow, in his judgment, said: "No argument can be drawn in the present case from internal evidence ; we must therefore refer to the rules of the Civil law." Similarly in interpreting the language of alleged trusts, the rules of the civil law are referred to[3]. Remains of the Roman doctrine of *beneficium inventoris* are traced in the time of Charles I., when an executor who had not exhibited an inventory was charged with a legacy after 20 years[4]. In the case of legacies for public uses Lord Thurlow said that the cases "had proceeded upon notions adopted from the Roman and Civil laws, which are very favourable to charities, that legacies given to public uses not ascertained shall be applied to some proper object[5]." And the same is true of charitable trusts[6]. But these rules were some-times applied with more zeal than discretion, as when Sir R. Arden, M.R., afterwards Lord Alvanley, entirely misunderstood the meaning of *exceptio doli*[7]. But Mr Spence's remark that "probably the same law as to legacies has continued in England from the time of Agricola to the present day[8]" shows too great a faith in the persistence of a highly developed system of law through centuries of barbarism.

The jurisdiction of the Chancery over Infants[9] is very similar to that exercised over guardians by the Roman *Praetor*, but Mr Spence is not able to say more than that the *Corpus*

---

[1] 5 Mad. 351, 357, 360.

[2] Cited in *Ridges v. Morrison*, 1 Brown, *Ch. C.* 389.

[3] *Knight v. Knight,* 3 Beav. 161, 172.

[4] Spence, I. 585, citing Tothill, 183 : 15 Car. I. which appears a wrong reference.

[5] *White v. White*, 1 Br. *Ch. C.* 15.

[6] Spence, I. 587.

[7] *Kennett v. Abbott* (1799), 4 Ves. 808.

[8] Spence, I. 523 note.

[9] Spence, I. 606—615.

Juris " has been occasionally consulted, if not resorted to as an authority" on the subject. We have already noticed Lord Macclesfield's preference for the Civil law rule as to the persons who should be guardians as compared to that of the Common law[1]. The Chancery jurisdiction over idiots and lunatics is also similar to that of the *Praetor* and may very possibly have been derived from it[2].

The English Law of Partnership is derived from three sources, the Common Law, the *Lex Mercatoria*, and the Roman Law[3]. Of the *Lex Mercatoria* we need only say here that it appears in itself to have been at least partly based on the Roman law[4]. Mr Justice Story has made an elaborate and detailed investigation of the relations of the Common to the Roman law, and finds great similarity between them[5]. Both laws recognize the difference between a partnership and a community of interest[6], and provide that no new partner can be introduced without the concurrence of the original partners[7]. But the Common law has refused to follow the Roman law in holding invalid an agreement that the personal representative of a partner should succeed him in the partnership[7]. Both laws require a partnership to be in good faith and for a lawful purpose[8]; and that all partners must contribute something, whether property or skill, to the common stock[9]. Both require community in profits among the partners and, to a more limited extent, community in losses[10]. In the absence of express agreement both laws require an equal division of profits[11]. The Common law formerly went beyond the Roman law in making persons who share the profits of a trade liable by operation of law, to third parties as partners[12], but this rule was overthrown in *Cox v. Hickman*[13]. Both laws recognize a division into universal, general, and special partnerships, though the chief Common law division is into public and private partnerships[14].

[1] *V. supra*, p. 130.
[2] Spence, I. 618—620.
[3] Collier on *Partnership*, Lond. 1840, p. 1.
[4] Spence, I. 665.
[5] Story on *Partnership*, Boston, 1881, 7th ed.
[6] Story §§ 3, 4.
[7] *Ibid.* § 5.
[8] § 6.
[9] § 15.
[10] § 20.
[11] §§ 24, 25.
[12] § 37.
[13] 18 *C. B.* 617. 8 *H. L. C.* 268.
[14] Story §§ 72—76.

Both regulate the duration of partnership by the consent of the partners, but the Roman law went further than the English, and prohibited partnerships extending beyond the life of the parties[1]. No particular forms for the constitution of a partnership were required by either law[2]. By the Roman law, the mere partnership relation conferred less extensive powers of disposition of the partnership property than are given by the Common law[3]. A Roman partner could not bind the firm by debts, nor alienate more than his share of the partnership property. But in the absence of express stipulation and with some limitations each partner of an English partnership may be taken by outsiders, as having an equal and complete power of administration over the whole of the partnership affairs[4]. Both laws admit a discharge of a debt to or by one partner to be good for or against the whole firm[5]. In the Common law, within the scope of the partnership, the majority have a right to govern, but in the Roman law the express or implied assent of all the partners is required[6]. Both laws make partners liable to each other for negligence or fraud, and require a withdrawal from the partnership to be in good faith[7]. Both laws consider a partnership for no certain period as dissoluble at the will of any partner[8]; but the Roman law went further than the Common law in requiring that the dissolution should not take place at an unseasonable time[9]. Both laws allow the Court to dissolve the partnership in case of positive or meditated abuse of it by a partner, or when its objects are no longer attainable, as in the case of a partner's insanity[10]. By both laws, the assignment of his interest by one partner, contrary to the will of the others, dissolves the partnership[11]. Both laws dissolve the partnership by death[12]; and many of the provisions in both laws for taking an account and winding up a partnership are similar, though the English sale is more convenient than the Roman division[13].

---

[1] Story §§ 85, 196.

[2] § 86.

[3] § 95.

[4] § 103.

[5] § 116.

[6] § 125 : noted by Blackstone, I. 484.

[7] §§ 135, 170, 176.

[8] §§ 268, 269.

[9] §§ 275, 276.

[10] §§ 288, 292.

[11] § 307.

[12] § 317.

[13] § 352.

Whilst English partners are liable to third parties *in solido*, by the Roman law they were only liable *pro parte*.

This enumeration shows a sufficient agreement between the two systems to justify the assertion that while the method of the introduction of so much Roman law in early times is not clear, in later times most of its leading principles have become incorporated into the Common law of Partnership[1].

Mr Spence and Lord Justice Fry[2] agree that the Equitable Jurisdiction to enforce Specific Performance is not derived from the Roman law, which only gave damages for breach of contract, and adhered to the maxim; "*nemo potest praecise cogi ad factum*[3]." Spence considers the jurisdiction a "clerical invention" and Fry doubts whether to attribute it to the Canon law, which said "*Studiose agendum est ut ea quae promittuntur opere compleantur*[4]," or to "the plain principles of morality and common sense of the Judges who founded and enlarged the equitable jurisdiction."

Besides the chief heads of its jurisdiction, the leading principles on which the Chancery administers justice show traces of clerical and Roman influence. The term "Conscience[5]," which is so involved in the decisions of the Court, though itself of clerical invention, is like the Praetorian notion of *bona fides*; but as to *mala fides* the English law has departed from the Roman principle, *lata culpa plane dolo comparabitur*, by holding that, "Gross negligence may be evidence of *mala fides*, but it is not the same thing[6]." The jurisdiction of the Chancery, in fraud, to cancel and deliver up deeds is analogous to the Praetorian *restitutio in integrum*, and *actio de dolo*[7]. Both *Praetor* and Chancellor had a power to relieve against Accident, grounded in the Roman law on *naturalis justitia*[8]. So the jurisdiction to relieve against Mistake, and the distinction between mistake of law, and of fact, both in the

---

[1] Spence, i. 665.

[2] Fry on *Specific Performance*, 2nd edit. Lond. 1881, pp. 3—8. Spence, i. 645.

[3] Pothier, *Des obligations*, i. 2, 2, 2.

[4] Decret. Greg. IX. i. 35, 3.

[5] Spence, i. 411. cf. *aequitas sequitur*

legem: (supra, p. 155).

[6] Ld. Denman in *Goodman v. Harvey*, 4 Ad. & E. 876. See also 1 Hare, 71. Spence, i. 425 note.

[7] Spence, i. 622.

[8] *Ibid.* i. 628. *Dig.* 27, 1, 13, 7.

Common law and Chancery, appear of Roman origin; though under Edward IV. the Roman maxim, "*nec stultis solere succurri sed errantibus*", was met by a clerical Chancellor with "*Deus est procurator fatuorum*[1]," and the "fool" was relieved. The injunctions of the Chancery are comparable to Praetorian Interdicts[2]; its jurisdiction in discovery to the *actio ad exhibendum,* and possibly to the early and obsolete *actio interrogatoria*[3]. The procedure for perpetuating evidence by examining witnesses *de bene esse* had also a parallel in Roman procedure[4].

Without proceeding to a more detailed examination enough has been said to show that though usually the details of the Equitable Jurisdiction were worked out by the Chancellors on English lines, the subjects of jurisdiction and the powers of the Court were largely derived from the functions of the *Praetor,* and that this was due in the main to the influence of the early Clerical Chancellors.

At present however the Courts of Chancery and Common law stand towards the Civil or any other law in no different relation. As Blackstone has said[5] "In matters of positive right, both Courts must submit to and follow ancient and invariable maxims......where they exercise a concurrent jurisdiction they both follow the law of the proper tribunal; in matters originally of ecclesiastical cognizance, they both equally adopt the Canon and Imperial law, according to the nature of the subject." But the nature of the subjects which come before the Chancery is more likely to call for its recourse to the Canon or Civil law, than those which are discussed in the Common Law Courts, and therefore Blackstone recognizes in 1763 that in the Chancery "the proceedings are to this day in a course much conformed to the Civil law[6]."

---

[1] *Dig.* 22, 6, 9. Cary's *Rep.* (ed. 1650), p. 17. Spence, I. 632, 637. Both editions of Cary that I have seen have the odd reading *est procurator futurus.*

[2] Spence, I. 669.

[3] Spence, I. 228, 678.

[4] *Dig.* IX. 2, 40. Spence, I. 681.

[5] Bl. III. 436.

[6] Bl. I. 20.

CHAPTER XII.

Of the Ecclesiastical Courts, Hale says[1]; " the rule by which they proceed is the Canon law, but not in its full latitude, and only so far as it stands uncorrected, either by contrary acts of Parliament, or by the common law and custom of England: when the canon law is silent, the civil law is taken in as a director, especially in points of exposition and determination touching wills and legacies." Their jurisdiction may be treated of under two heads: (1) that relating solely to the internal life and worship of the Church of England: (2) that affecting the whole realm, such as the testamentary and matrimonial jurisdiction.

The first head may be shortly dealt with. The separation of the civil and clerical courts under William I., ensured for the latter a peculiarly Roman and canonical law and procedure; the Conqueror's law provided; *"secundum canones et episcopales leges rectum Deo et Episcopo suo faciat[2]"*, and the procedure was that of the Roman Consistory. This tended to create a feeling of hostility on the part of the Courts of Common law and the English people towards Courts not ruled by the Common law of England.

The present ecclesiastical law consists of three portions[3]: I. Statutes, and enactments made in pursuance of, or ratified

---

[1] *Hist. C. L.* 28.

[2] Stubbs, *S. C.* p. 85.

[3] Brice, *Public Worship*, London, 1875, pp. 1—10. Phillimore *On Eccle-* *siastical Law*, London, 1873: i. pp. 12 —19. Coote, *Ecclesiastical Practice*, London, 1847.

by, statutes. II. Certain portions of the Canon law, and certain constitutions and canons issued by competent authorities. III. The Ecclesiastical Common law; ecclesiastical usages, not embodied in writing, except in some judicial decisions, but recognized as binding and supposed to be known by the Courts.

The Canon law as such is a body of Roman ecclesiastical law; but only such parts of it as are contained in the provincial constitutions[1], and in the general usages of the church, and are recognized in the Courts of this realm, are binding in England[2]. No canon contrary to the Common or Statute law or to the Prerogative is of any force; and no canons made since the reign of Henry VIII., and not sanctioned by Parliament, are binding on the laity: nor are canons binding made before that reign, unless adopted by the English church[3].

The position of Ecclesiastical law in England has been well described by Tindall, L. C. J. as follows[4]; "The question depends upon the Common law of England, of which the Ecclesiastical law forms a part...The law by which the spiritual Courts of this kingdom have from the earliest times been governed and regulated, is not the general Canon law of Europe, imported as a body of law into this kingdom, and governing those courts *proprio vigore,* but instead thereof an Ecclesiastical law, of which the general Canon law is no doubt the basis, but which has been modified and altered from time to time by the ecclesiastical constitutions of our archbishops and bishops, and by the legislation of the realm, and which has been known from early times by the distinguishing title of the King's Ecclesiastical law...That the Canon law of Europe does not, and never did, as a body of laws, form part of the law of England, has been long settled and established law." So also Sir John Nicholl[5]:—"Indeed the whole Canon law rests for its authority in this country upon received usage; it is not binding here *proprio*

---

[1] Collected in Lyndwood's *Provinciale seu Constitutiones Angliae.* Paris, 1505; Oxford, 1679.

[2] *Martin v. Mackonochie, L. R.* 2 Adm. and Eccl. 116, 153.

[3] *Bishop of Exeter v. Marshall, L. R.* 3 H. L. 17, 47, 55.

[4] *R. v. Millis* (1844), 10 Cl. and Fin. 534, 671, 678, 680.

[5] 3 Phill. *Rep.* 67, 78—79.

vigore." The Canon law of itself is not therefore part of English law, nor does the Civil law appear to enter into this branch of the Ecclesiastical Jurisdiction.

The Ecclesiastical Courts had jurisdiction affecting the subjects of the realm in three matters :—I. *Pecuniary,* in tithes, dilapidations &c., to which we need not further refer. II. *Matrimonial causes* ; validity of marriage, legitimacy, divorce, &c. III. *Testamentary causes,* and the administration of the estates of Intestates.

Matrimonial Jurisdiction.

The Judicature Act, 1873[1], transferred to the newly created Probate, Admiralty and Divorce Division of the High Court of Justice *inter alia,* all matters within the exclusive cognizance of the Court for Divorce and Matrimonial Causes, and applied to that Division all the rules, orders and procedure of that Court. The Court for Divorce and Matrimonial Causes was created by an Act of 1857[2], by which all causes and matters matrimonial, which should be pending in any Ecclesiastical Court in England were transferred to that Court, which was to possess all jurisdiction on the subject exercisable by any ecclesiastical court, and to proceed and act and give relief on principles and rules which in the opinion of the Court should be as nearly as might be conformable to the principles and rules, on which the Ecclesiastical Courts had heretofore acted and given relief. This law of the Ecclesiastical Courts in the matter of marriage had been based on the Canon law, though its authority was much restricted, and depended on its having been received and admitted by Parliament, or upon immemorial usage and custom[3]. This jurisdiction devolved upon the Clerical Courts from the conception of marriage as a religious sacrament and tie, the nature, validity, and dissolution of which were matters of clerical cognizance. The procedure was " regulated according to the practice of the civil and canon laws, or rather

---

[1] 36 and 37 Vic. c. 66 §§ 34, 70, 74. 38 and 39 Vic. c. 77 §§ 18, 21.

[2] 20 and 21 Vic. c. 85 §§ 4, 6, 22.

[3] Shelford *On Marriage.* London, 1841 : pp. 17—21.

according to a mixture of both, corrected and new modelled by their own particular usages, and the interposition of the courts of common law[1]." A well known instance of this is the way in which the law of England dealt with the Roman doctrine of *legitimatio ante nuptias*. But generally the greater part of the English law on matrimonial causes is derived from the Civil or Canon law.

Testamentary Jurisdiction.

The Testamentary jurisdiction was also in the hands of clerical judges[2]. The present Procedure and Practice of the Probate Division of the High Court of Justice are the same, (except as altered by rules under the Judicature Acts), as those in force in the Court of Probate before 1875[3]. This Court was created by the Act of 1857[4], by which the jurisdiction of all ecclesiastical Courts having power to grant probate of wills was transferred to it, and its practice, except as subsequently provided by rules and orders, was to be according to the then practice in the Prerogative Court of Canterbury[5]. Thus the present jurisdiction of the Probate Division is founded on this Ecclesiastical law ; but as to the origin of the Ecclesiastical Jurisdiction there is considerable doubt.

Wills were probably introduced by the clergy from Roman sources, and from early times the clerical courts had jurisdiction over suits as to the validity of wills, or in what is known as "*probatio solemnis per testes*[6]." But whether this jurisdiction dates from the separation of the Courts by the Conqueror, or was assumed by the English Church at a later period, there is no evidence to show. Lyndwood[7] expressly says "*cujus regis temporibus hoc ordinatum sit non reperio*," but the jurisdiction certainly existed at the time of Glanvil[8], and the absence of evidence appears to show that, when assumed, it was not

---

[1] Blackstone, III. 100.

[2] Coote's *Probate Practice*, 8th edit. London, 1878.

[3] 38 and 39 Vic. c. 77 §§ 18, 21. 36 and 37 Vic. c. 66 §§ 23.

[4] 20 and 21 Vic. c. 77 § 3.

[5] *Ibid.* §§ 29, 30.

[6] Bl. Com. III. 95. Coote's *Eccl. Practice*, pp. 22—86. *V. supra*, pp. 24, 25.

[7] Lyndwood, *Provinciale*, 3, 13, f. 176 (ed. 1679).

[8] Gl. VII. 8.

opposed by the common lawyers. As to the other branch of testamentary jurisdiction, the power of granting probate of a will in common form to an executor, and also as to the power of granting letters of administration of the goods of an intestate to his next of kin, we have more evidence[1]. The latter was, even in the time of Glanvil, in the hands of the king's courts, the next of kin having a right to succeed, subject to the claims of the lord, without any clerical intervention[2]. In the reign of Stephen, the jurisdiction over ecclesiastical persons and the distribution of their goods was placed in the hands of the Bishop, but this did not affect the laity[3]. Mr Coote attributes clerical control over wills to the study of the Civil law by the clergy after the teaching of Vacarius, although their attempts to obtain that control were resisted by the barons[4]. In 1191, the clergy in Normandy, who had previously been granted, as in England, the control of clerical wills and intestacies, received the control of all wills and intestacies. Magna Charta contains the provision[5] "*Si aliquis liber homo intestatus decessit, catalla sua per manus propinquorum et amicorum suorum per visum ecclesiae distribuantur, salvis cuicunque debitis, quae defunctus ei debebat.*" But this clause is omitted, not only, as Coote observes, in the Charter of 1225, but also, which he does not notice, in the reissues of the Charter in 1216, and 1217. He suggests that the omission is due to the hostility of the barons, but, if so, it is curious that the Articles which the Barons themselves put forward in 1215 should run[6], "*Si aliquis liber homo intestatus decesserit, bona sua per manum proximorum parentum suorum et amicorum, et per visum ecclesiae, distribuantur[7]*"; unless this was a concession to the church by the barons to secure its cooperation in the coming struggle. The Clergy were anxious to obtain control of intestacy that they might devote a share of the intestate's estate to pious purposes; the lords preferred to confiscate the property. The clergy protested "*Item mortuo laico intestato,*

---

[1] Coote, p. 22.

[2] Gl. VII. 6, 7.

[3] Coote, p. 27. Stubbs, S. C. p. 111.

[4] Ibid. p. 31.

[5] § 27. Stubbs, S. C. p. 292.

[6] Article 16. Ibid. p. 283.

[7] Note, that the clause as to payment of just debts is omitted.

dominus rex et caeteri domini feudorum bona defuncti sibi applicantes non permittunt de ipsis debita solvi, nec residuum in usus liberorum et proximorum suorum et alios pios usus per loci ordinarium cujus interest, aliqua converti[1];" thus the lords neither paid the debts, nor recognized the pious uses. The statute of Westminster charged the payment of the debts of the intestate on that third of the property which the ordinary destined to pious uses, instead of, as in previous practice, on the *rationabiles partes* of the widow and children[2]. A statute of 1357[3] commanded the ordinaries to appoint "*de plus proscheins et plus amis de mort intestat, pur administrer ses biens...et recoverer come executoures les dettes dues au dit mort...et soient accountables aux ordinairs si avant come executoures sont en cas de testament.*" The ordinary thus appointed one of the next of kin as administrator to distribute the effects in such proportions as the church following the system of the civil law should direct, and the Act also gave power to bring actions concerning the intestacy in the King's Courts, as well as in the Courts of the Ordinary, thus making the system more secure.

The Prerogative Court of the Archbishop, which dealt with wills and intestacies was established by Archbishop Stafford in 1443, who transferred the jurisdiction of the Court of Arches over those matters to the New Court, presided over by a Commissary[4]. The first Commissary was Alexander Provert, Bachelor of Canon law.

But the ordinary's power in intestacy became useless after the Reformation, owing to the refusal of the Common Law Courts to enforce the directions of the Ordinary, or the Ecclesiastical bonds for due performance of their duties which he took from administrators[5]. This unsatisfactory state of things resulted in the Statute of Distributions, which gave the Ordinaries and ecclesiastical judges, "having power to commit administrations of the goods of persons dying intestate", power to take bonds for the due administration of the estate, which should be enforceable in Courts of law[6].

[1] *Gravamina* and Articles of 1257, § 25. Coote, p. 39.

[2] Coote, pp. 44—47, (A.D. 1285).

[3] 31 Edw. III. c. 11.   Coote, p. 58.

[4] Coote, p. 81.

[5] Coote, p. 55.

[6] 22 and 23 Ch. II. c. 10, made perpetual by 1 Jac. II. c. 17 § 18.

We have thus traced, as far as the lack of evidence allows, the process by which the Clerical Courts acquired the jurisdiction over all matters connected with wills and testaments. This jurisdiction, once obtained, was exercised on the lines of the Canon and Civil laws: as Hale says[1], "where the Canon law is silent, the Civil law is taken in as a director, especially in points of exposition and determination touching wills and legacies," and these "directions of the Civil law" have been adopted by the Chancery in cases involving the construction of documents and wills[2].

The original jurisdiction of the Ecclesiastical Courts in cases *laesionis fidei*, over contracts not enforceable by the King's courts, and its influence on the works of Glanvil and Bracton have already been referred to[3].

---

[1] Hale, *Common Law*, p. 28.

[2] *V. supra*, p. 158.

[3] *V. supra*, pp. 77, 100.

CHAPTER XIII.

ROMAN LAW IN THE ADMIRALTY.

THE early history of the "Court of Admiralty proceeding according to the Civil law," as Coke terms it, is closely connected with the history of the Law Merchant, which will form the subject of our next section. From very early times merchants and mariners regulated their dealings by a set of customs and rules known as the Law Merchant, Law Marine, or Customs of the Sea. In the Domesday Book of Ipswich[1], it is recorded that "the pleas yoven to the law maryne, that is to wyte, for straunge marynerys passaunt, and for hem that abydene not but her tyde, shuldene be pleted from tyde to tyde;" and it is probable that similar courts existed in all seaport towns, and places where merchants resorted. This Law Merchant and Customs of the Sea came into prominence in the countries bordering on the Mediterranean; lands which had been under Roman rule continued to obey a modified version of the Roman laws, (which the Roman jurists themselves had borrowed from the Rhodian code,) adapted and altered to meet the new developments of commerce and civilization[2]. And by the middle of the thirteenth century a number of written codes of Maritime law came into existence in most of the principal centres of mercantile activity.

[1] Cited from a MS of 1289, in Twiss, *Black Book of Admiralty*, II. 23.

[2] Pardessus, *Collection des Lois Maritimes*, Paris, 1828, cited in Twiss, IV. Pref. 129. Godolphin's *View of the Admiral's Jurisdiction*, London, 1661, p. 13. Zouch, *Jurisdiction of the Admiralty of England asserted by R. Zouch, D. C. L., late Judge of the Admiralty Court*, p. 88: (written before 1663, published 1686). Malynes' *Lex Mercatoria*, p. 87, 1st edit. 1622; 3rd edit. 1685.

The *Consolato del Mare* represents the customs observed at Barcelona; the Laws of Oleron, the usages of Bordeaux and the Isle of Oleron; the Laws of Wisbuy, the rules of the Hanse Towns. The Italian version of the *Consolato* speaks of its contents thus[1]: "these are the good constitutions and customs which belong to the sea, the which wise men passing through the world have delivered to our ancestors."

The early history of the Customs of the Sea, and of the Admiralty Court in England may be gathered from a memorandum of 1339, entitled "*Fasciculus de Superioritate Maris*[2]," which recites that the Justiciaries of the King were to be consulted as to the proper mode of revising and continuing the form of proceeding instituted by the King's grandfather and his Council, for the purpose of maintaining the ancient supremacy of the Crown over the Sea of England, and the right of the Admiral's office over it, with a view to correct, interpret, declare, and uphold the laws and statutes made by the Kings of England, his ancestors, in order to maintain peace and justice amongst the people of every nation passing through the sea of England, and to punish delinquents, "which laws and statutes were by the Lord Richard, formerly King of England, on his return from the Holy Land, corrected, interpreted and declared, and were published in the Island of Oleron, and were named in the French tongue, 'la ley Olyroun'." There is no doubt that Richard I., on his return from Palestine did not visit the Isle of Oleron, and all that can be meant is therefore, that the Laws of Oleron, whose origin we have seen, were promulgated in England by Richard[3]. This account receives confirmation from the contents of the famous "Black Book of the Admiralty", which, having disappeared for many years, was at length found at the bottom of a chest of private papers in a cellar. It contains: (1) instructions for the Admiral's administrative duties in time of war; the first article of which is[4]: "when one is made Admirall", he must first ordain deputies, "some of the

---

[1] Cited in Zouch, p. 88. The original Spanish version (Twiss, IV.), has not the clause.

[2] On a roll of 12 Edw. III.; cited in

Twiss, I. Pref. pp. 32, 57.

[3] Twiss, I. Pref. 58.

[4] Twiss, I. 3.

most loyall wise and discreet persons in the Maritime law (*la loy maryne et anciens coustumes de la mer*)", (2) articles of war for the King's navy, and (3) an account of the Admiral's jurisdiction in 34 articles, of which the first 24 are identical with the most ancient version of the Rolls of Oleron, and the rest are peculiar to the English Admiralty, and probably the result of the conference of 1339. Another article in this part[1]: "Item any contract made between merchant and merchant beyond the sea, or within the flood marke, shall be tried before the Admiral, and nowhere else by the ordinance of the said King Edward I. and his lords," appears to furnish the origin of the Admiral's jurisdiction in civil suits, which probably were more often settled informally by the merchants in the seaport towns "*selon la ley merchant*."

The Admiral took his oath to make summary and full process "*selon la ley marine et anciennes coustumes de la mer*[2]." A subsequent treatise on procedure, entitled the *Ordo Judiciorum*, is Roman in character and terminology, and bears traces of being written by a civilian of the School of Bologna[3]. Indeed, as many of the judges in the Court of Admiralty, the deputies of the Lord High Admiral, were clerics, the procedure at any rate, if not also the rules of the Court, was likely to become Roman in character. The inquiry of 1339, already alluded to, was entrusted to three clerics, the Official of the Court of Canterbury, the Dean of *St Maria in Arcubus*, and a Canon of St Paul's[4]. By an Act of 1403, "*les dites admiralles usent leur leys seulement par la ley d'Oleron et ancienne ley de la mer, et par la ley d'Angleterre, et ne mye par custume, no par nule autre manere*[5]", while in 1406 under the Admiralties of the Beauforts, the jurisdiction of the Admiralty Court was much increased[6]. It is not therefore wonderful that under Edward VI. the answer was made to a French envoy[7] "that the English Ordinances for Marine affairs were no others than *the Civil*

---

[1] Twiss, I. 69.

[2] Twiss, I. 169.

[3] Twiss, I. 178. The title is Sir T. Twiss' invention.

[4] Twiss, II. Pref. 42.

[5] 5 Hen. IV. c. 7; 2 Hen. V. c. 6.

[6] Spelman, *Glossarium*, *sub voce* Admirallus, ed. 1687, p. 16.

[7] Zouch, 89.

Laws, and certain ancient additions of the realm." The Black
Book itself has an express reference to the Roman Law[1]: "It is
ordained and established for a custom of the sea that when it
happens that they make jettison from a ship, *it is well written
at Rome* that all the merchandise contained in the ship ought
to contribute pound per pound[2]," and many other clauses are
indirectly taken from the same source.

The foundations of Admiralty Law are thus to be found in:
(1) the Civil law, (*a*) as embodied in the Law Merchant,
especially in the Laws of Oleron; (*b*) as introduced by subsequent clerical judges, mainly in procedure : (2) in subsequent
written and customary rules, adopted in view of the developments of commerce. This view is borne out by the accounts
which text writers give of the nature of the Law.

Thus Sergeant Callis says (in 1622) "I acknowledge that
the king ruleth on the sea by the Laws Imperial, as by the Roll
of Oleron and other; but that is only in the case of shipping
and for merchants and mariners[3];" on which Zouch remarks[4]:
"I suppose no man will deny that the Civil and Imperial laws,
the Roll of Oleron and others...are of force in the Admiralty of
England," and again[5], "the kingdom of England is not destitute
of Special laws for the regulating of sea businesses, which are
distinct from the Common laws of the realm, as namely, the
Civil laws and others of which the books of Common law take
notice by the names of *Ley Merchant* and *Ley Mariner*"...
"Businesses done at sea are to be determined according to the
Civil law, and equity thereof, as also, according to the customs
and usages of the sea...for instruments made beyond the sea have
usually clauses relating to Civil law and to the Law of the Sea[6]."

This work of Zouch's was written in reassertion of the
privileges of the Court of Admiralty in opposition to the
encroachments of the Courts of Common law[7], who secured for

---

[1] Twiss, I. 127.

[2] *Lex Rhodia de jactu, Dig.* 14, 2, 1.
Twiss has a wrong reference.

[3] Reading on the *Statute of Sewers.*
1st ed. 1622.   Ed. 1686, p. 42.

[4] Zouch, p. 95.

[5] *Ibid.* p. 89.

[6] *Ibid.* p. 118.

[7] Coke, IV. 134; see also I. f. 11 b.
"Civil Law in certain cases, not only
in Courts Ecclesiastical, but in the
Admiralty, in which is observed la
ley Olyroun, 5 Rich. I."

their jurisdiction cases which properly fell within the cognizance of the Admiralty, by the fiction that the contract sued on was made in Cheapside, whereas, as the Civilians gravely remarked, a ship could not come to Cheapside because there was no water. The Common Law Courts also prohibited the Admiralty from trying certain classes of cases; on which Zouch says[1]: "It may be thought reasonable that such contracts being grounded upon the Civil law, the law amongst Merchants, and other maritime laws, the suits arising about the same should rather be determined in those courts, where the proceedings and judgments are according to those laws, than in other Courts, which take no notice thereof."

So Selden had said[2] "*Juris civilis usus ab antiquis saeculis etiam nunc retinctur in foro maritimo, seu Curia Admiralitatis*", and Duck[3]: "*Jus autem dicit Admiralitas ex Jure Civili Romanorum, et ejus Curia consuetudinibus[4].*" Godolphin writing in 1661, says "all maritime affairs are regulated chiefly by the Imperial laws, the Rhodian laws, the Laws of Oleron, or by certain peculiar municipal laws and constitutions, appropriated to certain cities bordering on the sea, or by those maritime customs...between merchants and mariners"..."The Court of Admiralty proceeds according to the known laws of the land and the ancient established Sea laws of England with the customs thereof, so far as they contradict not the laws and statutes of the realm[5]"..."A great part of this Fabric is laid on a foundation of Civil law...a law allowed, received, and owned as the law of the Admiralty of England[6]"...though "It is most true that the Civil law in England is not the law of the Land, but the law of the Sea...*a* law, though not *the* law of England, not the Land law, but the Sea law of England[7]."

Hale in 1676, with his usual strong feeling against the Civil law, sums this up thus[8]; "The Admiralty Court is not bottomed upon the authority of the Civil law, but hath both its power and jurisdiction by the law and custom of the realm in

---

[1] p. 103.
[2] *ad Fletam*, VIII.
[3] (1676), II. 8, 3, 24.
[4] Godolphin, p. 40.

[5] *Ibid.* Pref.
[6] *Ibid.* p. 123.
[7] *Ibid.* p. 127.
[8] Hale, *Common Law*, p. 40.

such matters as are proper for its cognizance. This appears by their process...and also by those customs and law maritimes whereby many of their proceedings are directed, and which are not in many things conformable to the Civil law...also the Civil law is allowed to be the rule of their proceedings, only so far as the same is not contradicted by the Statutes of this realm, or by those maritime laws and customs, which in some points have obtained in derogation of the Civil laws."

This opinion of Lord Hale's, though apparently inconsistent with the *dicta* previously cited is not, I think, so in reality; for all that he alleges is that the Civil law is only law in England by the authority of the English Crown, and that in many points it has been altered and modified by later decisions and enactments; and both of these propositions are recognized by previous writers.

Blackstone says of the[1] "maritime Courts before the Lord High Admiral", that "their proceedings are according to the method of the Civil law, like those of the Ecclesiastical Courts" ..."[2]The proceedings of the Courts of Admiralty bear much resemblance to those of the Civil law, but are not entirely founded thereon; and they likewise adopt and make use of other laws, as occasion requires, both the Rhodian laws, and the laws of Oleron: for the law of England doth not acknowledge or pay any deference to the Civil law considered as such, but merely permits its use in such cases where it judges its determination equitable, and therefore blends it in the present instance with other marine laws; the whole being corrected, altered and amended by acts of parliament, and common usage; so that out of this composition, a body of jurisprudence is enacted, which owes its authority only to its reception here by consent of the Crown and people."

On the criminal jurisdiction of the Court of Admiralty, Blackstone alludes to the disuse of its old procedure—[3]: "but as this Court proceeded without jury in a manner much conformed to the Civil law, the exercise of a criminal jurisdiction there was contrary to the genius of the law of England"; and

---

[1] Bl. iv. 68. [3] Bl. iv. 268.
[2] Bl. iii. 108.

as, owing to the requirements of two witnesses, gross offenders might escape, therefore " marine felonies are now tried by commissioners *oyer et terminer* according to the law of the land."

The procedure and practice of the Court of Admiralty was transferred by the Judicature Acts to the Probate, Admiralty and Divorce Division of the High Court of Justice, except as altered by subsequent Orders under the Act. This Division thus unites the three branches of English law in which the Civil law had most direct and acknowledged influence, the Testamentary and Matrimonial Clerical Jurisdictions, and the Jurisdiction of the Admiralty, which, as we have seen, was partly built up by clerical judges.

On the subject matter of Admiralty law, we may say more in the next section. The procedure *in rem* against a ship, analogous to "*Noxa caput sequitur*", the institution of average (*Contributio*), Bottomry, (*pecunia trajectitia vel nauticum foenus*), and probably charter parties, all bear traces of Roman origin.

CHAPTER XIV.

FROM the earliest times a summary mode of procedure appears to have existed, in which a kind of rough and ready justice was exercised in mercantile disputes according to the usages of commerce. As early as Bracton we find recognition of this; the solemn order of attachments need not be observed in such cases "*propter privilegium et favorem mercatorum*[1]"; and a summons with less than 15 days' notice may be adjudged lawful, "*propter personas qui celerem debent habere justitiam, sicut sunt mercatores, quibus exhibetur justitia pepoudrous*[2]." This "Court of Pipowder" is also mentioned in the Domesday of Ipswich, where besides the "pleas yoven to the lawe maryne," there are also "pleas between straunge folk that men clepeth *pypoudrus*, shuldene be pleted from day to day[3]." The Court of Pipowders in 1478 was a Court that sat from hour to hour administering justice to dealers in time of fair[4]; according to Coke, it was to secure "speedy justice done for advancement of trade," and there might be such a Court by custom without either fair or market[5].

Malynes, in his curious and interesting work on the *Lex Mercatoria*, speaks of "the law Merchant, that is according to the customs of merchants...which concerning traffic and commerce are permanent and constant[6]." Coke states that[7] "the merchant strangers have a speedy recovery for their debts and

---

[1] Br. f. 444.

[2] Br. f. 334 : so called because justice was done while the dust was still on the foot, or before it could be shaken off.

[3] Black Book of Admiralty, ed. Twiss.

Rolls Series, II. 23.

[4] 17 Edw. IV. c. 2.

[5] Coke, IV. 272.

[6] Pub. 1622, 3rd Edit. 1686: pp. 2, 3.

[7] Coke, II. 58; see I. 11, b.

other duties, *per legem mercatoriam*, which is a part of the Common Law." The Court of the Mayor of the Staple, he says[1], "is guided by the Law Merchant...merchant strangers may sue before him according to the law merchant or at the Common law....This Court is the Court in the Staple Market, and it was oftentimes kept at Calais, and sometimes at Bruges, Antwerp and Middlebro', therefore it was necessary that this Court should be governed by Law Merchant." Fortescue also mentions that in certain Courts, "where matters proceed by Lawe Merchaunt, contracts or bargains among merchants in another realm are proved by witnesses[2]" (because 12 men of a neighbouring county cannot be obtained).

Zouch goes into the matter more at length[3]. Sir John Davies, he says, owns the Law Merchant as a law distinct from the Common law of England in a MS. Tract, where he affirms "that both the Common Law and Statute Laws of England take notice of the Law Merchant, and do leave the Causes of Merchants to be decided by the rules of that law,...which is part of the Law of Nature and Nations," "whereby it is manifest," continues Zouch, " that the cases concerning merchants are not now to be decided by the peculiar and ordinary laws of every country, but by the general Laws of Nature and nations. Sir J. Davies saith further, 'That until he understood the difference between the Law Merchant, and the Common law of England, he did not a little marvel what should be the cause that in the Books of the Common law of England there are to be found so few cases concerning merchants and ships, but now the reason was apparent, for that the Common law did leave those cases to be ruled by another law, the Law Merchant, which is a branch of the Law of Nations.'"

Again Zouch says[4]: " For the advantage of those who use navigation and trade by the sea, the Law Merchant and laws of the Sea[5] admit of divers things not agreeable to the Common law of the realm," and he cites instances and continues : " It is

---

[1] Coke, iv. 237, 238.

[2] *De Laudibus*, p. 74, ed. 1616: Selden on Fortescue, *ibid.*

[3] Zouch, p. 89. See Godolphin, p. 128.

[4] p. 128.

[5] i.e. the written laws of Oleron, etc.

not hereby intended that the Courts of Common law cannot or do not take notice of the Law Merchant in merchants' cases, but that other things likewise considered, it might be thought reasonable to allow them the choice of that Court where the Law Merchant is more respected, than to confine them to other Courts, where another law is more predominant. Besides there may be danger of doubt thereof, because those things are not approved of for proofs at the Common law, which are held sufficient in the Admiralty among the merchants."

Blackstone defines very clearly the position of the Law Merchant in his time[1]; "for as the transactions of foreign trade are carried on between subjects of independent states, the municipal laws of one will not be regarded by the other. For which reason the affairs of commerce are regulated by a law of their own, called the Law Merchant or *Lex Mercatoria*, which all nations agree in and take notice of; and in particular it is held to be part of the law of England, which decides the causes of merchants by the general rules which obtain in all commercial countries, and that often even in matters relating to domestic trade, as for instance in the drawing, acceptance and transfer of inland bills of Exchange." And again: "thus in mercantile questions, such as bills of exchange and the like; in all marine causes relating to freight, average, demurrage, bottomry, insurances, and others of a similar nature, the law merchant, which is a branch of the law of nations, is regularly adhered to[2]."

Now this Law Merchant, thus recognized by the laws of England, drew part of its matter from the Civil law. Being "part of the law of nations," in that it was composed of the customs of merchants of all nations, it included a number of usages which were relics of the Civil law, continuing the practice of the coasts of the Mediterranean. Again, the Written laws of the sea, the *Consolato* and the laws of Oleron, which formed part of the Law Merchant, and the latter of which was expressly embodied in the laws of England, were based on the Civil law, with such additions as were necessary to meet the

----

[1] Bl. i. 273.   [2] Bl. iv. 67.

needs of the time. Thus Duck is justified in speaking of the "*Curia Mercatorum, in qua lites de contractibus mercatorum ex aequo et bono secundum jus civile Romanorum terminandae sunt*[1]." Indeed even at that time the Civil law was recognized as an authority, where usage was uncertain. Malynes records a case with which he was personally acquainted, where an unfortunate merchant unintentionally guaranteed the solvency of another, and "the opinion of merchants was demanded, whereon there was grand diversity, so that the Civil law was to decide the same," and it was decided by the *Digest*[2].

This *Lex Mercatoria* had therefore a Roman foundation; and the importance of this will be seen when we remember that Lord Mansfield, the father of modern Mercantile law[3], during the 32 years in which he was Lord Chief Justice of the King's Bench[4], constructed his system of Commercial law by moulding the findings of his special juries as to the usages of merchants (which had often a Roman origin) on principles frequently derived from the Civil law and the law of nations. One among Junius' bitter attacks on him expressly alludes to this feature of his[5]: "In contempt or ignorance of the Common law of England, you have made it your study to introduce into the Court where you preside, maxims of jurisprudence unknown to Englishmen. The Roman code, the law of nations, and the opinions of foreign civilians, are your perpetual theme"; a charge for which, says Lord Campbell[6], "there is not the slightest colour of pretence. He did not consider the Common law of England...a perfect code adapted to the expanded, diversified, and novel requirements of a civilised and commercial nation... but in no instance did he ever attempt to *substitute* Roman rules and maxims for those of the Common law. He made ample use of the compilations of Justinian, but only for a supply of *principles* to guide him upon questions unsettled by prior decisions in England; deriving also similar assistance from the

[1] II. 8, 3, 25.

[2] p. 69.

[3] Park on *Insurance*, Lond. 1787, 7th edit., Int. pp. 43—48. Lowndes on *Insurance*, Int. p. 27; Campbell's

Lives, Vol. II.

[4] 1756—1788.

[5] Cited in Campbell, II. 437.

[6] *Ibid.* p. 438, 439.

law of nations, and the modern Continental codes." The nature of his work was well described by Buller, J. in his celebrated judgment in *Lickbarrow v. Mason*[1], where he says concerning bills of lading: "thus the matter stood till within these 30 years; since that time the Commercial law of this country has taken a very different turn from what it did before....Before that period we find that in Courts of law all the evidence in mercantile cases was thrown together: they were left generally to a jury, and they produced no established principle. From that time we all know the great study has been to find some certain general principles...not only to rule the particular case then under consideration, but to serve as a guide for the future. Most of us have heard those principles stated, reasoned upon, enlarged and explained till we have been lost in admiration at the strength and stretch of the human understanding. And I should be sorry to find myself under a necessity of differing from Lord Mansfield, who may truly be said to be the founder of the Commercial law of this country." An example of Lord Mansfield's use of the Civil law will be seen in his exposition of the nature of the equitable action for money had and received, which can be traced, passage by passage, to the *Corpus Juris*[2]: and many of these usages of the merchants, which he thus harmonized, had their origin in the Roman law though their details were of modern growth.

Thus the law of General Average, as developed by the Courts, appears to rest upon a Roman foundation. Mr M°Lachlan even assigns a Roman origin to the name, deriving it from *actio ex aversione*[3], though this origin is challenged by Mr Lowndes and seems rather fanciful. The Rhodian law[4]: "*Si levandae navis gratia, jactus mercium factus est, omnium contributione sarciatur quod pro omnibus datum est*," really contains the whole principle of general average, though it restricts the

---

[1] 1787, 2 *T. R.* 63, 73; see also Lowndes on *General Average*, Pref. 3rd edit. p. 45.

[2] *Moses v. McFerlane*, 2 Burr. 1005. 1 W. Bl. 219; see this set out in Warren's *Law Studies*, pp. 1353, 1354 from Evans' translation of Pothier *des* Obligations, II. 379, 380.

[3] McLachlan's Arnould on *Insurance*, 5th ed., pp. 882—885. Lowndes, *General Average*, 3rd edit., pp. 270—272.

[4] *Dig.* 14, 2, 1. See Lowndes, *Int.* pp. 45, 46. *Ibid.* p. 256.

example to Jettison. The *Corpus Juris* expanded it to cover
other cases, such as cutting away the mast, "*removendi communis periculi causa.*" But these laws fell into desuetude,
though the practice of contribution may have survived in the
Mediterranean. Some slight reference to it appears in the laws
of Oleron, but the old Sea laws only recognize two cases of
average, jettison and cutting away a mast. The first express
definition of "*commune avarie*" appears in the *Guidon de la
Mer,* about 1560[1]: and a fuller one is found in the French
Ordonnance of 1681. In 1801 a Court of Common law first
recognizes and discusses the right to recover at Common law
general average contributions[2]. Lawrence, J. defines a general
average loss as "all loss which arises in consequence of extraordinary sacrifices made, or expenses incurred, for the preservation
of the ship and cargo," and this "must be borne proportionably
by all who are interested[3]." Since then the law on the subject,
probably founded on the Rhodian and Roman law, and expanded by mercantile usage in all countries, is still under-
going development in the Courts[4]; though in the last reported
case, the Master of the Rolls rejected the idea that the law of
England should be brought into consonance with the laws of
all other countries; "no English Court has any mission to
adapt the law of England to the laws of other countries; it has
only authority to declare what the law of England is[5]." But
the law of England on these points was originally the Law
Merchant, the same in all commercial countries; and the agreement of all foreign countries in a rule of the Law Merchant
would then have been evidence of its being part of the law of
England, or rather of a Code which the English Courts would
recognize and enforce.

Lord Mansfield's greatest work was done in the development
of the law of Insurance; and here, though he gave form and

---

[1] Lowndes, 275.

[2] *Birkley v. Presgrave,* 1 East, 228.
Lowndes, pp. 1, 276; Int. p. 48.

[3] *cf.* the Ordonnance; *les des-
penses extraordinaires faites, et le
dommage souffert, pour le bien et le
salut commun des marchandises et du*
*vaisseau sont avaries grosses et com-
munes.*

[4] *cf. Atwood v. Sellar,* 5 Q. B. D. 286,
Wright v. Marwood, 7 Q. B. D. 62,
Svendsen v. Wallace, 11 Q. B. D. 616,
13 Q. B. D. 69. 10 App. C. 404.

[5] 13 Q. B. D. 73.

coherence to the Law Merchant, it does not seem that that law can be traced to Roman sources. Its Roman origin has indeed been suggested ; Zouch, for example, says[1] : " Policies of Insurance are grounded upon the Civil law...which as Malynes affirms were taken up in this kingdom from the laws of Oleron": but the most recent authorities hold that, though there is almost an entire lack of evidence concerning it till the publication of the *Guidon* (circa 1560), it probably originated about 1200 A.D. with the Italians, and was introduced into England by Lombard merchants[2]. Under Queen Elizabeth a special Court was constituted to try London Policies of Insurance, and it is noteworthy that it was to consist of the Judge of the Admiralty, the Recorder of London, *two Doctors of the Civil Law*, two common lawyers, and eight merchants[3]. The Court fell into disuse, but its composition shows the view that Insurance was part of the subject-matter of the Law Merchant, which in its turn was connected with the Civil law. Apart from this, there is no trace of Roman influence in the English law of Insurance.

The Roman *pecunia trajectitia*[4] was a loan of money with which merchandise was bought and shipped, being at the risk of the lender till the goods reached their destination. The interest on the loan was originally unlimited but was restricted by Justinian to 12 per cent.[5] And though the Roman law fell into oblivion, the institution appears to have survived in the Bottomry and Respondentia of the Law Merchant. By a Bottomry Bond[6], the master under stress of necessity borrows money for the prosecution of his voyage on the security of the ship, to be repaid with maritime interest if the ship arrives in safety ; Respondentia is a similar loan on the security of the cargo, its repayment being also dependent on safe arrival. Neither of these is quite the same as *Pecunia Trajectitia*, which was rather an original venture by a merchant, dependent on the safe arrival of the ship, than a loan to the master, made under

---

[1] p. 102.
[2] Park on *Insurance*, Int. pp. 10—19. Lowndes on *Insurance*, Lond. 1881, Int. pp. 19—21.
[3] Park, Int. p. 40. 43 Eliz. c. 12.

[4] *Dig.* 22, 2, 1—5.
[5] *Cod.* 4, 32, 26.
[6] McLachlan, *Merchant Shipping*, 3rd ed. pp. 51—65.

necessity, to enable a voyage already begun to be prosecuted. But Malynes expressly calls Bottomry, *pecunia trajectitia*, while he also alludes to a transaction precisely similar to the Roman one, as "a deliverance of money of the nature of *Usura Maritima*[1]." The "darkness of an earlier age[2]" prevents us from tracing what connexion the later institution has with the Roman one, but it seems probable that the latter survived, and was modified and adapted into the Bottomry of to-day.

The Admiralty Court endeavoured to introduce the Civilian doctrine of a tacit hypothec of, or maritime lien upon, the ship herself for repairs or the supply of necessaries without any express Bottomry bond. Lord Stowell said[3]: "In most of those countries governed by the Civil law, repairs and necessaries form a lien upon the ship herself. In our country the same doctrine had for a long time been held by the Maritime Courts, but after a long contest, it was finally overthrown by the Courts of Common law, and by the House of Lords in the reign of Charles II.": and Lord Holt also, no opponent of the Civil law, held that[4]: "By the Maritime law every contract of the master implies a hypothecation, but by the Common law it is not so, unless it be so expressly agreed."

Zouch suggests that Charterparties are derived, through the Roman, from the Rhodian law[5]; "*Si quis navem conduxerit, instrumenta consignata sunto*," and Malynes, who cites other Rhodian rules as in force in the Law Merchant, also says that charterparties of his time (1622) commonly declared that they were in all things made according to the laws of Oleron[6]; the provision as to the forfeiture of double earnest by the Master, "if he repent," is clearly Roman[7]. But in this, as in most other heads of the Law Merchant, we can only speculate whether Roman customs, developed by Mediterranean nations, have furnished the groundwork on which the Courts and the merchants of England have built their Mercantile law. The law of Bills of Exchange, which owes most of its material to the

[1] p. 122.
[2] McLachlan, p. 65.
[3] *Zodiac* (1825). 1 Haggard, *Adm.* 325.
[4] *Justin v. Ballam* (1702). 1 Salk. 34. 2 Lord Raymond, 805.
[5] p. 102.
[6] pp. 98, 99.
[7] *V. supra*, pp. 76, 93.

Law Merchant, appears entirely free from Roman influence, the usages of merchants which it embodies being of much later origin. We must therefore rest content with pointing to the Law Merchant, as a probable source of Roman influence on the English law, while the lack of evidence does not allow us to estimate the amount of that influence.

The position of the Law Merchant, or of "the general maritime law," in this country has been under discussion in a series of cases, other than *Svendsen v. Wallace*[1], down to 1882. In 1801 Lord Stowell, discussing the powers of the master to give Bottomry Bonds, referred repeatedly to "the general maritime law," saying in one place[2]; "a very modern regulation of our own private law...has put an end to our practice of ransoming...but I am speaking of the general maritime law and practice, not superseded by private and positive regulation"; and again; "Adverting to the authority of the maritime law, as it has been for some years practised in this Court...adverting also to the position of what I may call the *Lex Mercatoria*[3]." In the *Hamburg*[4] (1864), also on the conflict of laws as to bottomry, Dr Lushington announced his intention of "governing his judgment by reference to the ordinary maritime law...no specific law being alleged as the governing law"..."I must take the law which ought to apply to this case to be the maritime law as administered in England," while the Privy Council on appeal[5] "entirely agree with the learned Judge that the case is to be decided by the general maritime Law as administered in England." This expression was criticized by Willes, J., in a case in 1865[6], where the "general maritime law, as regulating all maritime transactions between persons of different nationalities at sea," was suggested as one of the laws by which the decision should be governed; he said[7]: "We can understand this term in the sense of the general maritime law as administered in English Courts, *that*

[1] 13 Q. B. D. 69. *v. supra*, p. 182 note.

[2] *The Gratitudine*, 3 W. Rob. 240, 259.

[3] *Ibid.* p. 271.

[4] Br. and Lush, 259.

[5] *Ibid.* 272.

[6] *Lloyd v. Guibert*, L. R. 1 Q. B. 115, 119.

[7] *L. R.* 1 Q. B. p 123.

being in truth nothing more than English law, though dealt out in somewhat different measures in the Common law and Chancery Courts and in the peculiar jurisdiction of the Admiralty; but as to any other general maritime law by which we ought to adjudicate upon the rights of a subject of a country, which by the hypothesis, does not recognize its alleged rule, we were not informed what may be its authority, its limits, or its sanction" ..."It would be difficult to maintain that there is any general in the sense of universal law, binding at sea, any more than upon land, nations which either have not assented or have withdrawn their assent thereto"...and further on he speaks of "the general maritime law as administered in England, or (to avoid periphrasis) the law of England[1]." This series of cases came before the Court of Appeal in 1882, in a case[2] which Sir R. Phillimore had decided by "the general maritime law as administered in England[3]"; and in reversing his decision Brett, L. J. said[4]: "what is the law which is administered in an English Court of Admiralty, whether English law, or that which is called the Common maritime law, which is not the law of England alone, but the law of all maritime countries...The law which is administered in the English Court of Admiralty is the English maritime law. It is not the ordinary municipal law of the country, but it is the law which the English Court of Admiralty, either by Act of Parliament, or by reiterated decisions and traditions and principles, has adopted as the English maritime law."

It is not inconsistent with these decisions that the Law Merchant is recognized whenever a special jury "finds" a custom of merchants, which is acted on by the Courts; for the law of England recognizes such customs because they comply with rules it has previously laid down, and decides that they were law as complying with its rules, and not from any merit of the Law Merchant. But in this way the usages of merchants still influence the law of England.

[1] *L. R.* 1 Q. B. p. 125.   [3] *Ibid.* p. 4.
[2] *Gaetano e. Maria, L. R.* 7 P. D. 1,   [4] *Ibid.* p. 143.
137.

CHAPTER XV.

THE range of the English Common law is so vast, and its sources so voluminous, that we can only refer to one or two points on which Roman influences have affected it.

The English law of Bailments, and especially that part of it which treats of the liability of a common carrier, have been much discussed in relation to the Roman law. The present Master of the Rolls has said[1]: "No one who has read Story and Sir W. Jones on Bailments, and the judgment of Lord Holt in *Coggs v. Bernard*[2], can doubt that the Common law of England as to bailments is founded upon, though it has not exactly adopted, the Roman law. It is true that Lord Holt rests as for authority solely on Bracton; but the treatise of Bracton adopts all the divisions of the Roman law in the very words of the Roman text, and further adopts the exception of the Roman law, and the Roman reason for it...It is obvious that Bracton or English judges before him adopted into the English, the Roman law."

But this, the Roman theory of its origin, was expressly repudiated by Lord Chief Justice Cockburn, on appeal: he said[3]:—"it is a misapprehension to suppose that the law of England relating to the liability of common carriers was derived from the Roman law; for the law relating to it was first established by our Courts, with reference to carriers by land, on whom the Roman law imposed no liability in respect of loss, beyond that

---

[1] *Nugent v. Smith, L. R.* 1 C. P. D. at p. 28.

[2] 2 Ld. Raymond, 909.

[3] *Nugent v. Smith, L. R.* 1 C. P. D.: pp. 428, 430.

of other bailees for reward"; and in his view it was introduced as an exception to the more lenient English law, in the times of Elizabeth and Charles I.

With both these views Mr Holmes disagrees; he considers that the law of bailments is Teutonic, not Roman, in origin; and that the liability of carriers is not a stricter exception to the old rule, but a fragmentary survival of that rule, which has, in other parts, been mollified by time: while the changes in the old law were due partly to the introduction of the *action on the case*, and the *assumpsit*, partly to notions of public policy. All parties are agreed that Lord Holt in *Coggs v. Bernard* systematized and amplified Bracton, who in turn had copied the *Institutes* almost word for word. But it is not so clear how far Bracton or Lord Holt accurately represented the Law as it existed in their time.

The Anglo-Saxon procedure was based on the loss of possession against one's will, and was not open to the owner who had willingly parted with possession. Thus the bailee and not the bailor was the right person to sue for any wrongful dealing with a bailment; the bailee had the possessory remedies, and because he had the remedies, he was bound to sue the thief, and to hold the bailor harmless, even though, as bailee, he had committed no fault. These possessory remedies of the bailee were opposed to the Roman law[1], which held the agent, borrower, ordinary bailee, hirer and usufructuary, to have only Detention and not Possession, and therefore refused them the Possessory remedies though some of them had *actio furti*[2].

In process of time, the owner out of possession was allowed to sue the wrongdoer; but his suit against the bailee remained. The bailee had been liable because he only could sue: this reason was inverted to meet the new state of things, and it was held that the bailee could sue, because he was liable to his bailor. In Anglo-Norman law also the action to recover stolen property was based on possession[3], and cases in the Yearbooks show that the bailor had originally no remedy against third persons, but only against the bailee. The inverted explanation of the bailee's strict

[1] Moyle, on *Institutes*, I. 323.   [3] Bracton, f. 150, b.   Holmes, p. 168.
[2] *Inst.* IV. 1, 13—17.

liability was repeated, as thus[1]: "If a stranger takes beasts in my custody, I shall have a writ of trespass against him.. *because I am chargeable for the beasts to my bailor*, who has the property"; which is analogous to the Roman reason for allowing the *actio furti*, to the man *cujus interest rem salvam fore*, because he was liable over to the owner. The bailor acquired his action against third parties, though the possessory remedies of the bailee remained, and also his absolute responsibility to the bailor, if the goods were wrongfully taken from him. Thus Glanvil says: "*Sin autem res ipsa interierit vel perdita fuerit, quocunque modo in custodia tua, omnino teneris ad rationabile pretium mihi restituendum[2].*" Bracton has copied the *Institutes*, but owing either to imperfect absorption of his Roman materials or corruptness of the text, he has left the matter in doubt. The passage in Bracton, side by side with the corresponding passage in Justinian, is as follows :

BRACTON, f. 99, a. b.

INSTITUTES, III. 14, 2.

Is autem, cui res aliqua utenda datur, re obligatur, quae commodata est ; sed magna differentia est inter mutuum et commodatum, quia is qui rem *commodatam* accepit, ad ipsam restituendam tenetur, vel ejus precium, si forte incendio, ruina, naufragio aut latronum vel hostium incursu consumpta fuerit.

* * * * *

Ad vim autem majorem vel casos fortuitos non tenetur quis, nisi culpa sua intervenerit.

Is, cui res aliqua utenda datur, id est commodatur, re obligatur.... Sed is ab eo qui mutuum accepit longe distat ; namque non ita res datur, ut eius fiat ; et ob id de ea re ipsa restituenda tenetur. Et is quidem qui mutuum accepit, si quolibet fortuito casu quod accepit amiserit, veluti incendio ruina naufragio aut latronum hostiumve incursu, nihilominus obligatus permanet....

* * * * *

Sed propter maiorem vim maioresve casus non tenetur, si modo non huius culpa is casus intervenerit.

The first sentence in Bracton, as it stands, is consistent with Glanvil and with the old law; but it is contrary to the *Institutes*, and to the second quotation from Bracton, which follows the *Institutes*. This discrepancy has of course been noted

---

[1] Per Hankford, J., Y. B. 11 H. IV. 23, 24. Holmes, 170. Blackstone, *Com.* II. 453.

[2] Gl. x. 13 : see also x. 8. Holmes, p. 175.

by subsequent writers. Lord Holt in *Coggs v. Bernard* read "*mutuam*" for "*commodatam*," a reading which follows the *Institutes*, but makes nonsense of the words "*ad ipsam restituendam*," and is not supported by the MSS. Prof. Güterbock suggests[1]: "we must either understand '*nisi culpa intervenerit*,' or hold it to be an echo of the older English law." Sir W. Jones says[2] some MSS. of Bracton have a full stop at "*precium*"; and he suggests that at the completion of that sentence, a line has dropped out, viz.; "*at is qui mutuum accepit obligatus permanet*" (words in the passage from Justinian, though not consecutively)[3]. My own view, based mainly on the curious mistakes Bracton has made in copying Azo, through running two sentences into one[4], is this: Bracton's one sentence contains parts of three consecutive sentences in Justinian; in compressing them, and probably not quite understanding them, he has stated first the old law as found in Glanvil, and a little later has correctly reproduced in one sentence, the sentence as to *vis major* in the *Institutes*. I think his first sentence as it stands represents the true state of the law at the time, and the second is, like his passage on walls, and other Roman incorporations, inaccurate as a representation of English Law, and inconsistent with himself.

For subsequent decisions of the Courts[5], though Lord Holt treats them very lightly, thoroughly support the old law. For instance in the case of the *Marshal of the Marshalsea*[6], who was sued for the escape of a prisoner (being in the same position as a bailee of cattle), his defence was that enemies of the king by force carried off the prisoner: the Court held that, if these were alien enemies, the defence was good, for then the defendant "had a remedy against no one," but if they were subjects of the king he would be liable, for he had a remedy against them. And the law was stated similarly by Littleton[7]. In 1601 it was decided in *Southcote v. Bennett*[8] that a plea

---

[1] Güt. Coxe, notes, pp. 141, 175.

[2] *Bailments*, p. 64, note.

[3] I do not understand the first alternative suggested by Güterbock, while Sir W. Jones' suggestion seems to make the passage as to *rem commodatam* unmeaning.

[4] *v. supra*, p. 87.

[5] Holmes, pp. 176—180.

[6] Y. B. 33 Henry VI. 1, pl. 3 (1455).

[7] Y. B. 9 Edw. IV. 34, pl. 9. Holmes, p. 178.

[8] 4 Co. *Rep.* 83, b. Cro. Eliz. 815. Both reports agree that the obligation was founded on delivery alone. Holmes, 179.

of robbery was no defence to an action for a thing bailed by delivery, "for the bailee hath his remedy over by trespass or appeal, to have them again." Lord Holt[1] and, to some extent, Sir W. Jones[2] endeavour to show that this case is without authority, but it seems to be in accordance with the old law as stated by Glanvil, and found in the Teutonic sources. And if this is so it is unnecessary to consider, as Cockburn, C. J. does, its application to carriers as an exception to an early and more lenient rule, made from motives of public policy; while its agreement with Teutonic law frees it from the Roman origin suggested by Lord Esher.

Woodliffe's case[3], in 1596, is the first case of note, as to carriers. In that case Popham, C. J. and Gawdy, J. held a plea of robbery at sea, a bad defence as to goods entrusted to defendant "*pur merchandiser*," and Popham made the further distinction that the plea was bad for a carrier, because he is paid for his carriage, but that there was a difference between carriers, and other servants and factors. For servants had not control over the goods, and so were not bailees, while the distinction of paid and unpaid service shows the early stages of the doctrine of Consideration, which was referred to in *Southcote's Case*, five years later. The difficulty of a case of damage through omission to act was met both by the device of an *assumpsit;* i.e. that the defendant took upon himself a duty, for the breach of which he was liable in tort; and, if the defendant had a public calling, by the allegation that he was "a common carrier" etc., and therefore under a general obligation to carry on his public trade with skill. The carrier's liability might thus be rested either on the simple delivery of the goods, or on his *assumpsit*, or on his common or public calling, while Popham, C. J.'s distinction suggested that payment was material, and in this multitude of grounds of liability, the old law was lost sight of.

Rich v. Kneeland (1613)[4] was an action in the case against

---

[1] *Coggs v. Bernard.* 1 Smith, *L. C.* 8th edit. pp. 199, 208.

[2] Jones on *Bailments*, London, 1823, pp. 41—44.

[3] Moore, *Rep.* p. 462. Holmes, p. 181.

[4] Cro. Jac. 330. Cockburn, C.J. in *L. R.* 1 C. P. D. p. 430, 431. Holmes, p. 189.

a common hoyman; the writ of error assigned that "this action lies not against a common hoyman without special promise"... "But all the Justices and Barons held that it well lies as against a common carrier on the land." And for nearly a century after *Woodliffe's case*[1] the liability of common carriers was rested on *Southcote's case,* which as we have seen, stated the old law. In *Morse v. Slue*[2] (1671), the master of a ship from which a robbery of goods had occurred was held by Lord Hale not to be protected "by the rules of the civil law, by which masters are not chargeable *pro damno fatali,*" but to be liable because he took a reward, and because he took the goods generally without any special agreement; and this last position is that of *Southcote's case.*

The development of the doctrines of *assumpsit,* Common Calling, and Consideration led to the view that the strict liability of common carriers was something peculiar to themselves, and not applicable to bailees in general; and the judgments of Lord Holt during his tenure of office confirmed this opinion. In 1701[3], while suggesting that the liability of carriers and innkeepers was grounded on public policy, he had expressed his belief that "the principles of our law are based on the civil law": and this view was confirmed by his celebrated judgment in *Coggs v. Bernard* (1703)[4], which overthrew *Southcote's case* and the old Common law. In that case it was moved in arrest of judgment that the declaration did not allege a common calling or any consideration; it had alleged an *assumpsit,* and Lord Holt held this was sufficient, distinguishing bailees for reward exercising a public calling, who were within the rule of strict responsibility of *Southcote's case* on grounds of public policy, from other bailees who were not so strictly liable. But though he cited Roman passages from Bracton in support of his

[1] See *Symons v. Darknoll* (1628). 1 Palmer, 523: Holmes, 191, where "although no promise laid, the plaintiff should recover, and not alleging the defendant was *common* lighterman did no harm." Per Hyde, C.J., "delivery makes the contract" "*et in cest case Southcote's case fuit cite.*"

[2] 2 Keb. 866, 3 Keb. 72, 112, 135. 2

Lev. 69. 1 Vent. 190, 238. 1 Mod. 85. Sir T. Raym. 220. Holmes, pp. 192—194. Cockburn, C. J. at 1 C. P. D. 430. Brett, J. *ibid.* p. 31.

[3] *Lane v. Sir R. Cotton,* 12 Mod. 472, 482.

[4] 2 Lord Raymond, 909. 1 Sm. L. C. 8th edit. 199.

classification of bailments, the above position is far from being the adoption of the Praetor's Edict[1]: "*Ait Praetor: nautae, caupones, stabularii, quod cujusque salvum fore receperint, nisi restituant, in eos judicium dabo...nisi si quid damno fatali contingit.*" For the Roman class were excused by *casus fortuitus* or *vis major:* the English had a stricter liability. The English rule extends to all bailees for reward exercising a public calling; and of these two points the distinction as to bailees for reward is that of Popham, C. J. in 1596, and the conception of a "common calling" had also been in existence for the century before *Coggs v. Bernard.* The responsibility of carriers is precisely the same as that of all bailees under the old English rule, their exemption from liability for acts of God and the king's enemies being explained, as to the king's enemies by the Case of the Marshal[2], because there was no "remedy over" against alien enemies, as to the "Act of God," by the application of the general doctrine that all obligations were discharged if acts of God made them impossible of performance[3].

The general law of bailments up to *Coggs v. Bernard* was therefore Teutonic not Roman, all bailees being as strictly liable as carriers are now, and the alleviation of the liability of bailees other than carriers, though assisted by the Roman leanings of Lord Holt, was the result of the development of the doctrines of *assumpsit,* consideration, and public calling, of which two are distinctly English, and the third partly so. The present liability of carriers is not therefore an application of the Praetor's Edict, a more rigid exception to the lenient rule applied to other bailees, on grounds of public policy, but a survival of the older rule as to bailments which applied to all bailees universally.

A part of English law which can in all probability be traced back in a joint growth from Roman and German originals is the gradual development of the liability of a man for the acts of his children, servants, or agents, as to which I can only refer to Mr. Holmes' interesting work. The origin of the doctrine of consideration, and of much of the law as to acquisition of personal property has already been touched upon.

---

[1] *Dig.* IV. 9. 1, pr.   [3] Holmes, 202.
[2] v. *supra*, p. 190.

CONCLUSION.

This inadequate sketch of the influence of the Roman Law on the Law of England has now reached its close. We have seen that English law in its earliest stages is almost entirely Teutonic, and that those who claim for it descent from the laws and customs of the Roman occupation are unable to support their case by any satisfactory evidence. The most plausible of these theories is that which refers manorial institutions to a mingled Roman and South German origin, and even this at present lacks any certain foundation. The introduction of wills and charters comes from clerical and Roman sources, but except in this respect we cannot say that the influence of the Civil Law has in any way affected the Law of England until the coming of Vacarius.

The latter half of the twelfth century revives the study of Justinianean law throughout Europe, and England also shares in the revival. The Ecclesiastical Courts rule themselves by the Roman Law, and from their proceedings Roman influences affect the work of Glanvil. Bracton's great treatise contains much Roman matter and terminology, but his knowledge of the civil law was only that of every clerical judge, (and they were many), of his century. The full extent of their influence can only, even imperfectly, be traced by a detailed study of the Year-Books, a task far beyond our present powers; but it is clear that the revival was followed by a reaction. The Roman Law became not only a subject of distrust, owing to the conflicts between King and Pope; it even dropped into oblivion. With Coke, Hale, and Blackstone, while there is knowledge of the Law of Rome, there is also a clear definition of its position, as of no force in England, unless as adopted by the English law, or in particular courts where its authority was recognized by English jurisprudence. In those courts we have traced its history; in the Ecclesiastical Courts in their jurisdiction over marriages and succession at death, in the Admiralty Courts, proceeding according to the Civil Law and the Law of the Sea, and in the influence of the Law Merchant on both the Admiralty and the

Common Law; and we have referred though briefly to some of the points in which the Common Law itself has been affected by the Law of Rome.

That the history of Roman Law in England has yet to be written, no one is more conscious than the author of this Essay ; he can only hope for an indulgence, proportioned to the difficulties of the task, in the attempt to gather together some of the materials for such a history.

INDEX.

THE LAWS OF COPYRIGHT. An Examination of the Principles which should regulate Literary and Artistic Property in England and other countries. Being the YORKE PRIZE ESSAY of the University of Cambridge for the year 1882. Price 10s. 6d.

LONDON : JOHN MURRAY, ALBEMARLE STREET.

OPINIONS OF THE PRESS.

"An exceptionally good exposition and criticism. The plan is well conceived and consistently carried out; the statement is clear, concise, accurate and fresh. ....The author and the publisher will certainly find trustworthy guidance, and the general public an interesting history, and an impartial examination of an important question,...Mr Scrutton's lucid presentation and vigorous handling of the essential points of the subject invest his work with a distinct practical merit that deserves recognition."—*Spectator, July* 5, 1884.

"To write a new treatise upon the fruitful subject of copyright law, which is not rendered altogether superfluous by the prior occupation of the ground by such excellent authorities as Drone, Phillips and Copinger, is no very easy task. Mr Scrutton has achieved this feat...Mr Scrutton furnishes an exposition of the present state of our law which is supported by abundant references to statutes and cases, and generally trustworthy."—*Athenæum, Oct.* 18, 1884.

"The chapter on the 'History of the English Law of Copyright' is exceedingly well written. The examination of the general principles of each kind of copyright is thoughtful, independent, and well expressed, and shows a complete grasp of the subject...The index is as good as it could be."—*Solicitors' Journal, Dec.* 15, 1883.

"The Copyright lawyer will certainly find suggestive matter in Prof. Scrutton's exposition of the principles of his subject, and he ought at least to be interested in his animated sketch of the history of the legislation which has developed if not created it...For a clear and handy exposition of the provisions of the laws of this and other countries on the subject, readers are much indebted to the author. ...Eminently readable and suggestive."—*Scotsman, April* 15, 1884.

"Mr Scrutton's arrangement is good in this respect, he dominates the cases, and makes them subservient to his statement of the law. He gets from them and the statutes a clear idea of legal principles, which he expresses with accuracy...His volume is written scientifically with a view to set forth the principles of the law distinctly and clearly."—*Law Times, Dec.* 15, 1883.

"The most able and in some respects the most original book of its kind... His exposition of the present law is lucid and perspicuous...As a handy and most recent digest of the law the book is serviceable alike to authors and publishers...Both as a digest and commentary Mr Scrutton's work is of the greatest value."—*Bookseller, Feb.* 2, 1884.

"Mr Scrutton has succeeded in writing a book which, while it will be a trusty guide for the profession, will also be of service to publishers, authors, artists and others interested in the law of copyright...a very clear and careful account of the existing state of the law with regard to copyright."—*Tablet, March* 1, 1884.

"Mr Scrutton has produced a book which we expect to see run through many editions...We predict that it will be a standard authority on the laws of literary property...an elaborate Index, not the least meritorious part of a most meritorious work."—*Literary World.*

"A learned book, and one that augurs well for the future success of its author."—*Law Journal, Jan.* 19, 1884.

www.ingramcontent.com/pod-product-compliance
Lightning Source LLC
Chambersburg PA
CBHW032055080426
42733CB00006B/277